Quiet Politics and Business Power
Corporate Control in Europe and Japan

Does democracy control business, or does business control democracy? This study of how companies are bought and sold in four countries – France, Germany, Japan, and the Netherlands – explores this fundamental question. It does so by examining variation in the rules of corporate control – specifically, whether hostile takeovers are allowed. Takeovers have high political stakes: they result in corporate reorganizations, layoffs, and the unraveling of compromises between workers and managers. But the public rarely pays attention to issues of corporate control. As a result, political parties and legislatures are largely absent from this domain. Instead, organized managers get to make the rules, quietly drawing on their superior lobbying capacity and the deference of legislators. These tools, not campaign donations, are the true founts of managerial political influence.

Pepper D. Culpepper is professor of political science at the European University Institute. He was previously on the faculty at the Harvard Kennedy School. He is the author of *Creating Cooperation* and coeditor of *Changing France* and *The German Skills Machine*. His work has appeared in *International Organization*, *World Politics*, *Comparative Political Studies*, *Revue Française de Science Politique*, *Politische Vierteljahresschrift*, *West European Politics*, *Journal of European Public Policy*, *Journal of Public Policy*, and the *Oxford Review of Economic Policy*, among others. Culpepper was a Marshall Scholar at Oxford University and received his Ph.D. in political science from Harvard University.

Quiet Politics and Business Power

Corporate Control in Europe and Japan

PEPPER D. CULPEPPER

European University Institute

CAMBRIDGE
UNIVERSITY PRESS

CAMBRIDGE UNIVERSITY PRESS
Cambridge, New York, Melbourne, Madrid, Cape Town,
Singapore, São Paulo, Delhi, Mexico City

Cambridge University Press
32 Avenue of the Americas, New York, NY 10013-2473, USA

www.cambridge.org
Information on this title: www.cambridge.org/9780521134132

First published 2011
Reprinted 2012

A catalog record for this publication is available from the British Library.

Library of Congress Cataloging in Publication Data
Culpepper, Pepper D.
Quiet politics and business power : corporate control in Europe and Japan / Pepper D.
Culpepper.
    p.   cm. – (Cambridge studies in comparative politics)
ISBN 978-0-521-11859-0 (hardback)
1. Corporate governance – Europe. 2. Corporate governance – Japan. I. Title. II. Series.
HD2741.C94 2011
338.6094 – dc22   2010014153

ISBN 978-0-521-11859-0 Hardback
ISBN 978-0-521-13413-2 Paperback

To my mother

Contents

Tables and Figures

Tables

Figures

Abbreviations

ACCJ	American Chamber of Commerce in Japan
ADAM	Association de Défense des Actionnaires Minoritaires (French minority shareholders' defense association)
AFEP	Association Française des Entreprises Privées (peak association of large French enterprises)
BDI	Bundesverband der Deutschen Industrie (Federation of German Industry; peak political association of German employers)
BNP	Banque Nationale de Paris
CDA	Christendemocratische Partij (Dutch Christian Democratic Party)
CNPF	Conseil National du Patronat Français (name of the peak association of French employers from 1945–1998)
COB	Commission des Opérations de Bourse (the market-regulating authority in France)
CVSG	Corporate Value Study Group
EBC	European Business Council Japan
EU	European Union
FD	*Het Financieele Dagblad* (Dutch business newspaper)
FDI	Foreign Direct Investment
FFSA	Fédération Française des Sociétés d'Assurance (peak association of French insurance companies)
FSA	Financial Services Agency (Japan)
IDC	International Digital Communications
JSP	Japan Steel Partners
LDP	Liberal Democratic Party (Japan)
LPF	Lijst Pim Fortuyn (Pim Fortuyn List)
MAC	M&A Consulting
MEDEF	Mouvement des Entreprises de France (name of the peak Association of French employers since 1998)

MEP	Member of the European Parliament
METI	Ministry of the Economy, Trade, and Industry (Japan)
MoF	Ministry of Finance (Japan)
MoJ	Ministry of Justice (Japan)
MSP	Minority Shareholder Protection
MTFG	Mitsubishi Group
NBS	Nippon Broadcasting System
NLIR	Nippon Life Insurance Research Institute
NRE	Nouvelles Régulations Economiques (New Economic Regulations)
OECD	Organization for Economic Cooperation and Development
PEJ	Project for Excellence in Journalism
PFA	Pension Fund Association (Japan)
PR	Proportional Representation
PvdA	Partij van de Arbeid (Dutch Labor Party)
SDC	Securities Data Corporation
SEC	Securities and Exchange Commission (United States)
SER	Sociaal Economische Raad (Dutch Social and Economic Council)
SocGen	Société Générale
T1B	Thomson One Banker
TOB	Tender Offer Bid
UAP	Union des Assurances de Paris (insurance company taken over by AXA in 1996)
UMP	Union pour un Mouvement Populaire (French Gaullist Party)
VEB	Vereniging van Effectenbezitters (Dutch Shareholders' Association)
VEUO	Vereniging Effecten Uitgevende Ondernemingen (Dutch Association of Securities-Issuing Companies)
VNO-NCW	Verbond van Nederlandse Ondernemingen – Nederlands Christelijk Werkgeversverbond (Peak Association of Dutch Employers)
VVD	Volkspartij voor Vrijheid en Democratie (People's Party for Freedom and Democracy, the Dutch Liberal Party)

Preface

> If it is true that the result of political contests is determined by the scope of public involvement in conflicts, much that has been written about politics becomes nonsense, and we are in for a revolution in our thinking about politics.
>
> E.E. Schattschneider, *The Semisovereign People*, 1960[1]

Democracy is said to reflect the will of the voters. And in some policy domains, this is a reasonable approximation of reality. When governing parties and their opponents know that political issues are debated in the media – and that the people are watching – they have powerful electoral incentives to respond to the dictates of public opinion.

This book is about what happens in democracies when the people are not watching. Although the public cares about some issues most of the time, and many issues some of the time, certain issues receive little attention at all. These issues are often no less important to the public interest than their more sensational counterparts, but, for a variety of reasons, voters only dimly perceive the connection of such matters to their own welfare.

Political scientists describe these sorts of issues as having low political salience. And just as voters typically ignore issues of low political salience, so too do political scientists. Most models of politics simply assume that all issues are equally salient to voters, and that the electoral connection will force political parties to respond to the preferences of the voting public, or at least to interest groups representing these voters. Following the insights of E.E. Schattschneider, I argue in this book that the political dynamics of low salience issues actually differ dramatically from those of high salience issues. The latter are the stuff of which elections are won and lost, occasioning raucous debates in the media and on the floors of legislatures. The former give rise to what I call "quiet politics," in which highly organized interest groups dominate the policy process in arenas shielded from public view.

---

[1] Schattschneider (1960: 5).

This book focuses empirically on an area of policy making that affects the welfare of men and women in all democracies, but that nevertheless displays the hallmarks of quiet politics: the rules governing how easy it is for companies to be bought and sold. Where it is easy to take over firms against the will of senior management, companies are subject to dramatic changes of strategy that can result in plant closings and layoffs. Managers threatened by hostile takeovers must constantly be aware of their share price, limiting their capacity to pursue a long-term strategy. Hostile takeovers have momentous political and economic consequences, but the rules governing them seldom command public attention. The issue therefore provides an ideal terrain to investigate how political power functions under conditions of quiet politics.

The distinction between noisy and quiet politics also offers new purchase on an old question in the study of democracy, one that has attracted renewed interest in light of the recent international financial crisis: do the interests of big business always prevail? In the arena of noisy politics, organized business actually suffers many defeats, because these are the conditions under which politicians must cater to popular opinion if they want to be reelected. In the domains of quiet politics, though, public indifference means that politicians and the media are more likely to defer to managerial assertions of expertise. This is what allowed organized managers to achieve their goals in the area of corporate control in the four countries studied in this book: France, Germany, Japan, and the Netherlands.

A similar story can be told with respect to executive pay: as long as managerial compensation was an issue of low political salience, as it was at the dawn of this century, business organizations in France and the United States were able to maintain their preferred set of rules. But salience is not static. As public concern about executive pay began to rise in the wake of accounting scandals, business organizations in these two countries could no longer count on the deference of politicians. Managers were forced to cultivate allies within political parties in order to thwart government intervention, and they sometimes failed. This book thus affirms a dismal truth of modern democracies: politicians will indeed listen to the voters, but only when the volume of debate is dialed up to its loudest levels.

In the course of this project I have relied on a lot of help. At long last, it is a pleasure for me to thank the many friends and colleagues whose contributions shaped this work. For much of the past decade I have been fortunate to be part of a group of scholars interested in the political dynamics of corporate governance. We often disagree among ourselves about the best way to study these questions – indeed, much of this book speaks directly to these disagreements – but our interactions have taught me much about the politics of corporate control. Thanks to Ruth Aguilera, Helen Callaghan, John Cioffi, Michel Goyer, Gary Herrigel, Martin Höpner, Gregory Jackson, Mary O'Sullivan, Yves Tiberghien, and Nick Ziegler for their intellectual engagement. I would especially like to acknowledge the tremendous collegiality and friendship of

Peter Gourevitch, whose work with James Shinn has been at the heart of debates about the political dimensions of corporate control. Our views often differ, but my conversations with Peter have continually inspired me to improve my own ideas, and I am grateful for them.

Several scholars read an earlier version of the book manuscript and gave me valuable comments on it, including Rawi Abdelal (who first suggested the phrase "quiet politics"), Frank Baumgartner, Alex Keyssar, Curtis Milhaupt, and Gerhard Schnyder. Likewise, I received helpful reactions to parts of the argument from Matthew Baum, Suzanne Berger, Helen Callaghan, John Cioffi, David Coen, Giles Craven, Margarita Estevez-Abe, Michel Goyer, Eelke Heemskerk, Gary Herrigel, Torben Iversen, Patrick Le Galès, Stan Markus, Jacques Mistral, David Moss, Paul Pierson, Mark Roe, John Ruggie, Vivien Schmidt, Zenichi Shishido, Wolfgang Streeck, Christine Trampusch, Gunnar Trumbull, Steve Vogel, and Michael Witt. The book is far better as a result of their suggestions, and it might be better still had I heeded all their counsel.

Before the book went to press, it was the subject of a day-long workshop at Harvard University. This was an extraordinary intellectual opportunity, and I am deeply grateful to Keith Darden, Peter Hall, Peter Katzenstein, David Soskice, and Kathleen Thelen for their suggestions on sharpening the argument. Adelaide Shalhope organized the meeting, and the Weatherhead Center for International Affairs at Harvard supported it financially; I acknowledge both with gratitude.

At the risk of repetition, I recognize here a few friends who have tirelessly discussed these ideas with me over the years. Peter Hall read countless drafts, and his critiques have fundamentally improved the final product. David Soskice encouraged me from the beginning. His comments at critical junctures have had an important impact on the argument. Tarek Masoud was a tenacious critic and a stern editor, who constantly challenged me to be more precise about the role of salience in politics. He came late to the book, but the final version owes much to his relentless skepticism. Many lunches with Archon Fung have been devoted to discussion of the ideas in this manuscript. I acknowledge the indigestion this must have caused with profound appreciation. Larry Dagenhart, my father-in-law, read multiple drafts of many chapters. He has taught me much about the finer points of poison pill defenses and the art of clear exposition, among many other things.

This book draws together a wealth of new information on corporate control across the advanced industrialized countries, as well as on the political episodes of corporate control in the country case studies. I could not have assembled all of this information without the help of an outstanding group of research assistants: Hiroshi Amemiya, Ben Ansell, Gregoire de Chammard, Nathan Cisneros, Dilyan Donchev, Jane Gingrich, Tomohiro Hamakawa, Anne Gaëlle Heliot-Javelle, Orie Hirano, Guillaume Liegey, David Vermijs, and Chiaki Yamada. I appreciate the work of each of these people and acknowledge my gratitude to them. Elizabeth Steffen and Paul Yoon provided excellent administrative assistance over the years.

These final words are being written at the European University Institute, which is where the book was first born as a new project in 2003. Much of my time in between was spent at the Harvard Kennedy School. Both these institutions have proved congenial places to do research and to learn from colleagues and students. This research was supported financially by grants from the Weatherhead Center for International Affairs at Harvard University; the Mossavar-Rahmani Center for Business and Government and the Malcolm Wiener Center for Social Policy at the Harvard Kennedy School; and from the Abe Fellowship Program, which is supported by the Japan Foundation Center for Global Partnership and administered by the Social Science Research Council and the American Council of Learned Societies. For this financial support I am grateful.

The addition of the Japanese case has added much to this project, and even more so than for the European cases, I could not have done it without a great deal of support. Thanks to Nobuhiro Hiwatari and the Institute of Social Science at the University of Tokyo, and to RIETI, the Research Institute of Economy, Trade, and Industry, both of which provided institutional homes during my stay in Tokyo. Jun Kurihara was kind in assisting me in manifold ways with pursuing my research in Japan. On the personal side, I would like to thank Kay Shimizu, Shizuko Shimizu, and Michiko Shimizu for their unbounded generosity in introducing my family to the many delights of life in Tokyo, and for their help in navigating some of the unexpected challenges that arose during our stay there. Arigato gozaimasu.

I'd like to express my gratitude to Lew Bateman of Cambridge University Press for his support of the book and for his ideas to improve it, and to Margaret Levi for including it in the Cambridge Studies in Comparative Politics series. Jennifer Carey helped polish the prose, and Nathan Cisneros put together the index. Thanks to both. Parts of Chapters 2 and 3 originally appeared in my article "Institutional Change in Contemporary Capitalism," *World Politics* Vol. 57, No. 2. Permission from Cambridge University Press to reprint those sections is gratefully acknowledged.

My family has been gracious in tolerating challenging transitions between Cambridge, Tokyo, and Florence as this book has taken shape. I am forever grateful to my wife, Mary Louise, for her moral and intellectual support. Thanks also to each of our four children – Sophie, Sebastian, Savannah, and Saralynn – for the gusto with which they have embraced the leap into cosmopolitan living, and for their patience with the occasional absences the research for this book has entailed.

I dedicate this book to my mother, Lynn Watson, who will find it hard to believe that I have written a book in which the word "quiet" figures so prominently.

Pepper D. Culpepper

San Domenico di Fiesole, Italy

June 2010

Corporate Control and Political Salience

The hostile takeover is the signature act of no-holds-barred capitalism. While discussions of friendly mergers between companies are conducted in the language of cooperation and synergy, the discourse around unfriendly takeovers is replete with metaphors of war and violent conflict. The assets of conquered companies are treated as the spoils of war: the losing firm can be ransacked, reorganized, or liquidated, with grim consequences for its employees. Companies themselves are the site of many political compromises over fundamental issues such as wages, health care, and pensions. Hostile takeovers disrupt these compromises. After takeovers, companies become bundles of assets like any other, with some parts disposed of to pay off debts and others sloughed off in the name of strategic reorientation. The willingness of a state to allow hostile takeovers is therefore of no small political import.

In the United States and the United Kingdom, hostile takeovers are considered business as usual. These economies, where companies freely change hands, are described as having "active" markets for corporate control. In contrast, the coordinated market economies of continental Europe and Japan long opted for what are called "passive" markets for corporate control, in which hostile takeovers were extremely rare. In these countries, political and business leaders colluded to prevent large companies from being treated as simple commodities. At the beginning of the 1990s, as the implications of global financial liberalization were becoming clear, Michel Albert warned his fellow Europeans of the fundamentally different role of the company in an economy with an active market for corporate control:

> Buying a company, for the American capitalist, is no different from buying a property or a painting. It is therefore perfectly logical for the shareholder-kings to do as they please with the company they have just purchased, breaking it up and selling off the segments which do not interest them.[1]

---

[1] Albert (1993: 75).

Over the past two decades, the deregulation of capital markets around the world has challenged the institutional arrangements that formerly impeded hostile takeovers in Europe and Japan. Large companies have been forced to concentrate on ensuring a satisfactory rate of return for increasingly demanding shareholders. Foreign investors, particularly Anglo-American pension and hedge funds, have raised their ownership stakes in many domestic markets, demanding in return political and firm-level reforms to improve corporate performance.[2] These investors come with the promise of cheap and abundant capital, but there is a price. If investors are not satisfied with the performance of the existing management team, they may choose to sell their stakes to a bidder promising to make better use of the company's assets. Given the pressures of financial markets and the political demands of activist investors, many scholars predict the death of national models of capitalism.[3]

In France, for example, hostile takeovers have become far more common since the late 1990s. At the root of this shift were not legislative decisions, but rather institutional choices made by the managers of large companies, which stripped French firms of the defenses they had once enjoyed. Companies in France used to protect themselves from hostile takeovers through a system of high average shareholding concentration, in which a few owners controlled a large portion of the voting shares of a given company; these protections were reinforced by a network of mutual shareholding among French companies. At roughly the same time as their French counterparts, managers in Japan also abandoned the networks of stable share ownership that used to protect firms from takeover. These managers were also key players in making significant changes to Japan's legal system that have brought Japanese takeover law much closer to that of the United States.

Other countries in Europe have resisted the economic and political pressures to create active markets for corporate control. Most Dutch and German companies continue to enjoy the institutional protections that have for decades limited the frequency of hostile takeovers in these countries. German companies have perpetuated the patterns of concentrated ownership that their French counterparts have forsaken, which makes it exceedingly difficult to acquire a large German company against the will of its senior managers. Dutch companies continue to count on legal arrangements to discourage hostile takeovers, as they have throughout the postwar period.[4] Despite repeated political attacks on them between 1994 and 2006, these Dutch protections remain firmly in place as of this writing. In the Netherlands, as in Germany, the market for corporate control is largely quiescent.

Why did some markets for corporate control become more active in the face of financial globalization, while others remained passive? Existing explanations point either to partisan political entrepreneurs or to cross-class coalitions as the causal drivers of institutional change. The partisan account looks to political

[2] Tiberghien (2007), Ahmadjian (2007), Schaede (2008), Goyer (forthcoming).
[3] Hansmann and Kraakman (2001), Höpner (2003).
[4] De Jong and Röell (2005).

parties in general, and reformist politicians of the left in particular, as the likely motor of corporate governance reform.[5] The coalitional approach looks for the emergence of a transparency coalition, which brings together institutional investors with workers interested in ensuring shareholder oversight of their managers, as the most probable source of reform of systems of corporate control.[6] Although one of these theories stresses political parties and the other interest groups, they share the same underlying logic. A dominant political group seizes power through an election in which it wins the most votes; that group passes laws that secure or undermine institutions of corporate control; and these legal reforms destroy old institutions and replace them with new ones, born of legislative power. These two explanatory models, in other words, treat corporate control like any other high-profile battle in democracies, where public opinion and legislative votes are the most valuable currencies.

In this book, I argue that the outcomes observed in these four countries result not from variations in government partisanship or from different interest group coalitions, but from differences in the political preferences of managerial organizations. In all four countries, the rules favored by the managers of large firms are those that triumphed, often against substantial political opposition. The preferences of managers differed across these four countries, depending on the strength of labor organizations in their firms.[7] The globalization of international finance after 1990 offered firms in coordinated market economies the possibility of greater access to foreign capital. In return, foreign investors demanded that companies focus on their core competencies – that is, doing only what the firm does best – in order to increase shareholder value.[8] Focusing on core competencies requires that companies be able to reorganize rapidly, a process that frequently involves making workforce reductions. How managers responded to financial globalization depended on the shop floor strength of workers and their capacity to limit reorganizational initiatives. Where labor organizations were weak at the firm level, as in France and Japan, company managers pushed for radical reorganization and accepted active markets for corporate control as the price of doing business in a global economy.[9] Where works councils were entrenched enough to retain effective veto power over reorganizational plans, as in Germany and the Netherlands, managers found it too costly to abrogate their existing ties to other stakeholders.[10] They therefore

---

[5] Cioffi and Höpner (2006), Tiberghien (2007).

[6] Gourevitch and Shinn (2005).

[7] This argument about the source of managerial preferences draws on the work of Michel Goyer (2002, 2006a, forthcoming).

[8] Tiberghien (2007), Schaede (2008).

[9] Goyer and Hancké (2005), Schaede (2008).

[10] Jackson (2003), Goyer (2002, forthcoming). Strong firm-level labor is not only a constraint. Works councils can improve production by providing information from workers that management lacks. The cost, from a managerial and shareholder perspective, is the slower process of adjustment (Freeman and Lazear 1995). The devolution of autonomy to workers is a central part of Dutch and German production strategies, one that managers often consider an advantage in international competition (Goyer 2006a).

retained existing takeover protections in order to blunt the influence of institutional investors over managerial decision making.

Even though managerial preferences varied across these countries, managerial political power did not. In each case, managers got the regime of corporate control they wanted. What is interesting about the variation in regimes of corporate control is that they all shared this common cause. Why were managers always able to get what they wanted in the politics of corporate control, even when they wanted different things?

This book offers a framework for understanding the sources of managerial power in the politics of corporate control. This framework emphasizes the advantages of managerial organizations under conditions of *low political salience*. The political salience of an issue refers to its importance to the average voter, relative to other political issues.[11] Baldly stated, organized managers typically prevail in political conflicts over corporate control because those issues are of little immediate interest to most voters. Managerial organizations generally win under these conditions because they have access to superior weapons for battles that take place away from the public spotlight. Low salience political issues are decided through what I call "quiet politics." The managerial weapons of choice in quiet politics are a strong lobbying capacity and the deference of legislators and reporters toward managerial expertise. The political competitors of managers, be they liberalizing politicians or crusading institutional investors, lack access to equivalent political armaments, so long as voters evince little sustained interest in and knowledge about an issue.

Just as national armies use different strategies to fight other states than to fight guerrillas, so do managerial organizations rely on different resources under conditions of high and low political salience. Battles over issues of high salience force managers to seek interest group allies and persuade public opinion, which is why business organizations lose many high-profile political fights.[12] In low salience conflicts, on the contrary, the biggest army does not always win. Superior knowledge of the terrain and access to key decisionmakers are the most valuable resources in quiet politics, compensating for the small number of votes directly represented by senior managers in any democracy.

The importance of political salience in determining the political resources of interest groups has broad implications for our understanding of democratic politics. Much current work in political science looks to electoral politics and the competitive dynamics of parties and elections to explain major variations in policy outcomes. Such work emphasizes how political parties position themselves on a given issue with respect to the material interests of the voters for whom they are competing – notably, the "median voter," who sits at the very center of the preference distribution of the electorate.[13] Yet not all political

---

[11] Kollman (1998: 9).

[12] Smith (2000).

[13] Exceptionally, some scholars of public opinion – especially of American public opinion – do include salience in their models of public influence on policy (Kollman 1998, Jacobs and Page

competition takes place through high stakes elections, though political scientists often assume otherwise.

Many issues in capitalist democracies are not subject to a popular vote. Politics always involves conflicts among different groups, but the most effective weapons in those conflicts vary – depending, critically, on whether the issues at stake are of high or low political salience. Models of politics that assume a median-voter logic misrepresent the dynamics of some conflicts by failing to incorporate variations in issue salience. This is akin to assuming that the biggest armies always win guerrilla wars. The issue of corporate control, as an area of characteristically low political salience, constitutes a laboratory for the study of how political battles differ under these conditions.

Political Salience and Interest Group Politics

For political parties operating in a democracy, winning is about getting the most votes. But for interest groups, winning elections is not the only way to achieve political goals. Groups can also exercise other power resources: trying to influence legislators or parties on how to vote, or indeed, whether to put an issue to a vote at all.[14] Political parties take positions on high-profile issues, such as taxes and pensions, because voters care about their position on these issues and will hold them to account for it in future elections. These are the types of issues political scientists describe as having high political salience, in that most voters care and are at least minimally informed about them. But issues such as corporate control are, by virtue of their low visibility and technical opacity, much less likely to come back and haunt governments in an election. "Read my lips: No new poison pills," is an unlikely campaign slogan in any country. When an issue is of little interest to most voters, the press has little incentive to cover it and ambitious politicians gain little by acquiring expertise in it.[15] This creates an ideal political terrain for interest groups with a concentrated interest in the outcomes of the political process.[16]

It is well-known among students of regulation that issue areas with concentrated costs and dispersed benefits are prone to capture by an interest group that has much at stake.[17] Only those with very intense interests in the rules of corporate control pay attention to the complex area of corporate governance

2005, Soroka and Wlezien 2010). Perhaps for reasons of subdisciplinary specialization, these important insights have had little impact on the study of comparative politics.

[14] The "power resources" approach to politics, associated with the work of Walter Korpi (1974, 1985) and others, focused on how class solidarity among workers could lead to collective action through political parties of the left, which would then enact welfare state policies. That work concentrated attention on the power resources that are useful in the high salience arena of formal politics – votes. The power resources of managerial organizations emphasized in this book are different from those stressed in Korpi's work.

[15] Wilson (1973), Gormley (1986).

[16] Olson (1965).

[17] Wilson (1973).

regulation all the time. Managers care, because rules governing corporate control directly determine their autonomy. How easily a company can be taken over is a good indicator of how easy it is to replace that company's senior managers. Large shareholders also care, as they have a strong incentive to ensure that managers do not deviate too far from their preferences. Individual minority shareholders have a stake in these questions, but their holdings are often not large enough to compel them to inform themselves about corporate regulations, even though their collective benefit from a shift to active markets for corporate control might be substantial. Institutional minority shareholders, such as mutual funds, *do* care about the rules of corporate control, and they often oppose the political positions taken by managers. By contrast, workers with pension income invested in companies do not have this sort of interest. They are likely to be far more concerned about immediate issues of job protection and wages than the rules that govern companies in which their pension funds own shares. We should therefore expect that workers and their unions will be irrelevant voices in the politics of corporate control, both uninterested and unlikely to be heeded by politicians when they occasionally do express an interest in the rules governing hostile takeovers. This intensity of preferences leads three groups – institutional shareholders, managers, and large shareholders – to have a much more concentrated interest in the outcomes of policy reform than the other actors engaged in the corporate governance arena. Managers and large shareholders have closely aligned interests, and as we will see, their position as business insiders gives them political resources that are usually unavailable to institutional minority shareholders, which are typically seen as outsiders.

Managers have concentrated interests in corporate control, but those with concentrated interests do not always win the day in regulatory politics.[18] Business frequently loses political battles when the general public pays attention to them, because when the public pays attention to issues, political parties start paying attention to the opinion of the median voter and stop paying attention to powerful interest groups.[19] When interest groups think public opinion is on their side, they will frequently launch mobilization campaigns to draw public attention to their issue.[20]

How do previously ignored issues become politically salient? Two of the most common causes are a crisis or the mobilization efforts of political entrepreneurs, such as Ralph Nader.[21] Either force can make large numbers of voters aware of the implications of policies, even policies that have only a negligible benefit for them. James Q. Wilson argued that political entrepreneurs "can mobilize public sentiment (by revealing a scandal or capitalizing on a crisis), put the opponents of the plan publicly on the defensive (by accusing them

---

[18] Vogel (1987), Smith (2000).
[19] Schattschneider (1960), Baron (1994).
[20] Kollman (1998).
[21] Wilson (1980).

of deforming babies or killing motorists), and associate the legislation with widely shared values (clean air, pure water, health, and safety)."[22] Sometimes sudden events concentrate public opinion on a previously ignored topic and render it politically salient.[23] In the area of corporate governance, the Enron scandal in the United States created a broad upsurge of interest in the issue of corporate pay. That interest, to a considerable degree, arose because the existence of a scandal led the media to focus the spotlight of public attention on the issue.

The news media, indeed, occupies a central place in modern democracies. It provides politicians with an indicator of what information citizens are getting and what stories reporters think are newsworthy.[24] Politicians can pay attention to opinion polls to find out public *preferences* on political issues, but they have greater difficulty assessing the political *salience* of an issue: how much the average voter cares about this issue, relative to other issues.[25] Media coverage is one way for politicians to infer salience. Alexander Dyck and his colleagues provide a telling example of the impact of changing press coverage on the political influence of business in their study of votes in the U.S. Senate on the Seventeenth Amendment to the U.S. Constitution. The Seventeenth Amendment called for direct election of senators, rather than their appointment by state governments, and it was seen at the time as a way to limit the influence of big business on the Senate. The amendment failed in the Senate in 1902 but passed in 1911. Dyck et al. analyze the two roll call votes on it, looking in particular at how the votes of individual senators changed after the publication of a series of sensationalist articles in the muckraking magazine *Cosmopolitan* in 1906, entitled "The Treason of the Senate." As voters became informed about the issue of corruption and its connection to the direct election of senators – and as politicians became aware of the importance of the issue to the voting public – the ability of big business to get the vote it wanted from individual senators decreased.[26] When voters pay attention to an issue, politicians will start paying attention to public opinion. Media coverage is a key mechanism for bringing issues to public attention, and the media will publish more stories about issues that voters, as news consumers, will purchase.

Yet media outlets are not concerned primarily with making democracy work better. Their more immediate goals are to break big stories and to return a profit.[27] And the politics of corporate control is not an easy subject for reporters to sell – in part because its relevance to most citizens is uncertain, but

---

[22] Wilson (1980: 370).

[23] Contemporary theorists of the American policy-making process call this the phenomenon of issue intrusion (Jones and Baumgartner 2005).

[24] Patterson (1993), Tifft and Jones (1999).

[25] Kollman (1998).

[26] Controlling for partisan affiliation and regional political factors, Dyck et al. (2008) found a robust and significant correlation between the sales of *Cosmopolitan* by state and a switching of individual votes on the proposed amendment from "no" to "yes" between 1902 and 1911.

[27] Hamilton (2004).

also because the issues involved are complex. Corporate governance disclosure requirements, for example, are probably not of any lower political salience than are automobile inspection regulations. But the issues involved in car inspections are straightforward and easily grasped, even for those who are not mechanics. By contrast, disclosure requirements and hostile takeover defenses are complex matters, not easily translated into clear and concise prose that will hold the attention of a reader. It is easier to explain to voters, and voters can be made to care about these issues more easily, if the political stakes can be conveyed transparently. The combination of low salience and high complexity means that both journalists and political entrepreneurs have difficulty convincing the general public to pay attention to an issue.[28] This is an ideal combination of circumstances for managerial groups, which both understand the issues of corporate control and care about them a great deal, to wield disproportionate political influence.

The problem, it must be stressed, is not simply that the complexity of issues of corporate control makes it difficult for average voters to get a handle on them. When voters are faced with complex matters, they often use short cuts or informational cues to figure out their position.[29] In a California referendum on insurance reform, for example, voters who had little familiarity with the issue, but who knew the position of the insurance industry on it, voted the same way as voters with high knowledge of the issue.[30] In the case of corporate control, however, the complexity of the issues dissuades both the media and politicians from investing their limited capital in convincing voters to care.

Given low public salience and high policy complexity, senior managers and the political organizations that represent them have a strong incentive and the material and informational wherewithal to intervene in the politics of corporate control. To use a forensic metaphor, we have now established the motive for managerial intervention. We have also explained why the two forces that would normally police the managerial pursuit of self-interest – politicians and the media – have no incentive to oppose managers under conditions of low political salience. What we have yet to discuss are the particular weapons that managerial organizations use to achieve their political ends under quiet politics. The organizational advantages of managers – their weapons – flow from the low salience and the technical opacity of the issue of corporate control.

The Managerial Arsenal: Lobbying, Working Groups, and Press Framing

Low salience creates few incentives for political parties to mobilize in the area of corporate control. Even when there are political fights, managers can deploy three strong resources that make them the favorite in most contests over

---

[28] Gormley (1986).
[29] Lupia (1992, 1994), Sniderman et al. (1991). I am grateful to Peter Gourevitch for reminding me of the relevance of informational cues in this context.
[30] Lupia (1994).

takeover rules: lobbying capacity, the use of private interest committees, and influencing the tenor of press coverage. All three weapons acquire their force from the deference accorded them by politicians and the media because of their expertise in running the companies that serve as the productive engine of the economy.

The first advantage is in lobbying the government and members of the legislature. The strength of corporate lobbyists in the United States is a staple of American political discourse, but empirical research shows that the money of business lobbyists does not always translate to policy success, even in the United States.[31] The importance popular discourse places on money and politics actually distorts the understanding of the power of lobbying in most other advanced industrial countries. Companies have money, and money of course helps change minds. Yet managerial lobbying often derives most of its strength from the *expertise* of managers and their lawyers. Company managers know more about the effect of legal changes on their companies than do politicians, and politicians know this.[32] The high complexity of this field makes it difficult for politicians to challenge the expertise of business leaders, and the low salience of corporate governance lowers their incentive to invest in redressing their imbalance of knowledge.

A second advantage of managers is the fact that many governments grant significant agenda-setting capacity to informal working groups, in which managers have a preeminent voice. As in the case of direct lobbying, the power of managers in this context is the power to set the terms of the debate in an environment that is established with an explicit eye to protecting their interests. For example, the British Cadbury Committee was established by the Conservative government in 1990, with a mandate to elucidate best practices in corporate governance. By 2001, such codes had been drawn up in almost every member country of the European Union.[33] Following the structure of the Cadbury Committee, such informal codes were developed in private, "expert committees," where managerial interests were heavily represented. Obviously, such working groups are more likely to produce recommendations close to the ideal point of organized managers than is a legislative committee. But there is also a temporal dimension to the use of informal groups in public governance that should also be recognized. I have already observed that unexpected events can temporarily raise the salience of issues, thus creating a policy window for would-be entrepreneurs and a more level playing field for opponents of managerial incumbents. The institution of the private interest committee is a way for managerial interests to appear to relent to calls for greater regulation without transferring such regulation to an unpredictable forum like a legislature. Instead, a private interest body can move at its own speed, delivering its findings at a moment when the temporary rise in public salience has dissipated.

[31] Baumgartner et al. (2009).
[32] Bernhagen and Bräuninger (2005).
[33] Eberle and Lauter (2008).

Thus, the private interest committee is an institution that can support incumbent interest at any given time, but also one that allows managers to assert some control over the timing of new regulatory initiatives.

Managerial expertise can also allow business to influence the tone of media coverage. The voting public only pays attention to the issue of corporate control on rare occasions, as when a big takeover story suddenly makes headlines. This happened across Europe, for example, when the world's largest steel company, Mittal Steel, made a hostile bid for the European steel company Arcelor in 2006. During such moments, the public pays attention to the issue of corporate control, but the subject's underlying complexity remains. In such a situation – which is one of temporarily high salience – managers and managerial organizations can exploit the same informational asymmetries that allow them to be effective lobbyists in trying to frame press coverage in terms favorable to them. A situation of temporarily high salience differs in an important way from one of durably high salience. Durably high salience creates incentives for reporters to develop independent sources of expertise to understand issues they have to cover frequently, thus reducing the information asymmetry they face in a situation of temporarily high salience. The cause of high salience is also relevant to the influence managers can have on press framing. If a scandal such as Enron causes reporters to impugn the managerial reputation for competence, then managers will have a harder time dominating the framing of press coverage of the issue, because the very reason it came to public attention is due to a failure of management. Managerial organizations are especially likely to succeed in influencing the framing of press coverage of an issue when its political salience is only fleeting and when the cause of the temporary rise in public interest does not undermine their reputation for economic expertise.

Framing refers to the "subtle alterations in the statement or presentation of judgment and choice problems."[34] In such discussions, managerial organizations have a strong incentive to link their own interests with the broader interests of the national economy. For example, where managers are interested in blocking hostile takeovers, they will employ metaphors that highlight the "unfair" vulnerability of their firms to foreign competition and the consequent threats to national economic independence. Where they favor takeovers, they will speak of the benefits of market competition for the national economy. Such strategies are an occupational hazard for reporters, who always have to deal with the possibility that news sources are attempting to elicit sympathetic coverage, or that the desire to tell an interesting story leads journalists themselves to adopt a particular narrative frame.[35] Journalists are aware that

---

[34] Iyengar (1991: 11).

[35] See, for example, the study by the Project for Excellence in Journalism entitled "Framing the News" (PEJ 1998), which documented the variety of frames employed by American journalists in their coverage of news events. One finding of the study was that only sixteen percent of front page articles were written under a "straight news frame," i.e., without an identifiable interpretive lens.

business leaders have an interest in projecting a vision that favors them, and some scholars of press and public opinion are skeptical of the view that the media is a passive "conveyor belt" for elite opinion.[36] Yet journalists are constrained by their need to convey complex issues so that readers can understand them. This is an advantage for managers, and we expect them to try to deploy it when possible. As in political lobbying, being able to set the terms of press debate is no silver bullet to ensure managerial victory. But it is another weapon in a powerful arsenal.[37]

Salience, Managerial Power, and Informal Institutions

This arsenal includes formidable weapons that help managers influence formal political processes. Yet there is also an additional source of advantage for managerial groups in low salience political contests. Some battles in the area of corporate control are fought not over the wording of laws, but over patterns of behavior maintained by private actors. These I designate as informal institutions: regularized rules or practices that are not established by lawmakers or regulators.[38] Often these informal practices directly involve large companies, as in the case of cross-shareholding. Cross-shareholding refers to the practice by which companies hold each other's shares for some jointly agreed purpose, such as strategic partnership or protection against takeovers by third parties. Cross-shareholding is one of many informal institutions that can protect companies from a hostile takeover. Historically, these institutions may have been consciously developed with the consent of political parties, as was the case for Japanese and French cross-shareholding.[39] They are not, however, legal institutions, which governments can construct or abolish as they see fit.[40] Instead, these institutions depend on private decision making. I call those who decide the fate of informal institutions institutional incumbents: the current players in a given institutional regime. Where companies are the principals involved in these institutions, as is the case in cross-shareholding, the institutional incumbents are the managers of these large companies. If informal institutions play an important role in regulating the functioning of markets of corporate control, managerial power is strengthened further, because in such cases other managers are the most important actors for managers to influence in order to achieve their political objectives.

The fact that the area of corporate control often involves informal governance is not incidental to the properties that also make it typically a low salience area. Instead, low voter interest in the area means that politicians have little to

---

[36] Baum and Potter (2008).
[37] Guber and Bosso (2007).
[38] Cf. Helmke and Levitsky (2004).
[39] Schmidt (1996), Miyajima and Kuroki (2007).
[40] To be sure, government can pass laws that affect the costs or benefits associated with such institutions.

gain by intervening with public policy. So long as salience is low, institutional incumbents have little reason to fear that governments will step in and reshape the informal institutional order. The same deference that lawmakers extend to businesspeople in lobbying and law writing also works in favor of keeping informal institutions informal. As far as the economy is concerned, "if it ain't broke, don't fix it," is the likely mantra of many an ambitious politician.

To understand the politics of corporate control, therefore, we often need to be able to incorporate how informal institutions change. These are institutions that previous governments have allowed to function without direct government oversight. During episodes of institutional contestation, managerial organizations do not need to convince lawmakers to write laws that favor them; they just need to keep lawmakers from intervening in institutions that are privately maintained. Thus, the status quo favors managerial incumbents in the case of informal institutions. Moreover, unlike legislatures, informal institutions offer no venue in which opposition to institutional incumbents can be expressed. The decision making over informal institutions happens largely beyond the scope of direct public scrutiny.

If this reasoning is correct, it challenges the way many political scientists currently study institutional change, which is to ignore the informal institutions in the economy by assuming they are derivative of formal laws. Some scholars pursue this exclusive focus on formal institutions "because, to the extent that modern economies are *political* economies – that is, governed by politics – they are mainly controlled by norms and sanctions that are *formalized*."[41] Many social scientists who write about the politics of corporate control follow Wolfgang Streeck and Kathleen Thelen in writing only about the formal regulation of corporate governance, conflating regulatory and behavioral practice.[42] By adopting such a formalist definition, these scholars load the theoretical dice on behalf of the assumption that the cause of the difference in political outcomes lies in formal institutions. It is surely true that the politics of institutional change has distributional consequences, and that competing coalitions will advocate an institutional solution closer to their preferred outcome.[43] It does not follow, however, that coalitional bargains are necessarily pushed through legislatures or regulatory agencies.

Much of the action in quiet politics happens outside the legislative or regulatory arenas. Reforms of economic incentives to improve efficient market functioning often fail, as they are unable to change the incentive structure of preexisting informal rules, such as those of clientelism.[44] Many economists and most sociologists, in fact, focus on the role of informal institutions in stabilizing economic outcomes, whether as norms of reciprocity that lower transaction costs or as logics of appropriateness that constrain what choices

---

[41] Streeck and Thelen (2005: 10), emphasis in original.
[42] Gourevitch and Shinn (2005), Pagano and Volpin (2005), Höpner (2003).
[43] Amable (2003).
[44] North (2005).

actors reflexively make in structured interactions. If these institutions matter most for the functioning of political economies, then not only are Streeck and Thelen wrong to conflate politics with formal institutions, but empirical inquiry inspired by their approach will fail even to examine the institutions that matter most for actual changes in political economies.

Partisan and Coalitional Theories of Corporate Control

Focusing on the political advantages low salience creates for managers marks a significant departure from the way in which social scientists have previously studied the politics of corporate control.[45] Past scholarship has attempted to explain both the origins of ownership patterns and contemporary variations in systems of corporate control. Throughout this book I will compare the predictions derived from this existing work with those derived from the quiet politics framework laid out in this chapter. This section details the important contributions of this prior research, which can be summarized under the rubric of explanations based either on the action of political parties (partisan theory) or of interest group coalitions (coalitional theory).

Most scholarship on comparative corporate governance starts from the observation of variation between countries with concentrated and dispersed share ownership. In the United States, for example, the largest shareholder in a corporation usually holds a very small proportion of that company's overall shares. The ownership of the average company's shares is dispersed over a large number of shareholders. In Germany, by contrast, the largest shareholder in a company typically owns a significant proportion of that company's outstanding shares, meaning that share ownership is concentrated in few hands. Concentrated ownership is sometimes known as "blockholding," because the controlling owners possess large "blocks" of shares in a company. By dint of their ability to influence managerial decisions, blockholders are able to exploit minority shareholders. In countries with dispersed ownership, managers may be able to elude the monitoring of owners altogether, a point made by Adolph Berle and Gardiner Means in their foundational work on the subject.[46] It is this persistent divergence among countries in their patterns of ownership and control that political theories of corporate control generally try to explain.

---

[45] One important exception is the work of Lucian Bebchuk and Charles Fried, who have developed an approach known as the managerial power perspective, which they use with great success to explain the rise of executive compensation in the United States (Bebchuk and Fried 2004). Bebchuk and Fried emphasize the power of managers vis-à-vis shareholders and board of directors, rather than in the broader political sense in which I use it in this book. They also underscore the importance of arrangements for "camouflage" that keep the true extent of executive remuneration from being apparent to outsiders, which is an important element in whether or not executive pay triggers public outrage, thereby becoming politically salient. We return to the particular issue of executive pay in Chapter 6.

[46] Berle and Means (1932).

The difference between countries with and without blockholding is largely a product of politics. On this point, political scientists, legal scholars, and economists can agree. There are directly political causes of this divergence, such as the influence of the legislation that favors or impedes concentrated ownership. In addition, there are also other institutional relationships in the economy, such as those governing industrial relations, which indirectly facilitate or impede different patterns of ownership. These institutional relationships, too, have their origins in political deals. But the exact political mechanisms of institutional origins and persistence in patterns of ownership are a matter of dispute. Simplifying somewhat, we can distinguish two broad political approaches to explanation in previous work on corporate control. The first approach – partisan theory – emphasizes variation in the partisanship of governments as the ultimate cause of variation among countries.[47] The second view – coalitional theory – focuses not on parties and elections, but instead on interest groups and the coalitions they build to support their preferred corporate governance regime.[48] Below, I briefly consider the current state of the art in this field as represented, respectively by the contributions of legal scholar Mark Roe and political scientists Peter Gourevitch and James Shinn.[49]

Roe's important contribution was to reveal a fundamental flaw in a popular claim in the law and economics literature, which explains variation among countries through the origins of their legal systems. Civil law countries, such as those in continental Europe, generally have higher shareholder concentration than countries with common law, such as the United States and the United Kingdom. Civil law countries also tend to have a lower degree of "minority shareholder protection" (MSP) than do common law countries. MSP refers to the extent that the legal infrastructure enables small shareholders to hold managers and large shareholders accountable. Some scholars in the law and economics tradition have argued that the difference in the origins of legal systems accounts both for differences in equity market development and in the extent of MSP.[50] This view is a particularly stylized form of institutionalism, in which past legal histories entirely dominate contemporary politics and lock-in the expropriation of minority shareholders. The historical problem with this claim, as Roe and others have noted, is that the development of equity markets and of shareholder protections has varied over time within countries.[51] A constant – the origin of national legal systems – cannot possibly explain a variable – equity market development and MSP.

To explain this temporal variation, Roe identified instead a political cause: the rise of the "stakeholder society" and the political power of the left in the

---

47 Roe (2003, 2006), Cioffi and Höpner (2006), Cioffi (forthcoming), Perotti and von Thadden (2006).
48 Gourevitch and Shinn (2005), Rajan and Zingales (2003), Pagano and Volpin (2005).
49 Roe (2003), Gourevitch and Shinn (2005).
50 LaPorta et al. (1998, 1999).
51 Rajan and Zingales (2003), Roe (2006), Herrigel (2008).

countries of continental Europe and Japan after World War II. "Stakeholders" are all those actors that have a stake in the fate of a company, such as its employees, owners, customers, and local communities. Stakeholders are generally juxtaposed with "shareholders," which refers more narrowly only to those who own shares in a given company. Roe's central claim was that those countries that gave a prominent role to stakeholder views in politics adopted public policies that made it difficult for managers to respond to concerns about shareholder value.[52] Social Democrats chose a host of institutions, such as codetermination and labor market regulation, all of which created agency costs for shareholders. According to Roe, minority shareholders could not effectively monitor managers in these systems. Employment concerns would dominate efficiency concerns in the stakeholder society, and companies could not simply lay off workers in order to restructure in response to changes in market demand. So blockholding emerged as the only viable response to the agency problem facing shareholders in the stakeholder society.[53] Blockholders, because of their concentrated holdings, would have both the interest and the capacity to supervise managers closely, which dispersed shareholders would not.

Roe's work was pioneering in highlighting the connection between stakeholders and politics. Yet his use of social democracy as a conceptual umbrella for the stakeholder society is problematic, as political scientists have been prone to point out. Partisan theorists John Cioffi and Martin Höpner share Roe's fundamental emphasis on political parties as the driving force behind reforms of systems of corporate control. Yet they show in their work that, in places like Germany and Italy, the stakeholder society was also an initiative of Christian Democrats – that is, parties of the center-right.[54] In other words, the institutions supporting passive markets for corporate control were constructed not only by Social Democrats, as in Roe's theory, but also by conservative parties.

Among partisan theorists, there is therefore disagreement over whether we should expect political challenges to passive markets for corporate control to come from parties of the *right* or from parties of the *left*. For Roe, this challenge should obviously come from the opponents of social democracy, that is, parties of the right. For Cioffi and Höpner, by contrast, parties of the left are held to be some of the fiercest *opponents* of large blockholding. In their argument, recent economic changes have created incentives for a growing number of Social Democratic voters to prefer increased transparency and more active markets for corporate control. Thus, during the 1990s parties of the left in several countries passed reform legislation that challenged the institutions that supported passive markets for corporate control. Cioffi and Höpner, like Roe, have underlined important reasons why political parties might be interested in systems of corporate control. In later chapters I assess the empirical validity of

---

[52] Roe (2003: 24).
[53] Roe (2003).
[54] Cioffi and Höpner (2006), Höpner (2007).

these theoretical expectations by examining how parties of both left and right act during episodes of actual or potential reform.

For coalitional theorists, contrariwise, political parties are not the most likely agents of reform. Instead, scholars such as Gourevitch and Shinn argue that the political roots of corporate control are to be found in interest group coalitions, especially cross-class coalitions. The most likely source of passive markets for corporate control, by this logic, is neither Social Democrats nor Christian Democrats, as the partisan representatives of their respective social classes. It is instead a cross-class coalition, joining managers and workers, each of whom faces the potential of job loss if hostile takeovers become more prevalent. The big losers facing this cross-class coalition are owners – especially, minority shareholders – who do not get maximal shareholder value in order to allow these corporate insiders to expropriate part of the firm's profits. Just as political parties are not the agents of institutional origin in the coalitional perspective, neither are they agents of institutional change. The major threats to the corporatist compromise come from a defection of one of the groups involved in the compromise. Workers might decide that they prefer to have greater oversight of managers, especially as their pension income is increasingly invested in equity markets.[55] They could then join with minority shareholders in a "transparency coalition," which seeks greater accountability for any managerial choices. Alternatively, managers can defect from the corporatist compromise to join investors in an "investor coalition." The incentive for managers to do so is the possibility to increase their share of firm profits, at the expense of labor, even in the presence of strong minority shareholder protection. The coalitional explanation for blockholding, as one that results from a corporatist compromise, acknowledges that compromises are fragile things that can be easily broken.

For this reason, coalitional theorists also focus on the importance of electoral institutions through which social preferences are aggregated. In particular, proportional representation (PR) electoral systems facilitate the survival of the corporatist coalition between workers and managers.[56] PR electoral institutions work by slowing down the possibility of political change in the absence of broad political support for an initiative. PR thus makes possible a credible commitment among different partners to the coalition by limiting the likelihood of defection by one group.[57] The creation of other veto points in the political system, such as the requirement of corporatist consultation, further reinforces the credibility of the commitment to a corporatist coalition. Thus, the protection of passive markets for corporate control runs in part through the existence of political institutions that slow any efforts to defect from it by skittish coalitional partners.

[55] Gourevitch and Shinn (2005).
[56] Cf. Pagano and Volpin (2005).
[57] Gourevitch and Shinn (2005: 76–77), Hall and Soskice (2001), Wood (2001).

The great virtue of coalitional theory is that it breaks with the assumption that political parties are the major actors in the politics of corporate control. It focuses instead on the interests of specific social groups, which respond not to general political salience but to their own political preferences. Workers and managers may indeed have common incentives to promote passive markets for corporate control, even if their respective political parties do not share those ideological preferences. Coalitional theory, by recognizing the variation in the intensity and direction of preferences across social classes, provides a more realistic window into the formation of political interests. However, as in the partisan account, coalitional work assumes away the power resources of different interest groups, reasoning instead from the logic of preference aggregation embodied in the electoral system. In this model, interest groups only achieve their ends by engineering a political majority, given the electoral system of the country in which they operate.

Partisan and coalitional theories share two features. First, they emphasize winning national elections and the ability to make laws that go along with winning these elections. Their internal political logic hinges on the idea that the most important resource in a democracy is always the number of seats in the legislature. A second shared feature of the partisan and coalitional approaches is their focus on formal rules. Both models of politics suggest that controlling the character of public policy determines whether a country ends up with concentrated or diffuse shareholding. These models assume that changing public policy – that is, laws and regulations – is necessary and sufficient to change institutions of ownership. Both partisan and coalitional approaches simply assume that politics matters *because* of the public policy it produces, which then creates the incentives that lead to corporate governance outcomes.[58]

Neither approach admits a place for nonlegal rules of the game. Each theory acknowledges that such informal rules play a role in stabilizing systems of corporate governance. Yet their models of change, which are exclusively centered on public policy making, have little to say about how the dynamics of change may differ across formal and informal institutional arenas. Seizing a majority in a national legislature may allow opponents of an existing institutional arrangement to pass laws hostile to that arrangement. But institutional change is difficult to achieve via legislative fiat when many of the relevant institutional rules are informal.[59] It is not clear how a transparency coalition or a party of the left that opposes informal arrangements of stable shareholding can translate its support in the legislature into real institutional change, particularly when institutional incumbents favor the existing set of rules.[60]

Coalitional and partisan theories of corporate governance both offer convincing political accounts of the origins of regimes of corporate control. As befits their roots in legal and political science scholarship, though, they stress

[58] E.g., Gourevitch and Shinn (2005: 83).
[59] Aoki (2001).
[60] Culpepper (2007).

a world in which conflict happens in legislatures, and where votes are the most valuable currency. Enough of those votes can make laws, and it is laws and political institutions that are the major intervening variable between political forces and corporate governance outcomes. When corporate governance politics is highly politically salient, these theories are likely to be a helpful representation of reality. Under conditions of low political salience, though, neither votes nor formal rules are likely to be the most crucial variables in the political construction and maintenance of regimes of corporate control. To understand the dynamics of change in systems of corporate control, we need a theory that incorporates variations in salience and the role of power resources that are not ultimately tied to votes in a legislature.

Strategy of Research

The research for this book began with a question: faced with the common shock of financial globalization, why do some systems of corporate control change while others remain stable? As the outcomes in the different systems were not clear when I began this project, it seemed prudent to take as one starting hypothesis that different institutions for securing passive markets for corporate control might have different chances of surviving. Different countries use a variety of means to achieve passive markets for corporate control.[61] The largest coordinated market economies in Europe, France, and Germany, historically depended on high ownership concentration to provide companies with patient ownership. Some other countries have managed to secure inactive markets for corporate control even without high ownership concentration – Japan by using cross-shareholding networks, the Netherlands by using trust foundations anchored in law. Achieving variation on this potentially relevant variable was the origin of the selection of the four cases studied.[62]

Over the course of this research, it became clear to me that what was most remarkable about these cases was not the variation in outcomes, in which national markets of corporate control moved in starkly different directions in France and Japan than in the Netherlands and Germany. Instead, what was striking was the fact that, in all cases, the outcomes reflected the preferences of managerial organizations. This observation was puzzling in light of the theoretical expectations of partisan and coalitional approaches to the politics of corporate governance. Thus, the book became an inquiry into the mechanisms that drive political change over time within individual countries. In the succeeding chapters I confront the causal mechanisms associated with quiet politics against those of coalitional and partisan theories, which also try to explain contemporary changes in regimes of corporate control.[63]

---

[61] Franks and Mayer (1995), Gourevitch and Shinn (2005).

[62] In fact, these features of systems of corporate control proved not to be relevant to their durability, as the outcome in France and Japan were similar to each other, and different from the outcomes observed in Germany and the Netherlands.

[63] Cioffi and Höpner (2006), Gourevitch and Shinn (2005).

The methodological approach I use is primarily one of qualitative comparison. The partisan and coalitional accounts of concentrated shareholding are complex causal arguments that involve the interaction of political actors, political institutions, and the temporal discontinuity imposed by wartime destruction. The country-level data used to test these complex arguments seldom allow us to disentangle the effects of political and institutional mechanisms, which are heavily correlated. For example, it is consistent with the arguments in Gourevitch and Shinn that proportional representation electoral systems will make it harder to change systems of corporate control.[64] This claim works through a specific mechanism: coalition governments, which are by definition built from different interests in society, will have difficulty overturning complex social compromises between different social groups. By way of contrast, governments elected in majoritarian systems, as in France, are more likely to rule as single-party governments, and thus to be able to introduce changes that break with past social promises. Does this mean the French majoritarian electoral system accounts for the dramatic change in French markets? As I show in Chapter 3, that change had little to do with government policy, and much more to do with the changing actions of senior managers. Moreover, at the time of institutional rupture France was governed by a coalition government including Socialists, Greens, and Communists. Thus, the correlation of the French electoral system with systemic change in corporate control is spurious.

Within comparative political research, the problem of how to test complex theories with simple data is endemic. The approach adopted here is to take political processes seriously as a source of information for adjudicating between various mechanisms of political change.[65] This information was gleaned from primary and secondary sources, as well as from fifty-eight interviews with leading actors in the politics of corporate control in the countries studied.[66] Coalitional and partisan theories make predictions about the process we should observe empirically if their mechanisms are the most adequate explanations of the outcomes observed. I compare these predictions with those derived from the quiet politics framework. Methodologically, the approach draws on what Peter Hall calls systematic process analysis, in which "the point is to see if the multiple actions and statements of the actors at each stage of the causal process are consistent with the image of the world implied by each theory."[67]

---

[64] Gourevitch and Shinn (2005), Pagano and Volpin (2005).

[65] Cf. Hedström and Swedberg (1998), Mahoney and Rueschemeyer (2003), George and Bennett (2004).

[66] I conducted all the interviews cited in this book, with the exception of some of the Dutch interviews, which were conducted in Dutch and transcribed into English by my research assistant David Vermijs (based on a semistructured interview protocol designed by me). In Japan, some of the interviews were conducted in English. Others were conducted in Japanese with the help of a simultaneous translator. All interviews are cited in footnotes by the date of interview. In many cases – particularly in the case of senior leaders of managerial organizations – these interviews were conducted on the condition of anonymity. I am grateful to all interviewees for their candid discussions with me, and their anonymity is protected in all cases where it was requested.

[67] Hall (2003: 394).

The intuition behind such an approach is that much useful information is lost when we collapse political processes of change into country-year observations on a limited number of values on explanatory and dependent variables. In the chapters that follow, I attempt to use the available information to assess the success of coalitional, partisan, and quiet politics theories in explaining the change and continuity we observe across these four cases.

The best data on policy salience would come from repeated mass surveys across countries about the importance of corporate control, relative to other political issues. No such data exist. Survey researchers rarely ask questions about popular preferences about corporate control, let alone about how voters evaluate the importance of corporate control relative to other issues of political concern. Moreover, survey research has its own set of problems for assessing the political salience of various issues. Those surveys that try to measure salience typically include a question asking respondents to name the "most important problem" confronting their country. Christopher Wlezien notes that this measure conflates two analytically distinct issues: whether an issue is considered important, and whether or not it is considered a problem.[68] His empirical analysis shows that answers to the "most important problem" question fluctuate wildly, while views about the underlying "importance" of a policy issue are much more stable.

In the absence of public opinion data, I use newspaper coverage as the best available indicator of policy salience. Coverage from major national newspapers has the advantage of being a "reproducible, valid, and transportable measure" of citizen attention to political issues, according to Lee Epstein and Jeffrey Segal.[69] Other studies of the policy-making process also use press coverage as an indicator of political attention to issues.[70] Public opinion scholars have acknowledged the usefulness of such measures, but they have cited the lack of existing data for cross-country measurement as an impediment to using press coverage as an indicator of salience.[71] One objection to existing studies, which often use newspaper coverage in the *New York Times* as their benchmark, is that the *Times* will tend to bias coverage toward the presumably left-of-center political concerns of its editorial board.[72] To counter this concern, I use coverage from major newspapers across the political spectrum in each of the empirical chapters. These chapters also explain the detailed methods for conducting searches across multiple newspapers within each country. Because we expect that business organizations will try to influence the tenor of press coverage, Chapters 3 and 4 also report protocols for assessing the frames under which the media covered political issues of corporate control.[73]

[68] Wlezien (2005).

[69] Epstein and Segal (2000).

[70] E.g., Jones and Baumgartner (2005), Smith (2000).

[71] Netjes and Binnema (2006).

[72] Epstein and Segal (2000).

[73] Cf. Chong and Druckman (2007).

These techniques for assessing political salience of comparable issues across different political economies and the character of issue framing may be useful for other scholars in testing the propositions about political salience developed in this book.

Outline of the Book

The book's structure flows from the goal of evaluating competing causal mechanisms to account for different outcomes in regimes of corporate control. Chapter 2, thus, examines aggregate change and stability in the markets for corporate control in these countries. In the literature on comparative political economy, the institutions that contribute to the protection of passive markets for corporate control are known as patient capital.[74] To assess the overall degree of patient capital in the advanced industrial economies, Chapter 2 uses two different measures of ownership concentration – information on the largest single voting share and on the largest set of stable owners – as well as information on hostile takeover activity across eighteen advanced industrial economies. For the four countries examined in detail in this book, the chapter also examines the changes over time in nationally specific systems for securing passive markets of corporate control. As noted previously, Japan and the Netherlands used distinctive methods to prevent the emergence of an active market for corporate control: the "synthetic blockholders" of the *keiretsu* in Japan and the trust foundations in the Netherlands.[75]

Chapter 3 demonstrates that political parties are not big players in regimes of corporate control. The chapter examines developments in France and Germany from 1995 to 2006. Both countries saw governments of the left come to power during this time, and some scholars have looked at the political programs adopted by these governments as evidence of the importance of party politics for the reform of practices of corporate governance.[76] These party preferences were, in fact, soft, and they were reversed in the face of business lobbying. But equally important, those studies that look only at formal institutions fail to understand the big institutional changes that took place in France, because those changes took place in a set of informal arrangements among companies. As French managers reorganized to face international competition, they decided to abandon concentrated ownership and cross-shareholdings.[77] German managers of nonfinancial firms, meanwhile, were able to maintain their ownership networks despite the departure of many financial companies from those networks. *Pace* the partisan explanatory perspective, reformist governments played little role in these changes. *Pace* the coalitional perspective, labor unions and activist investors played little role in the French case, where

---

[74] Hall and Soskice (2001), Amable (2003).
[75] Gourevitch and Shinn (2005: 170, 183), Roe (2003: 92).
[76] Cioffi and Höpner (2006), Tiberghien (2007).
[77] Culpepper (2005), Goyer (2006a), O'Sullivan (2007).

the changes were driven largely by autonomous decisions at the top of the French industrial hierarchy.[78] So long as political issues are of low political salience, managerial organizations are likely to win political conflicts in both spheres. But their power resources are different in the informal and formal arenas, which is a distinction missed by scholarship focused only on formal institutional change.

Chapter 4 explores the politics of corporate control in the Netherlands. This is an important case for partisan and coalitional theories because the Dutch system does not depend on informal institutions supported by blockholders, as do systems in France and Germany. The protections of Dutch companies are politically constructed, and the battles over them take place in the formal arena. For Roe, these systems are stabilized by a political commitment to the stakeholder society; for Gourevitch and Shinn, these systems are stabilized by a corporatist coalition of managers and workers. From 1994 to 2006, the Netherlands was led by a coalition government that included prominent neoliberal reformers. At the same time, the country also saw a steep rise in the holdings of foreign shareholders. The managers of Dutch large firms, who have to win in the formal institutional arena in order to maintain their system of takeover protection, have a powerful lobbying organization devoted to the defense of these measures. This organization was successful in its major lobbying efforts because Dutch voters, and in turn Dutch political parties, do not care much about issues of corporate control. And even though Dutch rules are formally institutionalized, managers in the Netherlands still benefit from the proclivity of politicians to delegate the details of rule changes to informal bodies, in which managers are well-represented. Because of these political resources, at the end of a period when Dutch takeover protections came under repeated attack from neoliberals in the government, large companies in the Netherlands had successfully defended their passive market for corporate control.

The Japanese system of intercompany shareholding networks limited the possibility for hostile takeovers of most large companies until the late 1990s. As discussed in Chapter 5, Japanese managers did not dismantle this system intentionally, as did their counterparts in France. Instead, the network unraveled as a result of uncoordinated responses by managers to the challenges of the deep recession in Japan during that decade. Japan shared with the Netherlands two political factors emphasized by partisan and interest group theorists: a neoliberal group of reformers inside the ruling party (the Liberal Democratic Party, or LDP) and the dramatic growth in the ownership stakes of foreign institutional investors. In contrast to the situation in the Netherlands, organized employers were the reformist allies of these groups until 2002, actively favoring deregulatory reforms to support their own internal reorganization.[79] When the members of the reformist coalition clashed, as they did over a proposal to require independent board members for Japanese listed companies,

---

[78] Hancké (2002), Goyer (2006a).
[79] Schaede (2008).

organized employers were able to defeat the LDP reformers and institutional investors. After the first instances of takeovers that actually threatened large companies, in the summer of 2004 and January of 2005, organized Japanese managers turned decisively against the other members of the reformist coalition and pushed for new, formally enforced takeover protections. However, unlike in any of the other three cases, takeover politics became a high salience issue in Japan between 2005 and 2007. Thus, the tools of quiet politics were less useful to Japanese managers after 2005. They were only able to achieve their goals post-2004 by working through political parties, as partisan accounts suggest.[80] And they ultimately lost a battle to institutional investors over the issue of triangular mergers in 2007, as that fight played out in party politics under conditions of continued high salience.

Corporate control rarely achieves sustained political salience, as it did in the Japanese case. Using only the variation in political salience observed in Japan, which is consistent with the theory of quiet politics, would be a flimsy empirical foundation on which to rest broader claims about the distinctiveness of low salience politics. Because corporate control is rarely of high political salience, there is little variation in the salience of this area with which to test claims about the robustness of quiet politics. Chapter 6 remedies this shortcoming. It moves beyond the almost exclusively low salience cases of corporate control to consider what happens when the political salience of an issue changes from low to high. It looks at change over time in policy salience in a single policy area in two countries: the regulation of executive pay in France and the United States. In both countries, when the policy salience of this area was low, business groups tended to dominate through the mechanisms of lobbying and the deference of legislators and reporters. As salience rose, political parties became more sensitive to rising public wrath over executive pay packages, and business could no longer rely on its low salience resources of lobbying expertise and governmental deference. In the American press, Enron became a code word linking large pay packages with accounting malfeasance, and managerial expertise on this issue was discounted because the scandal raised questions about managerial competence. Under these conditions, the propositions of partisan theorists make sense, because under conditions of high salience, the success of business in repelling attempts to regulate pay depended on their proximity to parties in government. Where parties of the right were in power, business did substantially better in restraining government regulation of pay practices than when parties of the left were in power.

The final chapter of the book develops a general argument about the way in which the dimensions of political salience and institutional formality structure democratic politics. Business organizations often fail to get what they want on issues of high political salience, especially those contested in legislatures. By contrast, they very often succeed in achieving their political objectives in low salience issue areas, particularly those with a substantial degree of informal

---

[80] Tiberghien (2007).

governance. Understanding how these dimensions determine the likely arenas of political contestation in different issue domains illuminates several contentious issues in the study of politics. Chapter 7 explores two of these in some detail: the concept of business power and the character of institutional change in politics. Although the study of business power has been largely quiescent in political science since the mid-1980s, the practice of business influence on the state has been waxing. The global financial crisis of 2008, blamed largely on the deregulatory reforms fiercely advocated by business, has thrown into sharp relief the way in which business influence on deregulation has been an international phenomenon, not merely one limited to the United States. This chapter reflects on what we can now say about the role of business in politics, and of the relationship between business and the state, even as that relationship is in the midst of crisis-driven renegotiation around the world.

2

Patient Capital and Markets for Corporate Control

Corporate governance concerns the ways in which owners – that is, shareholders – control those who run the company for them – that is, managers. There are many dimensions of corporate governance, including transparency (the extent to which managerial decisions are subject to public scrutiny), accountability (the extent to which shareholders can discipline managers for the ways in which their decisions affect corporate performance), and incentive compatibility (the extent to which the goals of management and the goals of shareholders are aligned).[1] These are all problems of monitoring and sanctioning. The question for political scientists studying the politics of corporate governance is which dimensions of variation in national institutions of corporate governance are the most important, theoretically, in explaining the differences observed between liberal market economies (such as the United States) and coordinated market economies (such as Germany).

In recent years, scholars working in a variety of analytical traditions have come to focus on the market for corporate control as the key indicator of systemic distinctions among different varieties of capitalism.[2] The market for corporate control refers to the way in which the effective power over companies – that is, the ability to replace a senior management team – changes hands. There are two ideal-typical solutions to the problems of monitoring and sanctioning inherent in the corporate governance of publicly listed companies, both of which operate through the market for corporate control. In the first, the price of a company's shares serves as a public tool for dispersed shareholders to monitor and discipline managers. Markets pay close attention to the ability of a company to meet earnings expectations in each quarter, and a failure to meet those expectations causes some owners to sell their shares, and the share price of the company to fall. If the share price falls too far, the

---

[1] Berle and Means (1932).
[2] Hall and Soskice 2001, Amable (2003), Yamamura and Streeck (2004), Gourevitch and Shinn (2005).

company can be taken over by new owners, who will replace the management team and attempt to reallocate the company's resources more efficiently. In this first scenario, public information and the threat of hostile takeover discipline a managerial team. Thus, the market for controlling the corporation is said to be an active constraint on the ability of managers to misuse the company's assets.[3]

In a second ideal-typical scenario, some set of insiders controls a block of the company's shares.[4] These insiders have the incentive and capacity to monitor management's performance. Such controlling insiders also discipline management, but they are not dependent on short-term, publicly available performance metrics to do so. Thus, they are said to supply the firm with *patient capital*: ownership that allows for the realization of long-term management strategies.[5] The price mechanism cannot discipline management in such a system because holders of patient capital do not automatically sell their shares if the share price declines following a quarterly report in which a company fails to meet expectations. Instead, their investment in the company provides management with a bulwark against change, so long as the management is perceived to be satisfying the holders of patient capital.[6] The strategic shareholding of patient capital leads to a passive market for corporate control, because even though share prices may vary, outsiders possess no easy mechanism for dislodging management in the case of prolonged poor performance.

Although highly stylized, these two endpoints define a continuum that most scholars of comparative political economy see as differentiating the corporate governance of coordinated market economies, such as Germany, from those of liberal market economies, such as the United States.[7] But how do we distinguish an active from a passive market for corporate control, empirically? In other words, how do we measure patient capital? One reason it has been so difficult to develop a cross-nationally reliable measure of patient capital is because different countries use different institutional arrangements to secure functionally equivalent goals – namely, the protection of managers from short-term market pressures. This is a classic challenge of comparative research.[8] Compounding this difficulty is the fact that patient capital is a firm-level characteristic, but scholars of comparative political economy are interested in characterizing the degree to which companies across a national economy have access to patient capital. Thus, the problem of measurement is twofold: how do we identify patient capital at the firm level, and how do we describe the use of patient capital across a number of firms in a given economy at a given time?

An example may clarify the distinction between a firm-level and an economy-wide measure. In every country, there are some companies with large

---

[3] Höpner (2003).
[4] Franks and Mayer (1995).
[5] Hall and Soskice (2001), Amable (2003: 253).
[6] Hall and Soskice (2001).
[7] Hall and Soskice (2001), Amable (2003), Yamamura and Streeck (2004), Gourevitch and Shinn (2005).
[8] Cf. Locke and Thelen (1995).

shareholders whose controlling interest in the company gives its managers patient capital: Microsoft and Google are two American examples. Most large companies in the United States do not have shareholders with stakes equal to those of Bill and Melinda Gates in Microsoft. Most U.S. companies have instead a widely dispersed set of shareholders, or ownership by mutual funds that hold shares as portfolio investments. Unlike the Gates family, these owners have no long-term commitment to a company. Their goal is to earn a good rate of return on their investment, and they will happily sell their shares to a hostile raider if the company's management team is seen to be underperforming. This makes them impatient capitalists. By way of contrast, in economies where most companies have access to ownership groups with large stakes and long-term commitment to the company, we talk of a country having a system of patient capital.

This chapter develops a variety of indicators to make judgments about differences across countries and over time in the degree of patient capital. In the first section, I briefly explore the differences between patient capital and other measurements used in the literature on the politics of corporate control. I then use available data sources to construct an ordinal country ranking of nineteen advanced industrial countries on the likelihood that large firms in a given country can draw on patient capital. The measure has many limitations, which I discuss, but it nevertheless uses some of the best available data to provide a rough indicator of how the advanced industrial countries line up on measures of patient capital. However, the ranking is merely a current snapshot of country differences. To provide a perspective on change over time, the chapter then moves to a discussion of the evolution of regimes of corporate control in the four countries of interest for this study: France, Germany, the Netherlands, and Japan. France and Germany, which historically depended heavily on ownership concentration as the source of patient capital, are shown to have traveled divergent roads. France has moved away from the patient capital model, to a system in which companies have lower average ownership concentration and large firms can be taken over by their foreign competitors. Germany remains a country of highly concentrated ownership, where hostile takeovers are an exceptional event. The Netherlands retains an unusual combination of low ownership concentration and low hostile takeovers, thanks to the idiosyncratic legal measures that continue to protect most of its firms from hostile takeover. Japan, like France, has seen its institutional protections against hostile takeovers erode. However, it has not yet seen the same upsurge in successful hostile takeovers as in France, though hostile takeover attempts have increased markedly, which has in itself increased the pressure of share price considerations on Japanese managers.

Patient Capital in Scholarship on Corporate Governance

Patient capital is distinct from two other dimensions frequently discussed in research on corporate governance: that which runs between bank-based and market-based systems,[9] and that dividing countries with high and low owner-ship concentration.[10] There is a long history of scholarship on the important and distinctive role of banks in economic development in late industrializing countries, although this approach is not without its critics.[11] Much of this scholarship, and indeed some of the current research on finance and corporate governance, has attributed to banks a distinctive role in the maintenance of patient capital in Germany.[12] It is often the case that financial institutions, such as banks and insurance companies, hold large blocks of shares in companies in countries that are generally considered to have patient capital. At least based on the evidence of the 1990s, however, claims about the special role of banks as shareholders of German companies have not found empirical support.[13] During the 1990s banks held some large blocks of shares in Germany, to be sure, but they behaved no differently than did other owners of large shares in Germany.[14] Theoretically, this book assumes that we are interested in patient capital per se, not whether it is provided by banks, families, or other nonfinancial companies.

A second categorical difference dominates the law and economics literature on corporate governance: the distinction between countries with concentrated and dispersed ownership.[15] This distinction, too, is closely tied up with the identification of countries having patient capital. Indeed, in the following empirical section, I use ownership concentration as one important indicator of patient capital. This literature comparing systems of blockholding and of dispersed ownership has focused especially on the question of how large shareholders expropriate minority shareholders, and for such a theoretical task its simple metric (concentration) may be well devised. For our purposes, countries with very high ownership concentration – that is, where most companies have one owner who holds a significant number of shares – all have systems of patient capital. However, there are other ways, beyond straightforward ownership concentration, through which companies can acquire a powerful group of insiders that protect them from the possibility of hostile takeovers. One such way is to have several companies that own shares in each other (cross-shareholding) for strategic purposes. Such arrangements are commonly attributed to France and Japan, for example.[16] A second, related form of protection is through the strategic coordination of several shareholders, even without formal cross-shareholding arrangements.[17] A third involves legal measures

---

[9] Allen and Gale (2001), Barca and Becht (2001).
[10] LaPorta et al. (1999).
[11] Gerschenkron (1962), Zysman (1983), cf. Fohlin (1999).
[12] Höpner (2003), Jackson (2003).
[13] Jenkinson and Ljungqvist (2001), Windolf (2002: 45).
[14] Edwards and Nibler (2000).
[15] La Porta et al. (1999), Roe (2003).
[16] LaPorta et al. (1999), Morin (2000).
[17] Gourevitch and Shinn (2005).

that allocate special voting rights to some shareholders or that change the composition of shareholder meetings in the case of hostile takeovers, as exist in the Netherlands.[18] Although the institutional arrangements that secure patient capital may be idiosyncratic in some countries, it is the job of the comparativist to understand how different arrangements serve functionally equivalent goals across different countries. In more colloquial terms, there is more than one way to skin a cat. If cat skinning is the concept of interest, we need to find a measure that incorporates the different methods that countries use to flay a feline.

In the next section of this chapter I use different streams of information to shed light on how we might establish a country-level measure of the extent of patient capital. Although this measure does not include every possible method of cat skinning, it does show that the use of three distinct measures – ownership concentration, strategic shareholding, and hostile takeover frequency – produce ordinal outcomes whose endpoints are consistent with those described in the literature on comparative political economy for nineteen advanced capitalist democracies. Germany and Austria stand at one end of this index, and the United States and the United Kingdom stand at the other end.

Patient Capital: Cross-National Evidence

Any measure of patient capital must include an indicator of ownership dispersion. There are, however, multiple ways to measure the concentration of ownership and control in listed firms. One important debate among scholars in this area concerns whether one should only measure the voting rights of the single largest owner or instead try to include the interaction among large owners who typically vote their shares together.[19] In many countries, such as Austria, patient capital is the result of the predominance of single controlling owners with large individual blocks of shares. Those controlling owners may be families, states, or other corporations. In other countries, such as Japan, ownership is not concentrated in the hands of a single controlling blockholder. However, several owners may each own small shares, which they could use collectively as a way to protect managers from hostile takeover. In such cases, apparently diffuse shareholding – based on levels of absolute concentration, or on counting the percentage of blockholders in an economy – masks greater real levels of coordination among owners. An ideal indicator of patient capital would capture both these potential means of protection.

Below I use both sorts of data on the average concentration of control for large firms in the advanced industrial countries, using two independent

---

[18] De Jong and Röell (2005).
[19] For the first approach, see La Porta et al. (1999); for the second, see Barca and Becht (2001: 38–40). The first approach makes fewer assumptions about owners who work together, but La Porta et al. recognize that their method substantially understates the coordination through cross-shareholding in some countries.

measures.[20] One set of data, collected from a variety of public sources, shows the voting rights of the single largest owner among the largest companies in the advanced industrial countries in 2004. A second source, the Thomson One Banker (T1B) database, tracks the average stable ownership ratio – that is, the proportion of shareowners thought to vote together in support of management.[21] These data provide comparable indicators of where countries stand in terms of ownership concentration.

The first thing that jumps out from Tables 2.1 and 2.2 is that the rankings of ownership concentration and strategic shareholding are highly correlated. For the nineteen countries that are included in both tables, these two independent sources of data give rankings that have a correlation coefficient of 0.82.[22] Only Spain and Sweden move more than four places in the rankings when comparing tables. Whichever measure one uses for large firms, these tables confirm that the general finding of highly dispersed ownership in the United States and the United Kingdom continues to hold true. Canada and Ireland also appear toward the bottom of each table. Australia shows slightly higher stable ownership than the other liberal market economy/common law/English-speaking countries.

A perfect measure of hostile takeovers would be an ideal index of the existence of patient capital. However, hostile takeovers are extremely difficult to measure.[23] Walter Wriston, the former head of Citigroup, is reputed to have asked, "What is the difference between a hostile and a friendly takeover?" and then answered, "About $2 per share." Boards of directors of companies have an incentive, and indeed a fiduciary duty, to extract the highest possible bid from a potential acquirer. Thus, the standard definition of a hostile takeover – a proposal for acquisition initially rejected by the board of a company – may mask a friendly takeover negotiated by a savvy board.[24] An apparently friendly takeover, if only announced at the conclusion of long negotiations that started out being rejected by the board, may in fact be a hostile takeover in all but name.

Using several different metrics, William Schwert attempted to establish the percentage of all U.S. takeover bids that were hostile, examining listed firms in

---

[20] I follow LaPorta et al. (1999) in concentrating attention on the largest companies in each economy. Largest companies tend to be the most engaged in international markets, even when smaller firms remain more closely tied to the traditional institutions of domestic finance (Deeg 2009).

[21] I report data only for countries for which T1B contained data on at least fifteen large companies.

[22] Table 2.1 (Ownership Concentration) does not include data for South Korea. Table 2.2 (Stable Shareholding) does not include data for New Zealand. These countries are excluded from subsequent tables.

[23] Schwert (2000), Nuttall (1999).

[24] An influential formulation of this definition of a hostile takeover was put forward by Morck et al. (1988: 3): "We call an acquisition hostile if the initial bid for the target (which need not be a bid from the eventual acquiror) was neither negotiated with its board prior to being made nor accepted by the board as made. Thus initial rejection by the target's board is taken as evidence of the bidder's hostility, as is active management resistance to the bid, escape to a white knight, or a management buyout in response to unsolicited pressure."

TABLE 2.1. *Average Voting Share of Largest Single Shareholder, 2004*

Rank	Country	N	Largest Shareholder's Voting Share (percent)
1	Austria	23	41.3
2	Belgium	25	36.4
3	Germany	38	34.8
4	New Zealand	26	34.5
5	Portugal	19	34.4
6	Denmark	22	32.7
7	Italy	40	31.9
8	Norway	26	30.6
9	Sweden	24	30.0
10	Finland	25	29.9
11	Switzerland	20	26.7
12	Spain	19	25.9
13	Australia	24	23.8
14	France	40	22.4
15	Canada	24	19.9
16	Netherlands	21	19.1
17	Japan	40	17.1
18	Ireland	25	15.3
19	United States	40	10.9
20	United Kingdom	36	9.5
	MEDIAN	557	28.3

Note: For each country, N refers to the number of the largest companies by market capitalization for which these averages are calculated. I am grateful to Ben Ansell and Dilyan Donchev for research assistance. The data for Japan are taken from the Nippon Life Insurance (NLI) database, which classifies stable ownership (as of March 2005). Given the changes in Japan since 2005, these data probably overestimate the real concentration of ownership in Japanese large firms. This table does not include South Korea.

Source: These data were collected from publicly available data sources, including the Orbis, Osiris, and Amadeus databases; the Financial Times 500; and information from individual stock exchanges and companies.

the United States between 1976 and 1996.[25] The most conservative estimate of this percentage was seven percent, based on the number of bids characterized as hostile in the *Wall Street Journal* or *Dow Jones News Retrieval* system. The mid-range estimate, based on classifications of the Securities Data Corporation (SDC), put the figure at twenty-one percent (from 1980–1996). The high figure, based on the number of takeover bids involving at least one unsolicited offer, was forty-two percent of all takeover contests. Schwert's summary of his results is apt: "the phrase 'hostile takeover' means different things to different people."[26] However, on all three measures, Schwert found a statistically

[25] Schwert (2000).
[26] Schwert (2000: 2638).

TABLE 2.2. *Average Stable Concentration, 2006*

Rank	Country	N	Stable Shareholder's Voting Share (percent)
1	Austria	28	57.1
2	Portugal	18	52.8
3	Spain	40	46.1
4	Norway	25	45.5
5	Germany	40	44.9
6	Belgium	26	43.2
7	Italy	40	39.0
8	Denmark	28	37.4
9	Switzerland	40	36.6
10	Australia	40	33.9
11	Netherlands	40	32.6
12	France	40	31.0
13	South Korea	40	29.8
14	Finland	40	27.7
15	Japan	40	27.1
16	Sweden	40	25.1
17	Ireland	19	23.3
18	Canada	40	16.0
19	United Kingdom	40	12.1
20	United States	40	7.8
	MEDIAN	704	33.9

Note: For each country, N refers to the number of the largest companies by market capitalization for which these averages are calculated. Data are only included for which T1B had a minimum of fifteen companies. For this reason, New Zealand is not included in this table. I am grateful to Grégoire de Chammard and Anne-Gaëlle Heliot-Javelle for research assistance.
Source: Thomson One Banker (T1B) database.

significant decline in the frequency of hostile deals in the United States after 1991.[27] Other studies observe similar temporal trends.[28]

The relative fluidity of different conceptions of what constitutes a hostile takeover makes international comparison difficult. However, the Thomson One Banker database features information on hostile takeovers across most of the advanced industrial countries since 1990. T1B classifies a takeover as hostile if the board officially rejects an offer of acquisition, but the acquiring firm continues pursuing the offer by other means, such as a tender offer. If the board changes its mind and accepts the offer, then the transaction is relabeled

[27] This decline is probably a result of the clarification of laws governing antitakeover devices in the United States, such as poison pills.

[28] David North found that nine percent of deals were hostile in a sample of American listed firms between 1990 and 1997 (North 2001). Charlie Weir and David Lang found that about ten percent of deals in the United Kingdom were hostile during the 1990s (Weir and Lang 2003: 1752).

TABLE 2.3. *Hostile Takeovers Completed and Attempted and Friendly Mergers,*
1990–2007

Rank	Country	Hostile Takeovers Completed	Hostile Takeovers Attempted	Friendly Mergers Completed
1	United States	55	162	7853
2	United Kingdom	45	97	1748
3	Australia	27	38	448
4	Canada	19	50	697
5	France	9	17	786
T6	Italy	4	6	471
T6	Spain	4	10	331
T6	Sweden	4	11	276
9	Germany	3	5	678
10	Netherlands	2	6	321
T11	Belgium	1	1	112
T11	Denmark	1	3	91
T11	Finland	1	2	106
T11	Ireland	1	3	62
T11	Japan	1	4	508
T11	Norway	1	8	123
T11	Portugal	1	5	69
T11	Switzerland	1	6	160
19	Austria	0	1	54
	MEDIAN	2	6	321

Note: Based on all deals valued at $200 million or more in constant (inflation adjusted) dollars. T1B classifies a takeover as hostile if the board officially rejects an offer of acquisition, but the acquirer continues pursuing the offer by other means, such as a tender offer. If the board changes its mind, and accepts the offer, then the transaction is relabeled "friendly." The data on hostile takeovers attempted includes hostile deals classified by T1B as "withdrawn" or "intent withdrawn." Intended deals are those for which the acquirer has publicly announced the intention to make an offer but later retracted it (for example, in the face of an adverse reaction from the board of the company to be acquired). A very small number of transactions falls into this latter category.
Source: Thomson One Banker (T1B) database.

"friendly." As many offers start hostile and wind up friendly, the T1B data are almost surely a conservative estimate of the extent of hostile takeovers in an economy. Nevertheless, the T1B definition has the great virtue of being standard across countries, and thus allows us to see how hostile takeover activity in the advanced industrial countries compares to that observed in the United Kingdom and the United States, the general exemplars of liberal market capitalism. Hostile takeovers are comparatively rare, even in the United States and the United Kingdom, so I include for each country all hostile takeovers attempted and failed between 1990 and 2007, along with the number of friendly deals completed during this time.

TABLE 2.4. *Hostile Takeovers as a Proportion of Total Deal Activity, 1990–2007*

Rank	Country	Ratio, Hostile to Friendly Deals (percent)
1	Australia	6.03
2	Canada	2.73
3	United Kingdom	2.57
4	Ireland-Rep	1.61
5	Sweden	1.45
6	Portugal	1.45
7	Spain	1.21
8	France	1.15
9	Denmark	1.10
10	Finland	0.94
11	Belgium	0.89
12	Italy	0.85
13	Norway	0.81
14	United States	0.70
15	Switzerland	0.63
16	Netherlands	0.62
17	Germany	0.44
18	Japan	0.20
19	Austria	0.00
	MEDIAN	0.94

Note: See previous table for definition of hostile takeover. The denominator includes all deals classified as friendly in the T1B database.
Source: T1B database, based on deals valued at $200 million or more in constant (inflation adjusted) year 2000 dollars.

The United States has the most hostile takeovers in the world, as we might expect, given both the reputed functioning and the size of its market. However, according to the T1B database, if we consider hostile takeovers *in proportion* to the number of overall friendly deals in the economy, the United States' lead in hostile takeovers is largely a function of its very large economy. Australia, Canada, and the United Kingdom have far more hostile takeovers, as a percentage of overall deals, than does the United States (see Table 2.4).[29] Indeed, despite the relatively high level of stable ownership in the Australian economy – in which seventy-three percent of firms have at least a set of shareholders holding at least twenty percent of voting rights in the company – we see that some

[29] These data for the United States are surprising, given the reputation of its active market for control. I therefore compared the T1B data with the figures available from the Securities Data Corporation (SDC) Platinum Mergers and Acquisitions database. Those figures were very similar, showing the same low comparative figure for the United States.

TABLE 2.5. *Average Rank of Countries on Attributes of Patient Capital, circa 2005*

Country	Ownership Concentration, 2004	Stable Concentration, 2006	Inverse Combined Ranking, Frequency, and Absolute Hostile Takeovers	Average Rank
Austria	1	1	1	1.0
Germany	3	5	5	4.3
Belgium	2	6	7	5.0
Norway	7	4	6	5.7
Portugal	4	2	11	5.7
Denmark	5	8	9	7.3
Switzerland	10	9	3	7.3
Italy	6	7	10	7.7
Spain	11	3	14	9.3
Finland	9	13	8	10.0
Netherlands	15	11	4	10.0
Japan	16	14	2	10.7
Sweden	8	15	16	13.0
France	13	12	15	13.3
Australia	12	10	19	13.7
Ireland	17	16	13	15.3
Canada	14	17	17	16.0
United States	18	19	12	16.3
United Kingdom	19	18	18	18.3

Note: The final column of this table displays the average of country rankings on stable shareholding, concentrated shareholding, and incidence of hostile takeovers presented earlier in the chapter. The hostile takeover ranking is itself an average of the country ranking of overall frequency of hostile takeovers and the ranking of number of hostile takeovers relative to friendly deals. In order to be combined with the first two rankings, the hostile takeover data are presented in reverse order, such that low numbers means lowest incidence of hostile takeovers. Austria ranked first on all three indicators, and so its average rank is 1.0; the United Kingdom ranked last or second-to-last on every indicator among the nineteen countries, giving it the lowest average rank of 18.3.

concentration is not inconsistent with an active market for corporate control. The other English-speaking liberal market economy countries cluster at the top of the rankings, which is consistent with the expectations of the varieties of capitalism literature.

Each of the indicators reviewed here provides some information about the extent to which institutions of patient capital secure a passive market for corporate control across the industrialized countries. In Table 2.5, I average the country rankings on three indicators – the stable ownership rank, the concentration rank, and the hostile takeover activity rank[30] – to produce a relative

---

[30] To produce an overall ranking for the data on hostile takeovers, I averaged the rankings for absolute number of hostile takeovers with the ratio of hostile takeovers to friendly deals.

ranking of countries along the dimension of patient capital. This measure is
undoubtedly crude, for several reasons. First, it ignores local context in order
to rank countries according to common criteria; thus, there is no inclusion of
effective legal barriers to hostile takeovers, which are very important in the
Dutch political economy. Second, it combines recent snapshots of ownership
concentration with hostile takeover activity since 1990, and it fails to take
account of increases in the number of *failed* hostile takeovers in some countries, such as Japan. Finally, it is but an average ordinal measure, showing how
countries compare to each other on these indices, rather than an absolute indicator. Each of these is a serious drawback, and the next section of this chapter
attempts to correct for some of the weaknesses of this indicator by showing
data on change over time within individual countries.

Nevertheless, the data are worth summarizing in this admittedly imperfect
form to show that these rankings correspond well with the expectations of
existing scholarship in political economy. Those countries with the highest
average rankings – Austria, Germany, and Belgium – appear on almost any
short list of countries with passive markets for corporate control. The bottom
five countries are even less surprising. Australia, Ireland, Canada, the United
States, and the United Kingdom have the most active markets for corporate
control, as the scholarly literature on the varieties of capitalism suggests that
they would. In the next section, we turn to change over time in several of
the cases that fall at neither end of the two extremes in this ranking. It is
in these cases where knowledge of local context becomes more important
in establishing the current state of play in institutions of patient capital and
markets for corporate control.

Change Over Time in Patient Capital

In order to make comparisons across the group of advanced industrial countries, the previous section relied on a current snapshot of three characteristics associated with patient capital: concentrated ownership, stable ownership
groups, and limited hostile takeover activity. By these conventional metrics,
Germany remains a paradigmatic example of a passive market for corporate
control with stable patient capital. It is the large country that most thoroughly
combines high ownership concentration and minimal occurrence of hostile
takeovers. Since 1995, these traits of the German market have not changed.
This section considers German stability against the changes over time observed
in France, the Netherlands, and Japan. We first review some measures of the
changes in stable ownership groups across these cases. Then, we explore with
more contextual depth the evolution of these cases over time.

On the first measure of ownership concentration – average percentage of
stable shareholding among the forty largest companies in the economy – France
and Japan both experienced a sharp decline between 1997 and 2006. Germany
and the Netherlands experienced minimal change. The Netherlands, which
started with the lowest average ownership concentration of the four countries,

TABLE 2.6. *Change in Average Stable Concentration, 1997–2006 (Top Forty Companies)*

Country	1997 (percent)	2006 (percent)	Change (percent)
Japan	37.7	27.1	−28.1
France	37.6	31.0	−17.6
Germany	48.3	44.9	−7.0
Netherlands	34.0	32.6	−4.1

Source: T1B Database.

saw the lowest drop among them in the percentage of stable shareholding. The Netherlands, in fact, finished the period with marginally higher concentration than both Japan and France. Germany started and finished the period with much higher ownership concentration than the other three countries.

Table 2.6 includes both financial firms, such as banks and insurance companies, and nonfinancial companies, such as automobile and software companies. It is possible that the globalization of financial ties affects the two sectors differently, as financial firms may feel greater pressure to respond to calls for shareholder value, given their own large and diverse portfolio holdings. Moreover, because nonfinancial firms have historically led the political organization of business in most advanced industrial countries, it is worth examining the premise that the most important indicators of the real economy lie in the ownership of nonfinancial companies. Table 2.7 portrays the change over time for the twenty-five largest nonfinancial companies in these four economies between 1997 and 2006.

Table 2.7 confirms the impression that France and Japan have experienced much more sweeping change than have the Netherlands and Germany. These data show that changes in France have been especially large among nonfinancial firms, while the vertiginous change in Japanese shareholding is led by the decline in the ownership concentration of banks. Several large French mutualist banks, such as Crédit Agricole, have an ownership structure in which over fifty percent of the voting shares are controlled by groups sympathetic to management. This is not the case for French commercial banks, such as BNP/Paribas, but the

TABLE 2.7. *Change in Average Stable Concentration, 1997–2006 (Top Twenty-Five Nonfinancial Companies)*

Country	1997 (percent)	2006 (percent)	Change (percent)
France	34.0	26.7	−21.4
Japan	39.0	31.7	−18.7
Netherlands	39.0	35.9	−7.9
Germany	46.4	48.1	+3.7

Source: T1B Database.

inclusion of the mutualist banks in the data for the forty largest companies leads to an understatement of the degree of change in the real economy in France. In Japan, meanwhile, the bankruptcy of several banks between 1997 and 1999, combined with the low returns on bank stocks compared with the overall equity market, forced nonfinancial companies to unload their bank shares at this time.[31] In the Netherlands and Germany, by contrast, concentrated ownership in nonfinancial firms was stable, and in Germany the average concentration of shareholding ownership even increased slightly over this period.

It is clear from the evolution of the concentration of stable shareholding in these countries that France and Japan have experienced large changes. The Netherlands, like Germany, has not. Germany ends the first decade of the twenty-first century the same way it began the last decade of the twentieth: with a stable system of patient capital. However, even if there has been much *change* in France, there is not a big difference in the current *level* of stable shareholding in the Netherlands, France, and Japan. It is important to provide the political context of these three individual countries to understand why the changes in France and Japan have amounted to important institutional transformations of national markets for corporate control, while the market for corporate control in the Netherlands has not changed in any significant respect. The most central fact, as we will see in the next three subsections, is that cross-shareholding networks were important barriers to takeover in the first two countries, whereas the Netherlands enjoyed formal legal protections against hostile takeovers that did not depend on either cross-shareholding or high ownership concentration. This is a reminder that differences in national institutional context remain an important consideration for any discussion of change over time in comparative patient capital.

The Destruction of the French Institutions of Patient Capital

Three features characterized the French model of patient capital until the early 1990s: high levels of state ownership, concentrated ownership of those large companies in the private sector, and corporate cross-shareholding. For most of the postwar era, the state played a dominant role in the French economy, both by virtue of its direct ownership of many of the largest French firms and by the fact that many corporate elites moved to their jobs after long careers in the state bureaucracy.[32] In the early 1980s, the French government owned thirteen of the twenty largest firms in the economy, including virtually all the banks.[33] When a government of the right came to power in 1986, it inaugurated the privatization of many of the large state-owned companies, a program that would continue off and on for two decades. It was during the initial period of privatization that bureaucrats under Finance Minister Edouard Balladur built on existing patterns of cross-shareholding to construct networks of stable ownership

[31] Miyajima and Kuroki (2007: 89–90).
[32] Schmidt (1996).
[33] Culpepper (2006: 32).

(the so-called *noyaux durs*, or hard cores) to shield companies from the pressures of financial markets and from the prospect of hostile foreign takeovers.[34] The goal of the *noyaux durs* was to use the private sector to replace the state as a source of long-term industrial ownership, thus enabling privatization to take place while maintaining patient capital in France. The heart of the newly reinforced system comprised two networks of companies that held each other's shares for strategic reasons. One network was centered around the bank Société Générale (SocGen), the other around the Banque Nationale de Paris (BNP). As of 1997, these networks stood at the middle of an extended chain of strategic shareholding, which tied together most of the large companies in the French economy, to different degrees.[35] Figure 2.1 illustrates these ownership ties.

These ownership networks, stable between 1988 and 1996, collapsed suddenly in 1998 and 1999. Table 2.8 shows that the mutual voting shares held by companies at the center of the two "hard core" shareholding groups fell by about half in 1998 and 1999.[36] These interlocking French shareholdings among large French firms were replaced by the growing weight of foreign (mostly British and American) institutional investors, which by 2003 owned more than forty percent of the outstanding shares in CAC-40 companies.[37] Moreover, not all foreign institutional investors are alike: pension funds, for example, generally have longer time horizons than mutual or hedge funds. As Michel Goyer has demonstrated, the influx of Anglo-American institutional investors in France has been dominated by mutual and hedge funds, not by pension funds.[38] Thus, patient capital in France was replaced by the most impatient of capitalists.

The breakdown of the *noyaux durs* catalyzed the transformation of the French market for corporate control. As the large companies at the center of the network cast aside their cross-shareholdings in order to use the capital for expansion, other corporate owners across the economy rapidly followed. The destruction of these networks resulted in the dilution of concentrated ownership in France, which had been the foundation of French institutions of patient capital. In 1997, the average voting share of the single biggest shareholder of the forty largest French companies was thirty-seven percent; by 2005 it had dropped to twenty-two percent. An alternative metric of control – the number of these top companies in which the single largest voting share is twenty percent or higher[39] – fell from sixty-four percent in 1997 to forty-nine percent in 2005.

These transformed patterns of shareholding among French large companies made possible the spread of large hostile takeovers. Between 1990 and 1998, there were only three successful hostile takeovers in France, and the total dollar

---

[34] Morin (2000), Schmidt (1996: 123).

[35] Morin and Rigamonti (2002).

[36] Data on changes in French share ownership comes from the LEREP Database of the University of Toulouse.

[37] Goyer (2003).

[38] Goyer (2006b).

[39] Cf. La Porta et al. (1999).

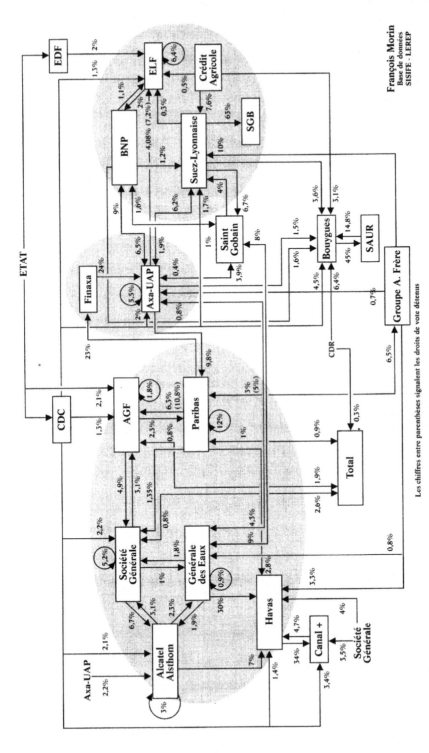

FIGURE 2.1. The French Hard-Core Shareholding Network, 1997
Source: François Morin, "Le Modèle Français de Détention et de Gestion du Capital," Rapport au Ministre de l'Economie, des Finances et de l'Industrie. Les Editions de Bercy, June 1998, Collection Etudes, p. 27.

François Morin
Base de données
SISIFE - LEREP

Les chiffres entre parenthèses signalent les droits de vote détenus

40

TABLE 2.8. *Breakdown of the Hard-Core Networks of French Cross-Shareholding*

	1996	1997	1998	1999	2000	Change, 1996–2000 (percent)
BNP Network						
BNP	16.8	16.1	11.0	8.2	8.6	−48.7
St. Gobain	22.6	22.3	22.3	13.5	7.6	−66.5
Suez/Lyonnaise des Eaux	8.4	8.4	8.4	1.7	1.4	−83.4
UAP/AXA	9.0	9.0	6.9	6.9	6.9	−23.0
Vivendi	16.5	15.1	14.1	8.7	4.9	−70.5
SocGen Network						
AGF	4.5	5.6	6.0	2.5	2.5	−44.2
Alcatel	7.0	6.7	8.4	5.0	4.4	−38.0
Aventis	11.5	12.3	14.4	7.5	6.9	−40.4
SocGen	23.0	24.7	28.8	15.0	13.7	−40.4

Note: Figures depict the proportion of a company's voting shares controlled by the other central members of its hard core network. These figures exclude some other stable and cross-shareholding ties, illustrated in Figure 2.1, which also fell in tandem with the core shareholdings depicted here. *Source*: Data from the LEREP database of the University of Toulouse. This table is adapted from Culpepper (2005).

value of all three deals was just under $7 billion. There were four successful hostile deals in 1999 alone, collectively worth more than $66 billion dollars. Three additional hostile takeovers took place between 2000 and 2004, which together were valued at $64 billion.[40] Two of these large deals involved French companies being acquired by foreign companies. The hostile takeover of the industrial giant Pechiney by the foreign company Alcan in 2003 symbolized for the French press the "ultra [neo]-liberal" turn of the French economy. Pechiney, once a state-owned company and the spearhead of French industrial policy, passed into foreign ownership with scarcely any political protest at all.[41] Such an outcome would have been inconceivable ten years earlier.

Takeover Defenses and the Market for Corporate Control in the Netherlands

Despite the lack of concentrated ownership that characterized France and Germany in the postwar period, the Netherlands has an inactive market for corporate control. There were no successful hostile takeovers in the Netherlands between 1990 and 2000. This is a result of the multiple protections against hostile takeovers introduced by Dutch companies. For example, one 1989 study found more than fifty such protective measures used by Dutch companies.[42]

---

[40] Dollar values of deals in this paragraph are taken from the T1B database and are expressed in constant dollar value, based on the year 2000.

[41] De Kerdrel (2003).

[42] Voogd (1989).

These measures allow managers to divorce the voting power of shares from the economic power of shares in a variety of ways. In this section I will focus on three of the measures most relevant to large listed companies in the Netherlands: preference shares, priority shares, and certificates. How do these work, and what is the distribution of these shares among Dutch companies?

Preference shares and priority shares differ in their purpose and structure. Preference shares allow managing boards to change the voting balance of shareholders in case of an attack, while priority shares are typically used to maintain special voting control in the hands of founding owners or families. Managing boards can issue preference shares without the consent of current shareholders, and these shares carry a high ratio of voting power to capital.[43] In the case of hostile takeovers, management can sell preference shares to a foundation, called a trust office – an organization created for the defense of the firm from takeovers – for twenty-five percent of their nominal value (not their market value). Depending on other takeover defenses at the company, the amount issued to the trust office can equal one hundred percent of shares outstanding at the time of issuance, thus creating an effective bulwark against hostile acquisition.[44] Priority shares, which are the second type of protective share available to Dutch companies, exist in other countries as well as in the Netherlands.[45] Priority shares give voting power disproportionate to economic value to certain shareholders – in the Dutch case, often to trust offices specifically tasked with protecting the company.

The previous two classes of shares are embedded in law. A third common type of protective device – share certification – is an informal (nonstatutory) practice that divorces voting rights from economic rights. In certification, the voting rights of shares issued to shareholders remain with a management-friendly trust office, while the shareholder has only a certificate for the economic value of the shares. As de Jong et al. characterize the device,

> the trust office is always friendly to existing management. The trust office is given responsibility for the ordinary shares. Through the process of certification, legal (not "economic") ownership of the ordinary shares is transferred to the trust office. . . . Certificate holders have dividend rights, can trade and attend the general meeting, but they cannot vote. . . . The trust office holds all voting rights including approval of the dividend policy.[46]

Each of these devices is in principle capable on its own of preventing a hostile takeover. Yet during the postwar period, many Dutch companies accumulated multiple protections as an insurance policy against being taken over. Table 2.9 shows that, during the period between 1993 and 2007, they reduced

---

[43] Heemskerk (2007: 56).
[44] De Jong et al. (2006: 356).
[45] The founders of Google, for example, have shares with special voting rights.
[46] De Jong et al. (2006: 356).

TABLE 2.9. *Takeover Defenses Used by Dutch Companies, 1993–2007*

	1993 (percent)	2001 (percent)	2007 (percent)
Preference shares	60	63	57
Priority shares	43	34	15
Certification	38	20	8
N	143	50	50

Source: Figures for 1993 are reported in De Jong and Röell (2005: 490); figures for 2007 are reported in Munsters and Abma (2007).

their reliance on other mechanisms while maintaining preference shares. Financial firms have been much more willing than nonfinancial firms to give up this protection in recent years.

Understanding the widespread use of protection mechanisms allows us to put the data on ownership concentration in the Netherlands into their political context. Unlike firms in Germany or France, Dutch patient capital does not depend on having concentrated owners. The existence of trust offices gives Dutch companies the protective benefits of ownership concentration without having concentrated owners because, with the activation of preference shares, most voting rights flow to the trust office in the case of a hostile takeover bid. To show how this affects the real degree of protection of companies, Table 2.10 compares *actual* ownership concentration of Dutch companies with the *effective* concentration provided through measures related to the trust office. The first row of Table 2.10 shows the average voting rights held by the largest shareholder. The second row shows the average voting rights held by the largest voter in the case of an attempted hostile takeover, which triggers the protective devices just discussed. As the table shows clearly, Dutch managers do not need the protection of a concentrated owner so long as they have the protection of a friendly trust office.

Table 2.10 shows not only the level of protection, but how that level of protection evolved between 1997 and 2004. As we saw earlier in the chapter, the degree of stable shareholding changed very little in the Netherlands. It is equally true, moreover, that the degree of effective protection also changed very

TABLE 2.10. *Concentration of Dutch Shareholding without and with Trust Offices*

	1997 (percent)	2004 (percent)
Actual concentration	18	19
Effective concentration	49	45

Note: These data are for the largest sixteen companies in the Netherlands (1997) and the largest twenty-one companies in the Netherlands (2001) based on market capitalization.
Source: Data collected from publicly available sources. Thanks to Ben Ansell and Jane Gingrich for research assistance.

little over this time. The relative dispersion of Dutch shareholding, which we observed early in the chapter, masks the fact that effective takeover protection in Dutch large companies appears as strong as the protection favoring German large companies. As in Germany, hostile takeovers remain a rarity in the Dutch large company universe. Whereas the basis of German stable shareholding is primarily the economic institution of concentrated shareholding, Dutch patient capital is a political construction. It depends on the ability of senior managers to use preference shares to defend their companies from hostile bids.

The Decline of Cross-Shareholding in Japan

In cross-national perspective, Japan has maintained dispersed shareholding throughout the postwar period. However, although the individual blocks of shares held by owners "friendly to management" are small, their cumulative weight was long regarded as an effective deterrent to hostile takeovers.[47] The conventional view of the postwar Japanese economy emphasizes the informal links among firms within individual networks, called *keiretsu*, organized around large banks or trading houses such as Fuji or Mitsubishi.[48] The term *keiretsu* is often used to refer both to horizontal links between allied companies as well as vertical links among supplier companies and their large customers.[49] Both sorts of shareholding networks could function as takeover protection. To assess patient capital in Japan, I rely on well-established public indicators of the degree of the long-term shareholding of listed Japanese companies, which include all types of owners considered unlikely to sell their shares on the basis of short-term fluctuations in share prices.

The most consistent data on ownership in Japanese companies has been assembled by Nippon Life Insurance Research (NLIR). NLIR tracks two measures of stable shareholding in Japanese companies. Its first measure, long-term ownership, includes all owners of a company's shares that are categorized as being held for long-term or strategic alliances. It includes ownership by commercial banks, perceived as being of long-term nature, but it excludes the holdings of trust banks, which maintain a portfolio approach and can change their holdings more rapidly. The second indicator, cross-shareholding, measures only the percentage of shares in company x held by other corporations in which company x also owns shares. The NLIR cross-shareholding figures are lower on average than are the long-term ownership figures. During the first half of the 1990s, both measures were stable among the largest companies. In 1996, the largest forty companies in Japan had on average about thirty-nine percent

---

[47] Dore (2000), Miyajima and Kuroki (2007). Cross-shareholdings were mainly built up during the 1960s, after the liberalization of capital flows led many Japanese managers to be concerned about the possibility of hostile takeover by foreign companies (Ramseyer 1987: 21–22; Gao 2001: 83–85; Miyajima and Kuroki 2007: 85).

[48] Pempel (1998), Jacoby (2005).

[49] On the functioning of *keiretsu*, see Pempel (1998: 70–71), Dore (2000: 39), and Gao (2001). Miwa and Ramseyer (2006) have recently challenged the prevailing wisdom about the strength of ties within the *keiretsu*.

Percentage Held

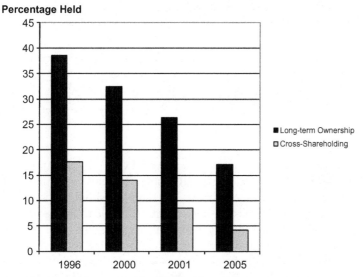

FIGURE 2.2. Decline in Stable Shareholding in Japan, 1996–2005
Source: Nippon Life Insurance Research Institute (NLIR).
Note: The vertical axis refers to the proportion of a company's shares held either by other companies identified by NLIR as having a strategic rather than a portfolio shareholding logic with respect to the given company (long-term ownership) or by other companies with which the company has reciprocal shareholdings (cross-shareholding). These data refer to the forty largest companies in the Japanese economy, as measured by market capitalization. I am grateful to Hiroshi Amemiya, Chiaki Yamada, and Orie Hirano for their help in research assistance and translation of the Japanese data.

of shares held by long-term owners, and about eighteen percent of shares held in cross-shareholding (the same percentages as in 1991).

The stability of stable shareholding in Japan rapidly disintegrated after 1996. Figure 2.2 illustrates this trend. Between 1996 and 2005, long-term ownership as measured by NLIR was reduced by more than half, falling from thirty-nine percent to seventeen percent of shares in the average large company. The drop was even sharper in cross-shareholding during this time, moving from eighteen percent of shares in 1996 to just four percent of shares in 2005.

The fall in Japanese stable shareholding coincided with the beginnings of a hostile takeover market in Japan. Between 1990 and 1998, only a single hostile takeover was attempted in Japan, and it failed. In 1999, the British company Cable & Wireless launched the first successful hostile takeover in Japan when it acquired International Digital Communications (IDC). This bid was followed by several others in the following years, but those bids generally failed. In Table 2.11, I show two different sources on the occurrence of hostile takeovers in Japan. The first is the comparative data from the Thomson One Banker Database (T1B), which I have used throughout this chapter. The T1B data show six hostile bids – all of which failed – between 2000 and 2006. The second

TABLE 2.11. *Activity in the Japanese Hostile Takeover Market, 1990–2007*

	1990–1998		1999–2007	
	Attempted	Successful	Attempted	Successful
Thomson data	0	0	7	1
RECOF data	1	0	24	4

Source: RECOF and Thomson.

data source is the hostile takeover database of the RECOF Corporation. The RECOF data, widely used in Japan, classify all unsolicited deals as hostile deals. The RECOF data are more inclusive than the T1B data and should probably be considered an upper bound on the possible extent of hostile takeover activity in the Japanese market. By this more generous measure, there were twenty-four hostile bids between 1999 and 2007, of which four were successful. Yet, even the more conservative data from Thomson show that the number of attempted hostile takeovers has increased substantially in Japan, confronting managers with a previously unknown market pressure. Hostile takeovers have become possible in Japan, but their success has been limited, at least as of this writing.

The period between 1996 and 2005 marked an end to the practice of widespread cross-shareholding among large Japanese companies and saw a sharp attenuation of the practice of stable shareholding. The disappearance of the old institution that protected companies from hostile takeovers prompted government officials to develop a proposal for the introduction of poison pill defenses, a process that I discuss in Chapter 5. Only ten percent of listed companies had adopted a poison pill defense as of 2008. Thus, from the perspective of straightforward protection, the ramparts of the Japanese model of patient capital have crumbled. Hostile takeovers have not yet proliferated, at least on the scale seen in the United States and the United Kingdom. Yet the balance of the evidence suggests that capital in Japan is far less patient than it was in 1995.

Conclusion

Patient capital has proved an elusive quarry for those who would nail it down empirically. In this chapter, I have used multiple indicators to establish a rough ordinal ranking of the activity of markets for corporate control. To do so, I have brought together measures of ownership concentration, strategic share-holding, and hostile takeover activity. While ownership concentration is the simplest of these measures, it also misses other forms of insider coordination, which can be used to protect managers from the threat of hostile takeovers. The T1B data provide information on strategic shareholding, which complements this data by making an assessment of the degree of stable ownership by country. Hostile takeovers are an important direct measure of the activity for market for corporate control, to be sure, but the data on hostile takeovers are suspect, because evaluations of hostile takeovers can vary widely between one source and another.[50] These three measures of patient capital come much closer to measuring the theoretical concept than do measures that look at distantly related (but easily available) measures such as the extent of stock market capitalization. Even so, the comparative empirical classification of degrees of patient capital remains a work in progress. It is to be hoped that future research will build on this effort to put together cross-nationally reliable data on the degree of patient capital.

These caveats notwithstanding, the ordinal ranking of countries in Table 2.5 confirms that Germany and the United Kingdom stand at opposite ends of the patient capital spectrum. As of this writing, Germany retains many of the barriers to an open market for corporate control that have led to its central role in the varieties of capitalism literature.[51] France, in marked contrast, is the non-English speaking country with the most active market for corporate control. The dissolution of concentrated ownership and cross-shareholding in France, and the burst of hostile acquisitions that followed in 1999, have radically transformed the once-staid market for corporate control in France. The political story of how the markets for corporate control in France and Germany came to such different points in the last decade is the subject of the next chapter.

The Japanese and Dutch cases – both formerly considered to be firmly in the camp of patient capital, despite their low ownership concentration and strategic shareholding – show the limits of the ordinal rankings established in this chapter. Both have recorded a low number of hostile takeovers, according to T1B, and each has historically enjoyed idiosyncratic measures of protection against hostile takeovers. Yet the institutions of protection fared very differently in the two countries. The Dutch measures of takeover protection, enshrined in preference shares that revert to trust offices in the case of hostile takeover, continue to be used by a majority of Dutch large firms. There has been no upsurge in attempted hostile takeovers in the country. The one outstanding case of an effective hostile takeover this decade – that of ABN-Amro by Royal Bank of Scotland in 2007 – only took place because ABN-Amro chose to renounce the measures that protect other Dutch firms. We return to the Dutch case in Chapter 4. Meanwhile, the stable shareholdings of Japanese companies collapsed between 1996 and 2005. This did not lead, as in France, to a series of successful hostile takeovers of large companies. It did, however, lead to a burst of attempted hostile takeovers, most of which failed. How managers have responded to this environment of lower patient capital is a question we take up in Chapter 5.

[50] Schwert (2000).
[51] Hall and Soskice (2001).

3

The Managerial Origins of Institutional Divergence in France and Germany

> I want to gather all our forces behind a veritable economic patriotism.
>
> Dominique de Villepin, French prime minister, 2005[1]

French politicians like nothing better than to proclaim their opposition to free markets. German politicians, contrariwise, generally profess a sober appreciation of the virtues of market regulation. Yet the reality of markets for corporate control is often far removed from the rhetoric of political leaders. Despite the openness to hostile takeovers expressed by Prime Minister Gerhard Schröder in 1999, hostile takeovers are a rarity in Germany, and the ownership concentration of German companies remains high. In France, by contrast, managers of large companies have embraced takeovers as an effective tool of internal reorganization and abandoned their strategic shareholdings, notwithstanding the periodic calls from political leaders like Dominique de Villepin for those managers to rally behind the banner of economic patriotism. In short, Germany has maintained the institutions that support its passive market for corporate control, while France has dismantled such institutions. This chapter explores the politics that led to these outcomes.

This surprising institutional divergence results from the different preferences of French and German managers of large firms, and from the political capacity of those managers to shape institutions of corporate control. During the 1990s, many French firms shifted toward a strategy of international growth powered by acquisitions abroad and at home. This change in company strategy led managers to dismantle the preexisting institutions of patient capital in France. These institutions were informal, so French managers did not have to act through Parliament to secure their preferred outcomes. In tandem with these moves in the informal arena, neoliberal managers also seized control of the political organizations of the French employers' movement. These organizations

---

[1] AFP (2005). This was de Villepin's response to rumors of a takeover bid for the French company Danone by the American company PepsiCo in July 2005.

would consistently push for laws that supported the newly active market for corporate control in France, most notably during debates over the European Union's takeover directive between 2001 and 2006.

In Germany, by contrast, firm-level representation of labor remained strong. The legal protection of German workers allows them to make rapid restructuring through takeovers impossible. Thus, German managers, supported by concentrated owners, saw little to like and much to fear in a transition to an active market for corporate control. As a result, such a market never came to Germany. The structure of German employers' associations, which excluded the financial companies most amenable to liberalizing the market for corporate control, reinforced the power of the managerial proponents of the existing German institutions. These groups would be instrumental in forcing Prime Minister Gerhard Schröder to reverse his political position and to protect the German passive market for corporate control in intergovernmental bargaining over the EU takeover directive.

How did these managerial groups succeed in defending their preferred political positions? Lobbying expertise, delegations of governmental authority to business-friendly working groups, and media framing capacity are important tools of managerial power where low salience institutional choices are made in formal arenas, such as legislatures. In a regime structured primarily by formal institutions, managers need to lobby political parties directly. Even when the rules are made in legislatures, the role of managers in informal working groups can set the agenda of legislation to be debated in Parliament. And, if public attention alights on the problem of corporate control – which is a rare happening – managers will also try to frame the public debate in a way that ties their interests to national interests, in order to influence public opinion in their favor. These tools of formal institutional influence were all in evidence during French and German debates over the EU takeover directive, which we explore in the later sections of this chapter.

Yet this chapter also highlights the fact that the use of informal institutions to regulate corporate governance reinforces the already strong hand of managers in the politics of corporate control. Some of the most important debates about French and German institutions of corporate control took place amongst managers and large shareholders at the end of the 1990s. The change of venue from formal to informal institutions converted politicians from manipulable players to interested spectators. Where the most important institutions of economic governance are primarily informal, it is not politicians who decide their fate. It is instead the institutional incumbents who currently maintain those institutions. When the institutions of patient capital are informal, as they were in France and Germany, then managers and blockholders directly control them. Under such conditions, they only have to worry about formal lobbying and public opinion if governments decide to try to pass laws influencing the functioning of these institutions.

This is a very different story than the one portrayed by existing theories of the politics of corporate control. Partisan theorists emphasize left-wing governments and political entrepreneurs as the force favoring the liberalization of corporate governance.[2] They suggest that parties of the left will try to break down patient capital. In Germany, this was true of Schröder's government only for a limited period of time, after which the government did an about-face under managerial pressure.[3] In France, the government of the left was a bystander during the breakdown of the stable shareholdings in the 1990s. When it was no longer in government in 2006, the Socialist Party actively opposed the transposition of the EU takeover directive, which the left correctly viewed as a law ratifying the liberalization of French markets for corporate control. The weakness of the partisanship argument lies in the fact that political parties of the left rarely have strong commitments in the area of corporate control. This chapter shows for the French case that left parties had little incentive to make corporate control a major political issue, because it was rarely of high political salience. The one time this issue did get some play in the press was in 2006, during the transposition of the European takeover directive, which coincided with Mittal Steel's high profile takeover of the French/Spanish/Luxembourgeois firm Arcelor. When the issue briefly became more salient, the left *opposed* liberalization rather than favoring it. Despite calls for economic patriotism on the right and stakeholder defense on the left, France adopted a neoliberal version of the takeover directive bringing it in the direction of American practice in the field of corporate control. Clearly, theories based on partisanship do not explain these outcomes, as neither left nor right parties adopted a consistent position on the desirability of hostile takeovers.

The second existing explanation, coalitional theory, places the preferences of social coalitions at the center of analysis, while also showing how different electoral institutions can make legal change easier or harder. Peter Gourevitch and James Shinn claim that German labor and business interests have begun to press for a more shareholder-centric system, while the corporatist veto points in the German political system provide many ways for opponents of change to derail reforms. This leads to the philosophical but untestable conclusion that "new alliances are possibilities, but by no means assured."[4] For the rapid institutional change in France, by contrast, Gourevitch and Shinn acknowledge that the changes in ownership structure of the late 1990s have resulted in a system of high managerial autonomy, which they call managerism. To account for such an empirical movement in a manner consistent with the coalitional account, they then fall back on a curious suggestion: "Overall, the decline of statist ideas on the left and the right seems plausibly to explain the movement of French policy."[5] This claim offers no explanatory mechanism connecting changes in the observed coalitions, the policy ideas they favor, and institutional practices regarding takeover protection. The clearest testable prediction

---

[2] Cioffi and Höpner (2006), Höpner (2007), Tiberghien (2007).
[3] Cioffi (2002).
[4] Gourevitch and Shinn (2005: 167).
[5] Gourevitch and Shinn (2005: 271).

one can derive from coalitional theory is that the majoritarian electoral system in France gives governments greater possibilities for effecting policy changes after a change in power than does the proportional representation system in Germany. If change does not happen in the arena of formal laws, though, no clear prediction emerges from coalitional theory. The possibility of informal institutional change that takes place outside of Parliament is rejected by assumption.

This chapter compares the mechanisms of quiet politics with those of partisan and coalitional theories of corporate governance. It does so by considering different episodes of institutional contestation in France and Germany between 1995 and 2007. The first section explains why managerial preferences diverged in France and Germany in the mid-1990s, and the second section explores the salience of corporate control over time in France. The remainder of the chapter then contrasts the battles over corporate control that took place in informal arenas, at the end of the 1990s, with the debate over the negotiation and implementation of the EU takeover directive, which occurred in formal arenas.

Why German and French Managers Have Different Preferences

All managers are acutely interested in the rules governing takeovers, but the managerial preference for takeovers varies across countries. If protection against takeovers were costless, all managers would want it – takeover protection is tantamount to a job protection law for senior managers. National managerial organizations always push for more takeover protection, when they can get it without giving up anything else. Yet managers also want to create the conditions that make their companies, and thereby themselves, most successful. Takeover protections may help company strategies or may harm them, depending on what managers have to trade away to get protection. To understand how managers think about the relative merits of takeover protection, I follow Gourevitch and Shinn[6] in focusing on *autonomy* as the primary criterion managers use in establishing their political preferences over regimes of corporate control. In coordinated market economies, where companies are engaged in a variety of networks with other firms and stakeholders, increasing the power of minority shareholders is often a way for managers to achieve greater autonomy vis-à-vis these existing stakeholders.

Faced with the deepening of global financial markets in the 1990s, managers in coordinated economies had two choices. They could embrace an influx of foreign capital, lowering the cost of borrowing and opening their access to other markets, but also exposing these companies to demands for internal reform from foreign investors. Or they could maintain barriers to active markets for corporate control, and thus the luxury of the longer term perspective associated with them, at the price of scaring away certain types of foreign investors. The first option was the choice made by managers in France. Yves Tiberghien

---

[6] Gourevitch and Shinn (2005).

has labeled this choice the "golden bargain."[7] Under the terms of the golden bargain, managers accept the higher level of takeover risk associated with more active markets of corporate control and the short-term perspective associated with reliance on quarterly earnings reports.[8] In exchange, access to the capital of foreign investors enables companies to pursue strategies of rapid internal reorganization or external growth.

The embrace of foreign investors in French companies required that managers be able to respond to calls from these investors for increasing shareholder value. According to Michel Goyer and Bob Hancké, French managers were able to make this choice because they faced no obstacle from organized labor within the firm and because it suited the core competencies developed by large French firms.

> [T]he lack of institutionalized labor influence within the firm provided management with ample room to introduce shareholder value practices inside French firms. Moreover . . . it complemented the organizational frameworks of large corporations. The concentration of power at the top of the firm, the ability to rapidly develop new strategic initiatives, the innovative design of products based on scientific research, and the virtual exclusion of labor from the corporate decision-making process characterize the business strategy of [French] large firms.[9]

French works councils are weak, so they lacked the power to impose costs on managers who unilaterally renegotiated contracts, as is sometimes demanded by investors seeking maximal returns. Thus, French managers could afford to allow a greater role for institutional investors, because managers possessed the power at the firm level to renegotiate or abrogate contracts if short-term market demands required it.[10]

German managers rejected the golden bargain in the 1990s, primarily because works councils in Germany retained a legislatively enshrined capacity for firm-level contestation.[11] The fact of works council power raises the potential cost of trying to reorganize through downsizing, as workers have formal representation and the capacity to challenge managerial strategies in court. Thus, the sort of radical reorganization associated with hostile takeovers faces an entrenched force for the representation of employee interests. Given that German managers are unlikely to be able to increase their autonomy at the expense of works councils, this creates an incentive for them to ensure that institutional investors do not encroach further on managerial autonomy. As Michel Goyer has shown, this choice influences the sorts of funds likely to invest in a given economy. U.S. hedge and mutual funds, which like to take large stakes in companies and to exert influence over managerial strategy, shy

---

[7] Tiberghien (2007).
[8] Albert (1993).
[9] Goyer and Hancké (2005: 185–186).
[10] Goyer (2002).
[11] Streeck (1995), Jackson et al. (2005).

away from the German market because of their limited ability to control companies, while they have moved aggressively into the French market.[12]

In addition to this fundamental difference in the strength of labor at the firm level, two other considerations also influenced the formation and expression of managerial preferences in France and Germany. First, with respect to company cross-shareholdings, concentrated ownership in Germany has a strategic logic, not merely a logic of takeover defense. The French hard core networks were built with political intent as the state privatized in the mid-1980s, with the aim of ensuring privatized companies did not fall into foreign hands.[13] German concentrated ownership has grown instead from family ownership and from firms taking an ownership stake in companies with which they have a long-term contracting relationship.[14] So while the assets tied up in the ownership of other companies had an opportunity cost in both countries, those costs were probably higher in Germany than in France.

Second, features of the political organizations of managers differed between the two countries. The foregoing description of the underlying interests of managers of large firms in France and Germany obscures the heterogeneity of views that existed among firms within each of these countries. Managerial interest associations are not only interest groups, but also forums for managerial conflict about the appropriate set of policies to strengthen national companies in international competition. We expect factional conflict within managerial organizations, just as we expect to observe factional conflict in political parties. As managerial preferences change within a country, we expect to see a competition of ideas play out through employers' associations, which represent the collective political interests of business.

These conflicts looked different in France and in Germany. French managerial associations were divided by debates about the commitment to the stakeholder model of capitalism. A faction of neoliberal managers took control of the peak associations in the late 1990s, and they shifted these organizations toward a much deeper embrace of foreign ownership and liberalization.[15] These same managers also led the destruction of the preexisting institutions that guaranteed the passivity of the French market for corporate control. In Germany, there

---

[12] Goyer (2006b, forthcoming). Works councils are not only a constraint on managerial strategies. Cooperation with the works council can be an asset in international competition. In German large firms, where works councils are represented on the supervisory board, there is great incentive for companies to negotiate major strategies with employee representatives. The presence of organized works councils at company level is therefore another resource for pursuing long-term strategies based on inter- and intra-firm cooperation (Hall and Soskice 2001). The role of works councils in German companies is reinforced by product market strategies that depend on extensive inter-firm cooperation. Hostile takeovers threaten long-term relationships that exist among firms with cospecific asset investments, just as they can challenge production methods that depend on delegating substantial autonomy to workers on the shop floor (Goyer 2006a, Börsch 2007).

[13] Schmidt (1996), Garrigues (2002).

[14] Goergen et al. (2004), Börsch (2007).

[15] Garrigues (2002).

were also divisions within managerial associations. But structural features of the German associations helped ensure the dominance of those managers who wanted to preserve takeover protections. The German peak association, the BDI, was dominated by industrial managers, who regarded prohibitions on the rights of managers to defend their companies during hostile takeovers as unacceptable. The BDI excludes many of the financial sector companies that favored the liberalization of German markets for corporate control.[16] And while German banks and insurers liberalized, the giants of German industry successfully maintained institutions of protection. Thus, the organizational characteristics of the BDI accentuated the influence of those managers in Germany who favored protections of the passive market for corporate control.

Salience and the Politics of Informal Institutions

Issues of low political salience are structurally more likely than issues of high political salience to be governed through informal institutions – that is, rules made by private actors outside of Parliament. When an issue area achieves sustained political salience, this means that voters consider it an important area, relative to the other political issues they care about. This creates a powerful incentive for politicians to develop the tools to intervene, so that they can be seen to respond to the concerns of voters. If business is seen to have captured a high salience policy domain characterized by informal governance, public opinion will push governments to intervene more heavily. Just as a monopoly distorts a product market, a monopoly of economic power invalidates the possibility for free contracting, which is the general condition under which democratic governments delegate to informal governance. One of the few ways for such issues to escape the reach of political regulation is when governments impose limits on themselves, constitutionally, to govern an issue area. This is the case, for example, in some European countries in the area of wage bargaining, where direct negotiation between representatives of workers and employers is often protected from direct state intervention.[17] Absent such government self-restraint, the combination of informal governance with high political salience is unusual.

By contrast, informal institutions in areas of low political salience are common. For political scientists, who thrill to the spectacle of a close vote in a legislature, informal institutions are hard to digest. Where is the political action in a set of agreements that no legislature or regulatory agency has ratified? Given this fixation on formal rule making, many eminent scholars have followed the intellectual lead of Peter Gourevitch in assuming that all informal institutions, to the extent that they are political, must have roots in Parliament:

---

[16] Callaghan (2004).

[17] In Germany this principle is called *Tarifautonomie*, and it gives unions and employers' associations the right to negotiate wages without state intervention.

TABLE 3.1. *Formality and Salience in Issue Domains*

	Informal Rules Primary	Formal Rules Primary
High Salience	Wage Bargaining Rules	Pension System
Low Salience	Takeover Protection	Vocational Training

"The regulatory system sustains the micro-institutional patterns of the economy. The regulatory systems are sustained, or changed, by choices made in a political process by policymakers."[18] This assumption is contradicted by many sociological studies of corporate governance, which emphasize that shared ideas among relevant market actors, rather than legal changes pushed through legislatures, determine the extent to which important practices of corporate governance actually change.[19] A political approach to institutional change that collapses informal institutions into the struggles we can see in Parliament thus risks obscuring some of the central political battles of modern capitalism.

Informal institutions are rules established outside legislative or regulatory arenas by nonstate actors. When an issue area is governed primarily by informal institutions, two aspects of informal governance further reinforce the advantageous situation of institutional incumbents. First, the incumbents do not have to convince politicians or regulators to decide in their favor, through lobbying or other exercises of expertise. They themselves are the decisionmakers, and they only need to ensure that state policymakers do not decide to intervene. This is a different arena than formal institutions, where state intervention is a given, and managers try to influence the direction of that decision. In other words, if an existing set of nonstate institutions already effectively governs an issue area, politicians must decide *whether* to intervene before deciding *how* they would change the rules. Second, in informal institutions those who oppose the incumbents lack guaranteed institutional conduits for their input. The question of institutional change and stability is not, "can we get this change past our opponents in Parliament?" Opponents in the legislature have no opportunity to rally others to their cause because there is no legislative or regulatory hearing process that structures political contestation over rules. Informal institutions generally have far narrower, less public forums for participation in the process of rule change than do formal institutions.

Table 3.1 represents the potential combinations of high and low salience issues with those governed primarily by formal and informal rules. Pension systems and vocational training are governed primarily through formal institutions: pensions because they are a politically important regime of state-supervised redistribution, and vocational training because school-based education is overseen by the state in every advanced industrial country, even those (such as Germany) where companies play a significant role in the firm-based

---

[18] Gourevitch (1996: 241); see also Streeck and Thelen (2005).
[19] Hirsch (1986), Davis and Greve (1997), Schneper and Guillén (2004).

components of apprenticeship training. The rules governing takeover protection and wage bargaining are primarily decided in informal arenas of decision making in many advanced capitalist countries, including France.[20]

Recall that the political salience of an issue refers to its importance to the average voter, relative to other issues. As noted in Chapter 1, press coverage from national newspapers is a robust indicator of political salience.[21] Figure 3.1 uses the press coverage received by these four policy areas as an indicator of their political salience.[22] The measures are based on LexisNexis searches of the original-language editions of the two most important general-interest newspapers in France: *Le Monde*, associated with the center-left, and *Le Figaro*, associated with the center-right. What do we learn about the political salience of takeover protection by looking at variations in press coverage over time?

From 1996 to 2007, takeover protection was an issue of very low political salience in France, averaging fewer than thirty articles per year combined in *Le Monde* and *Le Figaro*. If there were only one article *per month* on a subject in each of the two general newspapers, that would be equal to twenty-four articles per year. During this period, the systems governing pensions (formal rules) and employer-employee bargaining (informal rules) both received sustained press attention: 126 articles per year for pensions and 142 articles per year for wage

---

[20] The unusual regime of Dutch takeover protection, which is discussed in Chapter 4, is governed primarily by formal rules, which is what makes it so unusual among the coordinated market economies. Wage bargaining systems vary across the advanced capitalist countries in the balance of formal and informal institutionalization. They combine formally regulated areas, such as determination of the minimum wage, with recognitions of the right of social partners to negotiate outcomes, as in wage setting. However, in the countries studied in this book, wage setting is an activity that takes place between employers' associations and unions with the surveillance but not active involvement of the state. For this reason I designate it as primarily informal.

[21] The largest problem with using press coverage to measure salience is the assumption that newspapers cover issues in proportion to how much voters care about them. Absent better data, though, such a measure is a decent proxy (see Epstein and Segal 2000, who compare different measures of salience and come down in favor of newspaper coverage).

[22] In an attempt to create institutional categories that were as conceptually comparable as possible, the search relied on terms that would capture articles dealing with rules of governance in each issue area. The search terms used in Lexis-Nexis were the following (French original is followed by bracketed English translation):

Takeover Protection: "anti-OPA" [anti-takeover] OR (protection W/30 OPA) OR (protéger [to protect] W/30 OPA) [the construction w/30 OPA means any article containing the word protection within 30 words distance of the abbreviation OPA (takeover)].

Vocational Training: "formation par/en/d'alternance" [training by/through/of school/work combination] OR "contrats de qualification" [qualification contracts] OR "contrats d'apprentissage" [apprenticeship contracts].

Bargaining Rules: "accords de branches" [sectoral negotiated agreements] OR "accords collectives" [collectively negotiated agreements] OR "conventions collectives" [collective agreements].

Pension System: "régimes de retraite" [pension rules] OR "régimes spéciaux" [special pension rules] AND "retraites" [retirement] at least 5 times.

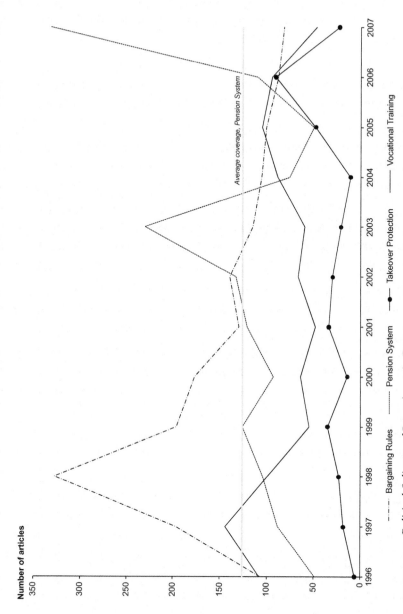

FIGURE 3.1. Political Salience of Issue Areas in France, 1996–2007

Source: LexisNexis search of *Le Monde* and *Le Figaro*. Definition of the search terms used for the issue areas is provided in footnote 22.

Note: The gray horizontal line shows the average number of articles per year published on the subject of the pension system, which is the less covered of the two high-salience issue areas depicted in this figure. This is one rough indicator of a minimal level of media coverage we might classify as being associated with an issue of high political salience.

bargaining. In the realm of economic policy, the dominant themes in the French press during this period were the changes to bargaining rules at the firm-level from 1997 to 2000, and the issues surrounding pension reform after the election of a government of the right in 2002. Vocational training was less salient than either one of these, garnering only eighty-two articles per year on average, which was still almost triple the average press coverage received by takeover protection.

How do we know high salience when we see it? Baseball players and fans often refer to the "Mendoza line" when they talk about a minimal level of batting competence. Mario Mendoza, a shortstop for the Pittsburgh Pirates, played tremendous defense but had limited offensive talents. His batting average – the ratio of hits to the number of at-bats – frequently fell below .200, or twenty percent. Players whose batting average does not reach the Mendoza line of .200, no matter how sparkling their defense, are not considered good enough to play major league baseball.[23] Given that every country has its own distinct political discourse and structure of print media, there is no obvious numerical equivalent of the "Mendoza line" in terms of the number of articles that must appear on a given subject for it to be considered of "high" political salience. In this chapter and the two that follow it, I try nevertheless to create a "Mendoza line" of political salience for each country, based on the relative frequency with which economic policy areas are discussed in the press. In France, the Netherlands, and Japan, bargaining rules and the pension system tend to receive much higher press coverage than do the less salient issues of vocational training or takeover protection. For each of these countries, I take the less well-covered of these high salience issues (i.e., whichever of the two that has fewer newspaper articles written about it), and use the average annual number of articles on that subject in a given country as the lower bound on when we might consider an issue of high salience. This is a very crude way of establishing where the threshold of "high salience" stands. Yet, it provides a useful point of reference for considering how coverage of takeover protection compares to other issues that are covered by the press and of concern to voters. This Mendoza line of political salience in France is represented by the gray horizontal bar in Figure 3.1.

Over this time period, takeover protection *never* reached the average level of coverage achieved by the pension system in France. When looking at the trends in comparative political salience in Figure 3.1, there is only one year – 2006 – when the issue of takeover protection received the same approximate level of coverage as the other subject areas. In March, 2006 the EU takeover directive was transposed into French law. As we will see later in this chapter, the spike in press coverage of this issue was driven both by coverage of parliamentary hearings on the new takeover law and by the attempt of the Indian steel company Mittal Steel to acquire the partly French steel company Arcelor. In terms

---

[23] Pitchers are excluded from this rule, as their value is derived almost entirely from their pitching (defense), not their batting (offense).

of institutional change, the dissolution of the *noyaux durs* was a much more significant institutional development than the transposition of the EU directive. But the fact is that the breakdown of the *noyaux durs* essentially took place out of the public eye. Major general interest newspapers in France ran fewer than one article per month on the topic of takeover protection from 1997 to 2000. French managers needed to convince neither politicians nor the broader public to support the breakdown of the old system of cross-shareholding. This transformation thus took place below the radar of politicians and the public, a process to which we turn now.

Informal Institutional Change at the Domestic Level: France and Germany in the 1990s[24]

Where institutions depend on intercompany coordination, what managers believe other managers believe may be as important to processes of institutional change as are legal reforms aimed at changing the rules of corporate control. As we saw in Chapter 2, patient capital in France was supported by concentrated owners combined with a set of strategic shareholders – the so-called *noyaux durs* (hard core) networks. One of those networks was centered on the bank Société Générale, the other on the Banque Nationale de Paris (BNP). At the beginning of the 1990s, many of the managers of large firms in the two networks shared the view that the future of French business had two components: the support of stable shareholders and their development as global, European companies.[25] In Bob Hancké's words, the system of stable shareholding "offered large-firm management the autonomy to restructure with a long-term perspective in mind, that is, without falling prey to the short-term profitability criteria that the capital markets imposed...."[26] Large French firms had used takeover protection as an external shield while they reorganized their internal structure and their external relationships with suppliers.

This reorganization had made French firms much more profitable, and it had both weakened firm-level works councils and reduced the labor costs of these firms.[27] By the mid-1990s, the senior managers of French firms viewed the expansion of global financial markets as both an opportunity and a threat. Old-style conglomerates would have to reorganize around their core competencies in order to attract the attention of international markets.[28] But if they were to compete at the scale of European and global markets, they also perceived a need to expand. Claude Bébéar, the chief executive of the insurance company

---

[24] This section draws on Culpepper (2005).
[25] Schmidt (1996), Levy (1999).
[26] Hancké (2002: 33).
[27] Employee compensation represented seventy-three percent of the value added by French non-financial firms in 1982, a figure which had dropped to sixty-four percent by 1989 (O'Sullivan 2007: 417).
[28] Goyer (2006a), Morin (1998).

AXA, pithily summarized the imperatives facing French managers in 1996: "either find a niche or get big and fight."[29]

The business objectives of focusing on core competencies and of expanding internationally were both facilitated by the weakness of labor at the firm level in France. Employees often favor a conglomerate structure, which works in several different product markets, as strong divisions of the company can subsidize weaker divisions. Moreover, a focus on core competencies in practice often involves substantial layoffs, and employees are well aware of this threat.[30] Where employees have the power to block this move, they will. But in France they did not, and in the mid-1990s many large firms began to shift their organizational strategy toward one of focusing on core business. Michel Goyer has shown that in 1990, seventy-seven percent of French large firms still had a conglomerate structure, but that by 1998 half of the large firms in France were focused in a single or dominant niche business.[31] One key part of expanding around core competencies involved strategies of external growth – in other words, buying other companies that made related goods for different markets. As Mary O'Sullivan's research has demonstrated, French managers were by the 1990s increasingly obsessed with how to expand through international acquisitions.[32] This, in turn, required substantial capital, and it raised the cost that many managers perceived of sinking investments in the protection of other companies through the *noyaux durs*.

With French big business focusing increasingly on core competencies and international expansion, the largest French firms collectively began to look more like the AXA of Claude Bébéar. Bébéar had succeeded as an entrepreneur by developing a regional insurance company into a global heavyweight by focusing solely on a single core competency: insurance.[33] Never a member of the state-trained managerial elite that had supported the system of the *noyaux durs*, Bébéar had long professed an unwillingness to engage in the long-term strategic shareholding favored by the establishment.[34] The structural change underway in French big business in the mid-1990s began to predispose more CEOs to adopt the neoliberal policy preferences of Claude Bébéar.

The tipping point in French business came in 1997, triggered by AXA's takeover of the insurance company UAP.[35] AXA's purchase of UAP meant that the company had purchased a place at the heart of the cross-shareholding network. Bébéar sent a public signal that AXA/UAP was abandoning the system of cross-shareholding in January 1997, saying that the company "had no intention of becoming the godfather of the French economy" and initiating a

---

[29] O'Sullivan (2007: 422).
[30] Goyer and Hancké (2005).
[31] Goyer (2006a: 88).
[32] O'Sullivan (2007).
[33] Abescat and Lhaik (1999).
[34] Schmidt (1996: 382), Garrigues (2002).
[35] Morin (1998).

token drop in its holdings of BNP, the bank at the heart of one of the two shareholding networks.

AXA/UAP's defection provided a shock to other members of the network. Bébéar's announcement did not trigger an immediate selling of shares by other companies. Instead, it stimulated a set of discussions among other managers in the hard core networks about the effectiveness of cross-shareholding as takeover protection, and experimentation with alternative modes to construct a hard core of ownership. For example, two of the members of the BNP network – Suez and Lyonnaise des Eaux – merged in March 1997, establishing hard-core shareholders in Groupe Bruxelles Lambert and Crédit Agricole that replaced the eventual loss of AXA-UAP.[36] AXA itself did not actually make any major sales of its nonfinancial shares until the end of 1997 (when it sold its small holdings in Alcatel) and near the end of 1998 (when it dropped its holdings in Saint Gobain and Vivendi).[37] The major fall in shareholding in the second hard core network, which clustered around Société Générale, did not occur until 1999, as shown in Chapter 2. Yet Bébéar's statement is widely regarded as the moment the system broke down. Frédéric Lordon echoes the general sentiments of French businesspeople when he identifies AXA's takeover of UAP as "the shock ... that overturn[ed] the organization of French capitalist control which, by stabilizing the ownership of capital, had in fact allowed for resistance against outside ownership. The bipolar structure [of French capitalism], essentially inherited from the days of Pompidou and built around the constellations of Suez and Paribas, found itself dismantled in a single blow."[38] The hard cores designed to protect French companies from hostile foreign takeovers were a dead letter by 2000.

Because the institution of stable shareholding was maintained privately and without legal support, there was no opportunity for nonmanagerial opponents of Bébéar's to rally opposition. In the formal political sphere, AXA's takeover of UAP took place the same year as the surprise election victory of a socialist/communist coalition government in 1997. The institutions of corporate

---

[36] Vincent (2004).

[37] AXA/UAP's combined shareholdings in nonfinancial companies in its network were all relatively minor (below five percent of their outstanding shares). As such, selling those shares alone would not have destabilized the existing network, absent selling by other shareholders. AXA/UAP's shares of financial companies were more substantial, as it held blocks larger than ten percent of the shares of both BNP and of Paribas. BNP merged with Paribas in 1999 (Vincent 2004).

[38] Lordon (2000). It is important to note that AXA's move to sell blocks of shares in the hard cores was not unprecedented, at least for AXA. The year before it bought UAP, AXA had significantly reduced its holdings in two large French companies in the hard cores: Alcatel and Suez. That sale of shares had had no effect on the behavior of other companies at that time, because at that time AXA was not a central member of the cross-shareholding network. It was only when it bought UAP and threatened to liquidate its shareholdings in 1997 that the other companies in French shareholding networks began to respond. The actions of AXA/UAP led them to reevaluate the idea (and costs) of using cross-shareholding as mutual takeover protection.

control were not an issue in the campaign, and indeed the victorious social-ist government had no position on the *noyaux durs*. In the economic sphere, the major question for the government was how to meet the macroeconomic criteria for European monetary union, the issue over which the election had been called.[39] In the social realm, the government's principal promise was to exhort the social partners to negotiate the conditions of a thirty-five-hour work week, which lies behind the extremely high salience of the issue of bargaining rules between 1997 and 2000 (Figure 3.1). The finance minister, Dominique Strauss-Kahn, thus had some latitude within the government, because the gov-ernment did not come to power with a clear economic agenda.[40] As a member of Strauss-Kahn's cabinet summarized the issue to me, "Jospin and the Social-ist Party had no precise idea about privatization.... And about the *noyaux durs*, I think that there was no precise idea of anybody, except Dominique Strauss-Kahn. Dominique Strauss-Kahn had very clear ideas."[41]

Strauss-Kahn's idea was that the state should act as a patient investor in strategic sectors to promote the development of European-wide industrial champions.[42] The finance minister thus shared the concern of French CEOs with how to get big enough to succeed in international competition. This is not surprising, because Strauss-Kahn was well-known for his proximity to the heads of French large firms. In 1993 he had founded the *Cercle de l'Industrie*, a group that brought together CEOs from the largest thirty-five companies in France. The group was both a lobbying organization, which tried to defend the interests of French companies in Brussels, and a collective thinktank for business leaders and politicians.[43] This cooperation with leaders of business did not come to an end when he was in government. As a member of his cabinet told me, "there were a few big CEOs, and they were the partners of Dominique Strauss-Kahn in thinking about strategy, industrial policy, etc."[44] Where Strauss-Kahn differed with some parts of the managerial establishment was in his view of what sort of ownership structure was necessary to sustain big European companies in which the state had a strategic interest: "He thought it was necessary to have a long-term ownership, or not necessarily a long-term owner, but a structure of the shareholder which could guarantee that in the long-term the company in those sectors could run a consistent and long-term strategy."[45]

Strauss-Kahn had a clear idea of the role of long-term ownership in the French economy, but the French government in 1997 possessed few instru-ments to act on this view. States have three main ways of favoring schemes

---

[39] Interview with Pierre Duquesne, chief economic advisor to Prime Minister Lionel Jospin, July 16, 2009.
[40] Tiberghien (2007).
[41] Interview with cabinet member of Finance Minister Dominque Strauss-Kahn, July 16, 2009.
[42] Tiberghien 2007: 76–81.
[43] Garrigues (2002: 277).
[44] Interview with cabinet member of Finance Minister Dominque Strauss-Kahn, July 16, 2009.
[45] Ibid.

of long-term ownership: owning shares themselves; determining to whom they sell those shares if they privatize state-owned enterprises; or using laws to change the costs and benefits of those private actors who own shares. These are important levers of influence. Yet by the mid-1990s, France had reduced many of its public ownership stakes, thus weakening the possible impact of the first lever of influence. The second lever – choosing ownership when privatizing – is one that French governments had used in the 1980s to build up hard core ownership networks for privatized companies, which were also among the largest companies in the French economy. When it comes to the third lever, however, the power of public influence is indirect. The government had no tools beyond privatizing the companies that remained in state ownership, and it was largely on the sideline as the *noyaux durs* were dismantled. At the beginning of 1998, Strauss-Kahn commissioned a report on the potential public responses to the changes in the ownership structure of large French firms.[46] The report was authored by François Morin, a long-time scholar of French ownership holdings and a close personal friend of Prime Minister Lionel Jospin.[47] Morin's report bemoaned the loss of coordination, which AXA's steps to dissolve the ownership networks had signified. The change had resulted in a "brutal rupture" with past methods of securing patient capital, and the new system was one in which French companies were increasingly constrained by the "dominant strategic model" characteristic of Anglo-Saxon markets: a focus on core businesses, a break-up of conglomerates, and an immediate reallocation of capital away from unprofitable business.[48] This public lament, however, was the only action of the government. A member of Strauss-Kahn's cabinet told me that the report "was not used, it was just for writing things."[49]

Bébéar's takeover of UAP in 1997 was followed the next year by the conversion of the old employers' association, the CNPF, to the MEDEF, a name change that signaled the triumph of the neoliberal wing of the employers' movement.[50] In 1990, Bébéar had also supported the elevation of Denis Kessler to the head of the FFSA (Fédération Française des Sociétés d'Assurance). Kessler would be the intellectual leader of the MEDEF's attempt to impose a new, more liberal set of social rules on the bargaining among French social partners after 1997.[51] Although the MEDEF was a publicly prominent representative of French companies, the organization itself has often been challenged by internal divisions,

---

[46] Morin (1998).

[47] Interview with Pierre Duquesne, chief economic advisor to Prime Minister Lionel Jospin, July 16, 2009.

[48] Morin (1998: 16, 44).

[49] Interview with cabinet member of Finance Minister Dominique Strauss-Kahn, July 16, 2009.

[50] MEDEF stands for *Mouvement des Entreprises de France*, a name change that signaled the newly activist line pursued by the organization under the leadership of Ernest-Antoine Seillière and Denis Kessler. CNPF stood for *Conseil National du Patronat Français* (Garrigues 2002: 274).

[51] Abescat and Lhaik (1999), Garrigues (2002).

particularly those between large and small companies.[52] French large firms began to rely increasingly on the lobbying capacity of the association of large firms, the AFEP, which represents only the ninety largest companies in France.[53] As an advisor to Prime Minister Jospin told me, AFEP has "excellent technicians, in particular for laws under consideration.... They do not merely take general positions, they try to have legislators add their own amendments, like real lobbyists."[54] From the managerial camp, an interview subject in charge of lobbying for one of the big employer organizations reiterated the same point: "AFEP is not a think tank which does big economic studies. They talk to their companies. They look at what works and what doesn't, and they make concrete propositions."[55] In 1999, Bébéar succeeded in pushing his candidate for the presidency of AFEP to replace Jean-Louis Beffa.[56] In short, although Bébéar had steadfastly refused to be the godfather of a French capitalism symbolized by the *noyaux durs*, by 1999 he was the incontestable leader of French senior managers, and his neoliberal policy preferences were those defended by the major representative associations.

Why Mannesmann in Germany Was Not Like AXA/UAP in France

The process that followed the AXA takeover of UAP triggered institutional change in the French system of corporate control. Yet an event that was viewed by some observers as similarly momentous for the German system of corporate control – the takeover of Mannesmann by the British company Vodafone in 2000 – did not trigger a similar selloff of cross-shareholding in German capitalism, as demonstrated in Chapter 2.[57] Why not? AXA was, like many other French companies at the time, focused on its core competencies and on strategies of freeing up capital for international expansion. In contrast, Mannesmann was unusual in the German context. Its shares were highly dispersed, and sixty percent of its shares were held by foreign investors, with two-thirds of the foreign owners being British or American.[58] Neither its ownership structure, nor the identity of its owners, was of the sort that could provoke other managers at large German companies to rethink their strategies, because Mannesmann's ownership structure was typical of large American companies, not large German ones. AXA/UAP sat at the heart of French capitalism, and its management faced a dilemma that was common to senior managers in the French ownership network: was the cost of refocusing on core competencies through international expansion strategies worth foregoing the collective takeover defense value of the *noyaux durs*? Mannesmann, in contrast, was an outlier, and its takeover

[52] Bunel (1995), Woll (2006).

[53] Interview with MEDEF official, July 4, 2003; Abescat and Lhaik (1999).

[54] Interview with Pierre Duquesne, chief economic advisor to Prime Minister Lionel Jospin, July 16, 2009.

[55] Interview with senior official of French managerial association, July 16, 2009.

[56] Abescat and Lhaik (1999).

[57] Cf. Höpner and Jackson (2001).

[58] Höpner and Jackson (2001: 25).

did not trigger a fundamental reevaluation of the system of stable ownership in Germany.

Unlike in France, works councils in Germany remained integral players in negotiating firm strategies through the legally protected institutions of codetermination.[59] One result of this continued firm-level strength is that the majority of large firms in Germany retained their conglomerate structure throughout the 1990s and beyond. In 2003, sixty-four percent of German large firms still had a divisional conglomerate structure, while only forty percent of French large firms did.[60] Indeed, when Vodafone announced its hostile takeover bid, the works council of Mannesmann particularly attacked the plan to end Mannesmann's conglomerate structure. Klaus Zwickel, the deputy chair of Mannesmann's supervisory board and also the president of the IG Metall union, denounced the deal on precisely these grounds.

> Mr. Zwickel said that Vodafone was interested only in cutting the "best fillet" out of Mannesmann – i.e., its extremely profitable mobile phones division. The other Mannesmann divisions would very likely be sold again and thereby the overall Mannesmann corporation would be disintegrated. The IG Metall president announced strong resistance to this scenario, which would threaten thousands of jobs and undermine the particular co-determination culture at Mannesmann.[61]

The production strategies of many German large firms, unlike those of their French counterparts, are organized around close cooperation of management with workers' representatives. As most German companies do not have the dispersed ownership of Mannesmann, managers and concentrated owners do not want to risk prolonged confrontations with empowered workers.[62]

What did happen in Germany during the second half of the 1990s was a split between the strategies of financial institutions and other nonfinancial corporations. German banks and insurers began to change their shareholding strategies, moving to become active players in European and global financial markets. The percentage of supervisory board representatives from financial firms fell continuously between 1996 and 1999, after having been stable (or even slightly increasing) earlier in the decade.[63] The number of substantial voting blocks of the top 100 German listed companies held by financial firms similarly decreased between 1993 and 2003.[64] However, the proportion of large blockholdings held by *non*financial firms remained stable over this period, and the proportion held by individuals and families – the largest set of blockholders in Germany – grew at a faster rate than the financial firm decrease. In other words, German banks and insurers began managing their assets more

---

[59] Jackson et al. (2005).
[60] Goyer (2006a).
[61] Schulten (1999).
[62] Goyer (2006a).
[63] Höpner (2003: 138).
[64] Wójcik (2003).

as portfolio holdings and less as strategic holdings, but German families and nonfinancial companies appear to have reaffirmed the value of patient capital as a way to blunt hostile takeovers.[65] The net effect was no change in the extent of patient capital.

This split between financial and nonfinancial companies failed to have important consequences for the institutions of patient capital in Germany because the core incumbents of the system – nonfinancial companies and the families controlling their shares – did not defect from them. This was important in the German context because there was a strong push in the formal institutional arena to challenge the system of stable shareholding. The Social Democratic coalition government of Gerhard Schröder, elected in 1998, was decidedly more hostile to institutions of patient capital than was the Socialist coalition elected in France one year earlier. Its most important policy instrument for liberalizing share ownership was the passage of a tax reform in 2000 that abolished the fifty percent capital gains tax for companies selling shares in other companies. This was a deliberate attempt by the government to use its policy tools to undermine the patient capital network among German large companies.[66] However, the informal institutions of protection held because a majority of German manufacturing firms continued to prefer the advantages of the system. A 2002 survey of managers at the large listed companies in Germany found that fifty-nine percent of those managers still had no plans to change their strategic holdings of the shares of other companies.[67]

The Schröder government's attack on stable shareholding created a backlash among managerial elites. At this juncture, the lobbying structure of German associations also revealed an important difference from those in France. The German employers' lobby, the BDI, did not incorporate the voice of financial institutions.[68] Those companies that had largely opted out of the system of patient capital – financial companies – were not important players in the German managerial lobbying organization. Thus, there was no dramatic reorientation of the political organizations of German managers that corresponded to the neoliberal shifts in the MEDEF and AFEP in France after 1997. The different orientations of the two groups, and the opposing demands they made on their governments, were virtually diametrically opposed in the debate over

---

[65] Höpner and Krempel (2003). German industrial companies appear to value controlling shareholding heavily, as their stakes are much larger than those held by banks: "the median size of blocks held by industrial firms is 70%, which is substantially larger than for both individuals and banks (18 and 15%, respectively). This finding suggests that firms, banks, and individuals have very different motives in holding voting blocks. Firms appear to value majority control, while individuals generally own only a minority block. We find further that industrial firms control the largest percentage (26%) of all officially listed shares" (Becht and Boehmer 2003: 13).

[66] In John Cioffi's words, the tax law was "animated entirely by corporate finance and governance concerns. The anticipated effects of the law were tax neutral" (Cioffi 2002: 379).

[67] Börsch (2007: 69).

[68] Callaghan (2004). BDI stands for Bundesverband der Deutschen Industrie, the Federation of German Industry.

formal, international regulation that would affect both France and Germany: the takeover directive of the European Union. It is to this formal political fight that we turn now.

Formal Institutional Change at the International Level: The EU Takeover Directive

We often think of formal political rules as being set at the level of the nation-state. International treaty commitments are also formal rules with consequences for domestic interest groups. In the European Union, which plays an active role in passing and policing common rules of market regulation for its member states, this is especially true. At the international level, national managerial lobbies are as interested in how the rules affect their foreign competitors as how they affect the domestic rules of competition. Helen Callaghan has called this a "constrain-thy-neighbor" effect.[69] This means that international treaty obligations, such as those in the EU, may be relatively more costly to competitor firms in some countries than in others. Managers will prefer rules that limit their competitors more than they limit themselves. And their domestic preferences for allowing institutions that impede hostile takeovers will depend in part on how the adoption of such regulations might affect companies in other countries. Managerial organizations are politically pragmatic, not ideologically consistent. They may prefer one set of institutions at a domestic level – those that make takeovers easier – while pushing their governments to shape international rules in ways that allow some measures of protection. But we also expect managers to be cognizant of the costs of maintaining domestic takeover protections if this allows other countries to maintain them as well.

The EU Takeover Directive ultimately failed in its attempt to harmonize takeover regulations across the countries of the European Union. Scholars take this failure as evidence that, in political conflicts between national models of capitalism and European harmonization, national economic interests continue to be the dominant line of cleavage.[70] In the course of negotiations over the directive, representatives of different European countries adopted a view that was more likely to reflect the preferences of national companies, and national managerial organizations, than the harmonizing imperative favored by the European Commission. In this section I will show that the positions taken by national governments were consistent with the views favored by national managerial organizations in France and in Germany.

Throughout the 1990s, the European Commission, which has responsibility for drafting legislation in the European Union, advocated a framework directive that would harmonize takeover regulations throughout the EU. After a long period of negotiation, the Council of Ministers approved the directive and submitted it to the EU Parliament for approval. There, opposition to the

---

[69] Callaghan (forthcoming).
[70] Callaghan and Höpner (2005), Clift (2007).

TABLE 3.2. *Voting in the European Parliament on the Takeover Directive, 2001*

	Yes (pro takeover directive) (percent)	No (contra takeover directive) (percent)
France	63	37
Germany	1	99

Source: Callaghan and Höpner (2005: 24). Numbers refer to the percentage of each country's delegation to the European Parliament which voted for (or against) the draft takeover directive in 2001. (In absolute numbers, the voting for EPs from France was 45 yes, 26 no, and in Germany 95 yes, 1 no.)

directive was led by the German Christian Democratic rapporteur for the bill, who argued that the directive would put German and European firms at a disadvantage relative to their potential U.S. competitors.[71] The directive was sent to a conciliation committee, which produced a new version of the directive and resubmitted it to the Parliament. On July 4, 2001, the directive vote failed to pass the European Parliament in a tie vote: 273–273, with twenty-two abstentions.[72]

The European Parliament consists of families of national parties that often vote together: the European People's Party brings together Christian Democratic and Conservative parties, while the Party of European Socialists includes most center-left parties. These two major party groups split down national lines in voting for the takeover directive in 2001. As shown in Table 3.2, two-thirds of French members of the European Parliament (MEPs) voted in favor of the directive, while only a single German MEP (from a delegation of ninety six) voted in favor.[73]

The leading lobbying organization of German business, the BDI, strongly opposed the takeover directive. German managers particularly objected to the neutrality clause (article 9), which would have required company directors and senior managers to maintain a neutral position in the face of a potential hostile takeover. One of the leaders of the management lobbying offensive against the takeover directive was Wendelin Wiedeking of Porsche, who observed that it was "grotesque to condemn the management board to neutrality during a takeover bid. It cannot be true that a manager should be forced to watch without recourse to help while his company is taken over.... Openness of the German economy, yes, but not at any price."[74] German managers also complained that the takeover directive was effectively discriminatory within Europe because it did not eliminate the double voting rights available in France

[71] Cioffi (2002: 383–384).

[72] Callaghan and Höpner (2005).

[73] Eighty percent of French MEPs from the main center-left and center-right groups voted for the directive. Most of the "no" votes from French MEPs came from the Greens and the far left groups, which voted unanimously against the bill (Callaghan and Höpner 2005).

[74] Callaghan (2004: 23).

or the trust office foundations available in the Netherlands.[75] While executives of some large German banks favored the directive, these banks are not represented by the BDI and remained a quiet voice in the discussion.[76] Though the German party of the left, the SPD, was divided on the issue, organized labor swung solidly behind the position advocated by managers.[77]

French managerial organizations, in contrast, favored the passage of the directive. The director general of the AFEP, the association of large French firms, claimed that the large majority of AFEP members favored passage of the takeover directive.[78] After the directive's defeat, AFEP pushed for a new directive as quickly as possible.[79] Daniel Bouton, the head of Société Générale, responded similarly when asked about the defeat of the directive: "any harmonized system would have been preferable to the current, non-harmonized system.... Let's not lose sight of the most important thing, and I am sure this is also the point of view of the MEDEF: the European construction has just run into a major defeat."[80] French companies had embarked in the late 1990s on an economic strategy predicated partly on growth through international expansion. The defeat of the takeover directive in 2001 appeared to close off options for French firms, which strongly favored such a measure.

French corporate leaders wanted to make takeovers in Europe easier, but they did not want to lose double-voting rights or voting pacts that helped protect some French managers from international challengers.[81] This is an example of the "constrain thy neighbor" political strategies observed by Callaghan.[82] This stance became a political issue as the German and French governments negotiated with other EU governments over the appropriate revisions to the takeover directive in the wake of its defeat in the EU Parliament. An expert commission proposed a new article, the breakthrough rule (article 11), which would have rendered all takeover protections invalid after a specified length of time, once an acquirer crossed a certain threshold of ownership. Germany refused to accept the breakthrough rule unless it also banned French double voting rights. The French government, following the preferences expressed by managerial associations, refused to allow double-voting rights to be affected by the breakthrough rule.[83] Faced with the Franco-German deadlock, the Council ultimately adopted a compromise version of the takeover directive that left open to member-states the choice of whether or not to incorporate the two controversial articles, on board neutrality (article 9) and the breakthrough rule (article 11). Twenty-one of the then twenty-five member-states ultimately opted

---

[75] Cioffi (2002).
[76] Callaghan (2004).
[77] Cioffi (2002).
[78] Mauduit (2001b).
[79] Callaghan (2004: 25).
[80] Mauduit (2001a).
[81] CCIP (2002).
[82] Callaghan (forthcoming).
[83] Callaghan and Höpner (2005: 311).

out of article 11.[84] The European Union could not achieve a qualified majority behind harmonized takeover regulations, and the potential for opting out of its two central articles reflected a tacit admission that member-states would retain a diversity of national takeover protection regimes.

Formal Institutional Change at the Domestic Level: Adopting the Directive in France

In Germany, the government followed the preferred position of managerial organizations in opting out of articles 9 and 11 of the European Takeover Directive. In the Netherlands the neoliberal coalition government tried to incorporate article 11 against the wishes of managerial organizations, and it lost (see Chapter 4). This section analyzes the transposition of the takeover directive in France, where article 9 was incorporated directly and parts of article 11 were incorporated, but with the simultaneous creation of poison pill-like devices (the *bons Breton*) in 2006. Much of the political discussion in France actually revolved around article 12 – the reciprocity clause – which allowed firms under attack to use the same defenses allowed to the attacking firm, from whatever legal jurisdiction. The debate turned this way in France because the large French firms were interested not so much in domestic liberalization of takeover regulations – which they had already achieved through the dismantling of the *noyaux durs* – but in ensuring the opening of other markets for takeovers by French firms. The ultimate outcome, which Finance Minister Thierry Breton summarized as allowing French firms to compete "*à armes égales*" [with equal weapons] in the international economy, reflected the same line that Claude Bébéar had consistently advocated for French business.[85]

Unlike in the late 1990s, though, the debate did not take place within the informal context of institutions supported by managers. Instead, it took place in the formal legislative venues of French politics, where the directive's fate was debated and ratified. How did the conventional strengths of managers – the delegation of power to informal bodies favorable to business, lobbying expertise, and framing effects – come into play in the formal environment of the debate over the European directive? That is the subject of this section.

There were three significant coalitions involved in the discussions over transposition of the French takeover directive. The first group, which (following Gourevitch and Shinn) I call an investor coalition, united minority shareholder activists, led by Colette Neuville[86] and the few neoliberals in Dominique de Villepin's UMP government, such as the chairman of the finance committee

---

[84] Buck (2006).

[85] Clift (2009: 26).

[86] Colette Neuville was the president of the best-known minority shareholder group in France, ADAM (Association de Défense des Actionnaires Minoritaires: Minority Shareholders' Defense Association).

in the National Assembly, Hervé Novelli.[87] This investor coalition favored a straight transposition of the takeover directive, including articles 9 and 11, and the most limited interpretation of the reciprocity clause. At the opposite end of the spectrum from this group was the stakeholder coalition, which united the Socialist Party and the labor unions.[88] Members of the stakeholder coalition favored opting out of articles 9 and 11, which they viewed as neoliberal in inspiration. In between these two groups stood the managerial coalition. The managerial coalition had a powerful ally in government: Finance Minister Thierry Breton, who was ideologically close to Claude Bébéar and who as a CEO had belonged to Bébéar's exclusive managerial club, *Entreprise et Cité*. The managerial coalition wanted to transpose the takeover directive in a way that would open other markets to French firms. This group advocated an aggressive interpretation of the reciprocity clause (article 12), along with transposition of articles 9 and 11. Within the managerial coalition, there was disagreement over the extent of allowable defense mechanisms. Some managers of large firms insisted they needed no protection at all, other than their high share price, while the MEDEF and AFEP initially favored legal language that would allow managers to offer preferential terms to white knights in the case of a hostile bid. Neither the investor coalition nor the stakeholder coalition would have any impact on the contours of the law that transposed the European takeover directive. The stakes quickly turned into the relatively technical question of what sort of market-conforming measures could satisfy the Bébéar/Breton group of managers (which wanted no protections) and the MEDEF/AFEP group (which wanted the transposition to create some form of legal protection mechanisms for French companies in order to provide teeth to the reciprocity clause).

---

[87] Novelli was the leader of the reformers (les reformateurs), a group of more than 100 neoliberals within the principal center-right party (UMP), a group which also includes the former presidential candidate Alain Madelin. The current website of the reformers is http://lesreformateurs .com/blog/.

[88] Dominique de Villepin, the prime minister, had advocated a position of economic patriotism during the summer of 2005, when there were rumors that PepsiCo might acquire the French company Danone. There was, however, no apparent opposition to the transposition of the takeover directive within the center-right government, and no prominent politician of the right adopted the economic patriotism position during the debates over the directive as a reason to reject articles 9 and 11. The "economic patriotism" episode was almost entirely hot air. The government issued a decree with a list of strategic industries that could not be taken over without government approval, but after negotiations with the European Commission it failed even to be able to include Danone on this list. The one legislative product of the period was a law passed during the summer of 2005, which forced would-be acquirers to announce their intentions in the case of widely rumored takeovers. This law included the so-called Renault amendment, which required that any takeover of a French company must include a takeover of any foreign subsidiaries it controlled. At the time, Renault controlled Nissan, which had a market capitalization that was twice that of its French parent company, and was thus a very expensive prospect for a would-be acquirer. In the press analysis below, economic patriotism is included as a distinct category from stakeholder defense.

One strength of managerial associations under quiet politics is their involvement in working groups to which governments refer political decisions. Such a group was named by then-Finance Minister Nicolas Sarkozy to develop recommendations for how the French government should transpose the EU directive into French law.[89] The commission, called by the name of its leader Jean-François Lepetit, the former head of the market-regulating authority (COB), included one legal expert, one representative of the insurance companies, and one representative of listed companies. The latter role was filled by the CEO of Saint Gobain, Jean-Louis Beffa, a senior figure in the AFEP.[90] The commission excluded any union representation. In its report, the Lepetit Commission called for the following transposition:

- Article 9 (neutrality): Direct transposition
- Article 11 (breakthrough): Opt out of the restriction on shareholder's pacts, but accept measure calling for suspension of voting ceilings
- Article 12 (reciprocity): Adopt reciprocity clause, such that French companies attacked by companies outside France that have not adopted articles 9 and 11 can also suspend the restrictions of articles 9 and 11[91]

The bill as presented to the Senate in October 2005 followed the Lepetit report in every major detail, stressing the *"armes égales"* interpretation of reciprocity. The baseline proposal, including the major decisions on which member states had alternative possibilities, was determined by a private group composed of representatives of business and a market regulator.[92] The thrust of the transposition was to insist that France was open to full competition so long as foreign companies were equally available for takeover. Although the discursive point may seem minor, consider the difference between the trope adopted by French managers – equal weapons – and that stressed by Dutch managers in their national debate – a level playing field. As we shall see in the next chapter, Dutch employers used the language of the level playing field to emphasize the threat to the independence of Dutch firms. As *Le Monde* made clear for its readers, though, the French principle was one of opportunity, not threat: "The leaders of French companies have until now largely profited from a national law in favor of assailants. Numerous members of the CAC-40 built themselves out of stock-market battles.... Today, they tend to be predators."[93] Readers of the business paper *La Tribune* got the same message that economic patriotism was to be observed only in the breach, as "the philosophy of the text, of neo-liberal

---

[89] As finance minister, Sarkozy established the working group in November 2004. Once elected president of the ruling center-right party, the UMP, he resigned and was replaced as finance minister by Hervé Gaymard in November 2004. Gaymard, in turn, resigned almost immediately after a housing scandal in February 2005, when he was replaced as finance minister by Thierry Breton.

[90] Garrigues (2002).

[91] Lepetit (2005).

[92] Lepetit (2005).

[93] Ducourtieux (2005).

origin, [is] to effect 'multilateral disarmament' in the question of cross-border takeovers in the Union. Any sign of chauvinism would in any case be out of place at the time when France is the European league leader for cross-border acquisitions."[94]

The proposed bill thus entered the legislative process on the terms proposed by members of the managerial coalition. The investor coalition wanted to minimize the impact of the reciprocity clause, because its interest was in getting the best deal for shareholders, not in securing the most favorable conditions for French managers. By contrast, some members of the AFEP and MEDEF wanted to reinforce the reciprocity clause by establishing legally valid takeover protections that could be invoked in situations where foreign acquiring firms had some sort of protection.[95] This position was argued by the government's rapporteur for the takeover law, Etienne Blanc, in the National Assembly debate in December 2005. The problem facing the managerial coalition was that there was not unanimous support among managers for a measure that pre-identified a white knight to whom extra shares could be sold in the case of a takeover. The liberal members of the coalition, such as Finance Minister Breton, opposed such a measure. The internal division of the managerial coalition, between the Breton/Bébéar reformist wing and the Beffa traditionalist wing, opened the way for a procedural victory by the investor coalition, which was led by Hervé Novelli, who chaired the Finance Committee in the National Assembly. Novelli used an amendment to the bill in December 2005 to limit the conditions under which reciprocity could be invoked in the case of multiple bids.[96] If the December version of the bill represented the final version of the law, this would disconfirm the hypothesis that low salience politics always favors business because Novelli was able to move legislation in his direction when there was no press attention on this issue at all and the managerial coalition was internally divided.

It is at precisely this intermediate point in the law that the two other levers of business influence kicked in: lobbying strength and press framing. The MEDEF and the AFEP sent a joint letter complaining about the Novelli amendment to Finance Minister Breton in January 2006. The following month, the Senate reversed Novelli's amendment, reinstating the government's original language. The MEDEF and the AFEP also negotiated with Breton the adoption of a defense mechanism they could use when invoking the reciprocity principle. Breton was willing to countenance the creation of American-style poison pills,

---

[94] Raulot (2005).

[95] Recall that the reciprocity clause would allow target firms to use any defenses available to acquiring firms.

[96] At issue was the question of whether reciprocity could be invoked if there were multiple potential acquiring firms, some of which followed the neutrality and breakthrough rules, and some of which did not. The government's version allowed for the reciprocity clause to be invoked if any of the would-be acquirers were not governed by article 9. Novelli's amendment said that reciprocity was to be invoked only if *all* acquiring firms were not subject to article 9 (Raulot 2006).

known as *bons de souscription*, or as they became known, the *bons Breton*. The choice of the poison pill protection was in effect a compromise between Breton and the Bébéar group of liberal CEOs, who simply wanted to ensure the passage of articles 9 and 11, and the traditionalist wing of the MEDEF and AFEP, which had wanted the stronger protection of specified white knights. Frank Riboud, CEO of Danone, summarized the appeal of the compromise among managers: "the government's proposition seems to me to go in the right direction, giving French companies merely the same means of defense as their counterparts abroad, as in the United States, for example. It is also in the interest of the shareholders."[97]

The French press is seldom described as having either a probusiness or neoliberal bias. To assess the ability of the managerial coalition to derive advantage from press coverage in France, I created a sample of every quotation appearing in articles about takeover protection in 2005 and 2006 from four leading French newspapers (see Table 3.3 note for description of the coding procedure).[98] French managers favored the adoption of neoliberal rules. Yet they also faced a challenge from the investor coalition, which advocated even more neo-liberal rules, particularly opposing the adoption of poison pill legislation. To compare the weight of different actors in the tenor of press coverage, I coded quotations from all the articles in my sample into four different categories, corresponding to the three different coalitions as well as the position of economic patriotism associated with Dominique de Villepin. To distinguish between the neoliberal views of the investor coalition and the managerial coalition, the coding focused on the distinction between the market as a tool of company competition (managers) and the market as a tool of shareholder supremacy (investors). The view generally favored by managers was that competition through hostile takeovers was good for them, and the only defense they needed was a high share price. French managers did not emphasize the vulnerability of French firms, but instead their opportunities for growth through takeovers. Three months before Mittal's bid was announced, Arcelor's French CEO, Guy Dollé, was quoted in *Le Figaro* warning against state intervention in the hostile takeover market: "The protection of a company against hostile takeovers is the responsibility of management. It has to convince its shareholders that its strategy is the good one."[99] The CEO of Legrand, a large French company that specializes in electrical installations, summarized the view of takeovers in the press that was presented by many French managers

---

[97] Julien (2006).

[98] I coded individual quotations because they provide the most illustrative, and usually value-loaded, terminology within articles. Thus, the predominance of certain quotations provides the best cue of the tenor of a given article. In the coding for the Netherlands (see Chapter 4), which was performed first, entire articles were coded. In that group of articles, quotations from key actors were the key determinants of the overall tone adopted by individual articles.

[99] Bembaron and Martin (2005). Arcelor had been created in 2002 from the merger of French steel company Usinor with Spanish and Luxembourg steel companies. It was based in Luxembourg but continued to operate plants in France.

TABLE 3.3. *Frequency of Normative Viewpoints on the Market for Corporate Control in the French Press, 2005–2006*

Pro-Active Market for	Market Competition	37%
Corporate Control	Shareholder Supremacy	25%
Anti-Active Market for	Economic Patriotism	13%
Corporate Control	Stakeholder Defense	25%

Note: A LexisNexis search of articles in the area of takeover protection yielded 421 articles from 2005 and 2006 from *Le Monde*, *Le Figaro*, *Les Échos*, and *La Tribune* (the two major general interest newspapers plus the two newspapers focused on economic affairs in France). This table takes as a sample all quotations from nonstate actors that appeared in these articles; if multiple quotations appeared in an article, we coded each quotation separately. This led to a sample of 241 total quotations (many articles were short factual accounts and included no quotations from nonstate actors). Two research assistants, both of whom are native French speakers, independently coded the quotations in one of four categories (or in none of the above): Market Competition, Shareholder Supremacy, Economic Patriotism, and Stakeholder Defense (the coding protocol for this exercise is included as an appendix). The initial coding decisions were identical between the two coders for eighty-one percent of the quotations; the kappa intercoder score for these initial coding decisions is 0.74. In all cases of disagreement between the two coders, I coded the quotations independently. The three of us then decided the final coding together to ensure consistency of practice. We coded forty-nine quotations as Market Competition; thirty-four as Shareholder Supremacy; thirty-three as Stakeholder Defense; and eighteen as Economic Patriotism; the remaining quotations were coded none of the above (thus, the actual number of coded articles used for the table is 134). We coded as Economic Patriotism any quotation that characterized the takeovers as being a question of national or European-level interests, vis-à-vis either actors from other countries or the impersonal functioning of the market. We coded as Market Competition any quotation that characterized takeovers not as a threat for French (or European) firms, but as an opportunity for growth, or to quotations that noted that a high share price is the best defense against hostile takeover. We coded as Shareholder Supremacy any quotation that referred to the stakes in takeovers as affecting shareholder rights, equality of shareholders, shareholders as the ultimate owners of the firms, or transparency as a value for shareholders. We coded as Stakeholder Defense any quotation that characterized takeovers affecting a broader group than just shareholders, including employees, unions, long-term owners, customers, and local communities (but not the whole country, which we characterized instead as Economic Patriotism).

during the transposition debate. "Concerning hostile takeovers, I consider the best defense is to be outstanding and conquering. We are more an actor than a target in global consolidation."[100] This sort of view was coded as favoring Market Competition in takeovers.

Table 3.3 compares the use of Market Competition frames in press articles about takeover protection, in comparison with views associated with the investor coalition (Shareholder Supremacy), Stakeholder Defense, and Economic Patriotism. In the first half of 2006, takeover protection briefly became a relatively prominent issue in French politics, as depicted already in Figure 3.1. Although the overall number of quotations is small (241 over a two-year period), this table shows that, over the whole period, the viewpoint favored by the managerial coalition was the single most frequently evoked

---

[100] Amedeo and Bembaron (2006).

view of takeovers by journalists in the major French press. And, more broadly, views in favor of an active market for corporate control clearly exceeded those favoring a passive market for corporate control.[101]

Until the Novelli amendment passed in late-December 2005, the managerial coalition had largely achieved its aims in working directly with the government in drafting the takeover bill. From January to April, 2006 – a period when the managerial coalition succeeded in passing a version of the law very close to its ideal point and reversing Novelli's amendment – the competitive viewpoint espoused by managers continued to be the single most visible perspective featured in French press coverage, because the press relied heavily on managerial perspectives to convey these issues to the French public. Whether such coverage influenced anyone is difficult to demonstrate conclusively, but the messages in the press were at the very least consonant with the view of takeovers propounded by the managerial coalition.

The poison pill was a tool adopted against the objection of both the neo-liberal coalition, which wanted no protections, and the stakeholder coalition, which wanted greater protections and opposed transposition of articles 9 and 11.[102] Shareholder activist Colette Neuville acidly asked: "this new procedure, is it not going to work especially to protect management?"[103] During the final debate over the bill in the National Assembly, the Socialist Party decried what Arnaud Montebourg dubbed the triumph of "government by shareholders." His party colleague, Eric Besson, argued similarly that "hostile takeovers cannot be decided by shareholders alone. This situation is unbalanced and harmful." Speaking on behalf of the government (and close to the view of large companies), Thierry Breton responded, "contrary to what certain people think, a takeover is not an act of war: it is that which has allowed most French companies to become global companies." Indeed, Breton's opening comments to the Assembly drew the parallels between French and American poison pill regulation: "this is an option known and used in countries like the United States, which cannot be accused of shackling the right of enterprise nor of injuring the interests of shareholders."[104]

---

[101] Note that the coding procedure I used understates the total support in the French press for the market-competition framing of the Breton proposal because it limited the coding to quotations from nongovernmental actors. Research on the press and politics has shown that governments are likely to quote governmental decision makers especially heavily (Baum and Potter 2008), and I wanted to remove this effect in order to consider the weight of business versus other social actors (including even opposition political parties).

[102] Novelli amended the bill to impose a two-thirds vote threshold for the *bons Breton* to be adopted, which was the threshold preferred by minority shareholders' organizations. The final version of the law accepted the two-thirds threshold, but then nullified that decision by allowing shareholders' meetings to use a simple majority vote to delegate the choice of whether or not to use the poison pill to the board of directors.

[103] Lechantre (2006).

[104] National Assembly debate, March 6, 2006. During the final debate on the bill in the French Senate, Senate rapporteur for the bill, Franco Marini, used the competitive trope to attack the stakeholder views expressed by socialist Senator François Marc: "Firms with French capital and French headquarters must not, obviously, be held back by the market in their attempts

Two points are worth underlining about the opposition of the Socialist Party in Parliament as leaders of the stakeholder coalition: first, it directly contradicts the claims of Cioffi and Höpner that the French "center-left tak[es] the side of shareholders against managers."[105] Instead, the French center-left pushed against shareholders *and* against managers, and it lost. Second, it is worth noting that the minority shareholders (on the antiprotection side) and the Socialist Party (on the proprotection side) exercised little influence on the final bill. The policy reached was a compromise between two factions of management, and available evidence suggests that the outcome would have been the same in the absence of both minority shareholder activists and the Socialist Party. There was no rush by French companies to adopt poison pill protection after the measure was adopted. The spike in "market competition" quotations in April 2006, shown in Figure 3.2, was generally a product of French company managers announcing they did not need the poison pill protection.[106] Poison pills were adopted as a way to give teeth to the reciprocity clause, not to shield French companies from takeover, any more than American companies with poison pills are shielded from takeovers. It was a compromise premised on the importance of hostile takeovers as a tool for French companies in their attempt to compete globally.

Conclusion

This chapter has illuminated two aspects of the politics of takeover protection. First, where institutions are informal, we should look at the interests of institutional incumbents to understand why institutions change or remain stable. Institutional change in such contexts is unlikely to be driven by governmental action, but by the preferences of institutional incumbents. In other words, where managers are in charge of systems of patient capital, the political stake lies in understanding how they define their interests in those institutions, not in the posturing of politicians or the clamoring of shareholder groups.

Second, where institutional governance moves into the domain of formal legislation, managers will rely heavily on their advantages in lobbying capacity, their role in informal law-writing bodies, and their ability to influence press coverage. In both the French and the German cases, the position of national governments hewed closely to the line pushed by national managerial organizations. In the German case, this forced Gerhard Schröder to change his views substantially and surprised his EU negotiating partners, who had thought they had a deal on the takeover directive in 2001.[107] When it came to national transposition of the directive in the French case, the government allowed an

at external growth. The narrow vision put forward by Mr. Marc would have precisely the consequence of handicapping them in their external growth operations" (Senate final reading, March 23, 2006).
[105] Cioffi and Höpner (2006: 470).
[106] As of June 2008, only seven firms in the CAC-40 had adopted poison pills.
[107] Cioffi (2002: 383).

informal body sympathetic to large companies to develop the key elements of the French transposition of the directive. This is especially noteworthy given the temporal conjuncture: the Danone case in July 2005 and the Mittal/Arcelor affair in early 2006 had both provoked governmental calls for economic patriotism. In practice, the political posturing was toothless. As the press analysis in the previous section showed, the framing wars in discussions of takeover protection were dominated by those highlighting France's interest in neo-liberal takeover laws rather than those favoring economic patriotism. The passage of that law, with American style poison pills, confirmed the triumph of the aggressively liberal stance that Claude Bébéar had favored in pushing for the breakdown of the *noyaux durs* in the late 1990s.

France and Germany made different institutional choices during this period because the interests of managers of large firms in the two countries diverged. As Michel Goyer and Bob Hancké have shown, the different preferences of French and German managers were a product of the different role of labor at the firm-level in the two countries. During the 1980s, French large companies had restructured and undermined the role of works councils.[108] This restructuring had taken place behind the protective institutions of concentrated ownership and cross-shareholding networks, which large company managers had favored. As French companies emerged from this restructuring process in the 1990s, though, their predominant concerns were how to get big enough to compete on international markets and how to focus on core competencies.[109] These were priorities that increasingly inclined French companies toward reliance on international capital markets, which favored company deconcentration. French labor, meanwhile, was in no position to oppose this move. This is in contrast with Germany, where the power of works councils remained strong and statutorily protected. German managers are accountable to their blockholders and their works councils more than to small shareholders. Their primary goal was to maintain this autonomy vis-à-vis small shareholders and pension funds. When Mannesmann was taken over by Vodafone, there was no tipping effect at all – because Mannesmann was an unusual company by German standards. It already had dispersed shareholding. There was no political movement among German managers corresponding to the neoliberal tendency led by Claude Bébéar in France. For this reason, the Mannesmann takeover had no effect on the shareholding patterns of other German large firm.

In short, this chapter has argued that both informal and formal domains of hostile takeover protection were dominated by the views of managers in France and Germany between 1996 and 2007. Against a partisan analysis, this chapter has shown that left parties did not have a consistent view about the desirability of takeover protection, nor did governments have tools to secure their preferred regimes of corporate control. The disinterest of the Socialist

---

[108] Hancké (2002).
[109] Goyer (2006a), O'Sullivan (2007).

Party allowed Finance Minister Dominique Strauss-Kahn to influence positions of the government, as Yves Tiberghien has argued, but Strauss-Kahn's views about the desirability of long-term ownership in strategic sectors did not translate into the government's ability to create long-term shareholding arrangements.[110] The major action in French shareholding was in the informal arena, and government has few effective tools in this sphere. The limits of governmental interest were especially clear in Germany, where the Red-Green coalition government did try to undo the strategic shareholding among German companies. The backlash this provoked, from the managerial lobby, caused Gerhard Schröder to reverse his position on takeover protection.[111] His switch of position at the European level led to the severe dilution of the EU takeover directive. Its two controversial articles – the neutrality rule and the breakthrough rule – were both made optional for national governments. German managers lobbied for opt-outs from these clauses. French managers, by contrast, viewed themselves as the likely winners from a more neo-liberal framework of European takeovers. They lobbied for a common directive at the EU level, and at the national level they fought (against the Socialist Party) for a transposition of article 9 and parts of article 11. To be sure, French managers were not pushing for shareholder supremacy. They defeated shareholder advocates and neoliberals in the National Assembly in adopting the possibility of poison pill protections.

The evidence is entirely consistent with an argument that highlights the power of interest groups, as coalitional theory does. Yet the role of electoral systems in stabilizing coalitional compromises, discussed by Gourevitch and Shinn, is not borne out by the Franco-German comparison. During the 1990s, both France and Germany had coalition governments of the left. But the composition of the government was immaterial to the changes in the informal sphere, as the preferences of institutional incumbents drove these processes. Governments have little incentive to intervene in the functioning of informal institutions of low structural salience, such as corporate control. And where they do try to intervene, as in Schröder's tax reform, they are likely to be unsuccessful without the active support of institutional incumbents. Where institutions are formal but an issue continues to have low salience, governments generally will take their cues from managerial interest groups about the course of legal reform. This dynamic operates at the international level, as in the case of debates over the EU takeover directive, but also in the domestic debate about the conditions of transposing the directive in France. French managers wanted and got terms of transposition that would favor their international growth strategies. The managerial alliance had a powerful ally in Finance Minister Breton, a once and future CEO himself. But, as we will see in the next chapter, managerial lobbying over the terms of law making does not depend on the good fortune of having a close ally of business in the government. Rather,

---

[110] Tiberghien (2007).
[111] Cioffi (2002).

when managers are able to mount both powerful lobbying initiatives and to influence the framing of press coverage of their political issues, they can find allies across the political spectrum. The power of coalitions should therefore be judged not only by the number of their voters, but by the effectiveness of the political weapons they can bring to a given political fight.

Appendix 3.1: Coding Scheme for French Newspapers, 2005–2006

There are four potential codes, as well as "none of the above":

Economic Nationalism
Market Competition
Shareholder Supremacy
Stakeholder Defense

Coding Protocol

Economic Nationalism: any quotation that characterized takeovers as being a question of national or European-level interests, vis-à-vis either actors from other countries or the impersonal functioning of the market.

> Examples:
> "It is only natural that the French government assures that certain firms remain in French hands."
>
> "A European-level fund for supporting national champions is not inconsistent with the market rules of the EU."
>
> "When national interests and market considerations diverge, the government will ultimately pursue national interests first."

Market Competition: any quotation that characterized takeovers not as a threat for French (or European) firms, but as an opportunity for growth, or to quotations that noted that a high share price is the best defense against hostile takeover.

> Examples:
> "The best defense against takeovers is maintaining a high share price."
>
> "French firms have been the beneficiaries of cross-border competition. We take over foreign firms more than they take over ours."
>
> "The best way to grow is in this economic environment is by buying other firms in other markets."

Shareholder Supremacy: any quotation that referred to the stakes in takeovers as affecting shareholder rights, the equality among shareholders (including minority shareholders), shareholders as the ultimate owners of the firms, or transparency as a value for shareholders.

Examples:
"Shareholders are the ultimate owners of the firm, and they should be able to decide which sort of takeover bid they wish to accept."

"Poison pills are made to protect managers, not shareholders. It is shareholders whose rights must ultimately come first."

"Transparent rules are the best guarantee that shareholders can monitor the managers, who are supposed to be working for them."

Determining the difference between market competition and shareholder supremacy: references to share value as a strategy (of management) for avoiding takeover are market competition; references to the shareholder decision process and selecting the highest offer per share for a takeover are shareholder supremacy.

Stakeholder Defense: any quotation that characterized takeovers affecting a broader group than just shareholders, including employees, unions, long-term owners of the firm, customers, and local communities (but not the whole country, which we characterized instead as Economic Nationalism).

Examples:
"A firm belongs not just to its shareholders, but to the workers."

"There is a group of owners who have demonstrated a commitment to the long-term strategy of the firm. Their view must carry a lot of weight in such decisions."

"The major criteria for evaluating the effect of a takeover must include the potential unemployment effects of a merger, which can have major ramifications for local communities."

"Savage liberalism is not the way we do things here. These bids should be negotiated with workers' representatives."

Examples of quotations that fit none of the above:

"The law seems like a good law overall."

"We are not interested in poison pills for our firms."

"This law is a minor question. We must stay focused on the major problems of the economy, not technical details."

"When one says the directive is neoliberal inspiration, this ignores the fact that the United Kingdom and the United States, both neoliberal countries, have very different rules for takeovers."

.nds and the Myth
ratist Coalition

The 1990s was the era of the Dutch miracle, when international observers lauded the ability of the consensual corporatism of the Netherlands to produce dramatic job growth without introducing the levels of inequality seen in the American labor market. In their well-known study of the Dutch miracle, Visser and Hemerijck highlighted the important role of unions and employers' associations, cajoled by political reformers, in crafting the political compromises that underlay job growth and welfare reform.[1] This recent story is consistent with the long-prevailing understanding of the Netherlands as an exemplar of liberal corporatism, in which the Dutch economy adjusts to international pressures for change through continuous negotiations between employers and labor unions.[2]

In the area of takeover protection, however, the Netherlands was neither corporatist nor reformist in this period. Instead, a well-organized managerial lobby consistently defeated reform measures supported by both the Liberal Party (VVD) and the lobbying organizations of institutional investors. Despite a twelve-year stint in government between 1994 and 2006, the VVD was unable to effect change in the Dutch market for corporate control. This chapter is an inquiry into the reasons why liberalizing reformers were so unsuccessful in the Netherlands.

Unlike in the French and German cases examined in the previous chapter, Dutch managers do not benefit from the direct economic power of concentrated shareholdings. The shares of most Dutch-listed companies are widely held in comparative perspective, as we saw in Chapter 2. The passive market for corporate control in the Netherlands is therefore not the product of informal norms of behavior among a limited group of shareowners. It depends instead on the existence of solid legal defenses against takeovers. To defend such legal instruments requires doing battle in parliament and in bureaucracies, the preserve of formal rules. We would expect there to be powerful

---

[1] Visser and Hemerijck (1997).
[2] Katzenstein (1985).

political interests on the other side of this fight, and indeed there were. Foreign direct investment is much higher in the Netherlands, as a proportion of GDP, than in France, Germany, or Japan. If institutional investors are a force in politics in any coordinated economy, we would expect them to be powerful in the Netherlands.[3]

This chapter explores how the managers of Dutch large firms successfully defended takeover protections from the attacks of neoliberal politicians and institutional investors. First, the chapter demonstrates empirically that takeover protection is an issue of low political salience. Most Dutch voters do not care about the issue, most of the time. For the leaders of political parties, even those with a strong and ideologically founded view about the importance of changing the rules governing takeover protection, the disinterest of general voters creates a disincentive to invest too much political capital into a project of eliminating them. For managers, in contrast, takeover protections matter a great deal. Their elimination would fundamentally threaten managerial autonomy, forcing them to pay close attention to short-term variations in their stock price. In a country where works councils have defined prerogatives that are difficult for business to challenge, and where cooperative labor relations are considered one of the strengths of the Dutch economy, managers prefer to retain their autonomy vis-à-vis institutional investors rather than to submit themselves to the discipline of an active market for corporate control. With a concentrated interest in the political outcomes of corporate control, and a press and public largely indifferent to the issue, the stage was set in the Netherlands for the managers of Dutch large firms to use the tools of quiet politics.

These tools all stem from the deference that politicians and the press show managers, given their presumed expertise in the needs of Dutch companies. The first advantage is in lobbying the government and members of Parliament. In the Netherlands, where private money plays a negligible role in electoral competition, lobbying is about expertise, especially legal expertise. As one prominent figure in Dutch corporate governance debates said in an interview, "the Netherlands is small and [you] do not realize how close we are to politics, as individuals. So a lot of lobbying is going on. The Netherlands is more a city than a country."[4] In this small environment, the managerial organization has built close ties with the best corporate lawyers, and these ties are important in influencing legislators. Moreover, as in other countries, Dutch politicians have been willing to grant significant agenda-setting capacity to informal working groups, in which managers have a preeminent voice, and in which unions have no voice at all. Finally, the expertise of managers also gives them a tool to deploy in shaping press coverage of hostile takeovers. When legal measures are introduced to parliament, the ability to influence press coverage improves

---

[3] Engelen et al. (2008).
[4] Interview with Morris Tabaksblat, chairman of the 2003 Corporate Governance Committee, October 11, 2006.

the odds of lobbying. Subsequent sections of this chapter explore each of these propositions.

The tools of quiet politics are not emphasized in existing research on corporate control. Such studies tend to assume that the generally corporatist policy-making features of the Netherlands also apply to the governance of corporate control in that country. In the coalitional approach of Gourevitch and Shinn, the corporatist compromise describes the situation in which workers join managers to limit the rights of shareholders, maintaining defenses against hostile takeovers.[5] Yet I will show that Dutch unions have played little role in the politics of corporate control. The shifting positions of the Dutch Labor party are also inconsistent with the partisan logic of Cioffi and Höpner, who claim that leftist parties are stalwart opponents of the arrangements of coordinated capitalism.[6] In fact, the Labor party changed position on the issue, and whether it was for or against takeover protection, the position of managers in protecting takeover defenses consistently prevailed. The preferences of Dutch managers are indeed influenced by the existence of strong institutions of employee representation at the workplace, but that is not the same thing as saying that interest groups representing workers are active players in the politics of corporate control. As this chapter will show, they are not. If the labor-half of the corporatist coalition is unnecessary for political victory, either in the guise of union activity or Labor party support, then the causal mechanism of political success is not the cross-class coalition itself, but the political tools available to managerial organizations under conditions of low political salience.

The Political Narrative of Dutch Corporate Control, 1994–2006

The major stake of Dutch corporate protection politics between 1994 and 2006 was the extent to which legal protections against hostile takeovers, particularly preference shares, could be eliminated or made temporary. The managers of Dutch large companies have fought to defend these protection mechanisms since the mid-1980s when they first came under threat. Like their German counterparts, Dutch managers face well-established works councils representing labor. The "structure regime" of 1971 gives labor representatives important input on the structure of the supervisory board of Dutch companies.[7] The managers of large firms in the Netherlands are already constrained to work with labor at the firm level, and rapid reorganization without labor cooperation would be difficult in the context of Dutch codetermination. This situation has created incentives for these managers not to cede autonomy to investors.[8] Also, as in Germany, Dutch managers use works councils as a resource for

---

[5] Gourevitch and Shinn (2005: 178).

[6] Cioffi and Höpner (2006).

[7] The structure regime was revised in 2004, but works councils received in the reform the right to propose one-third of the supervisory board members (Schnyder forthcoming).

[8] Poutsma and Braam (2005).

negotiating strategies of firm-level change during mergers or reorganizations.[9] Both because they cannot reorganize rapidly without the acquiescence of works councils, and because cooperation with works councils is considered an advantage in international competition, Dutch managers have fought to maintain the autonomy from investors provided by takeover defenses.

The first political challenge to these defense mechanisms came in 1986, after a series of blocked takeovers led the Amsterdam Stock Exchange to appoint an expert committee to study the issue of takeover protection. This committee, dominated by established managers, recommended against making any significant changes; however, a minority on the committee favored liberalization of the takeover market.[10] The Amsterdam Stock Exchange attempted to incorporate regulation of takeover protections into its listing rules. This event is largely important for Dutch takeover protection because of the political countermobilization it provoked within the employers' organizations. Rather than delegating this issue to the existing peak federations of employers, the VNO and the NCW, managers of the largest listed companies in 1988 founded the Association of Securities-Issuing Companies (VEUO).[11] In the Netherlands, famed for its polder model and corporatist consensualism, this was surprising: "Creating a new lobby association of this kind was a remarkable initiative, as it seemingly bypassed the bodies in which managers and employers normally dealt with each other."[12] The VEUO would orchestrate all major managerial offensives against takeover liberalization over the next two decades. Because the organization was founded to defend takeover protections, its internal logic tends to favor the proponents of takeover protection, even when there are neoliberal opponents of protection measures in the VEUO.[13]

With the election of the first purple coalition in 1994 – uniting the red (left-wing) Labor Party (PvdA), the blue (right-wing) Liberal Party (VVD), and the centrist D'66 party (socially liberal, economically neoliberal) – the Christian Democrats were out of government in the Netherlands for the first time since 1918. The leader of the VVD at the time was Frits Bolkestein, who would later become the EU commissioner who drafted the EU takeover directive. His successor as VVD party leader, Finance Minister Gerrit Zalm, would hold office for all but ten months between 1994 and 2006. During this time, Zalm

---

[9] Goodijk (2003), van den Berg et al. (2008).

[10] Frentrop (2002: 339–344).

[11] VEUO stands for the Vereniging Effecten Uitgevende Ondernemingen. The two peak associations of all employers – the VNO (Federation of Netherlands Industry and Employers) and the NCW (Dutch Federation of Christian Employers) – merged in 1995 to form the Confederation of Netherlands Industry and Employers (VNO-NCW). Throughout the remainder of this chapter, the organization is referred to by its post-merger name.

[12] Frentrop (2002: 344).

[13] As one leader of the VEUO told me in describing the organization's decision making, "we function very much in an undemocratic manner" (interview, October 11, 2006). The VEUO's position on the questions of takeover protections is thus heavily influenced by the composition of its governing board, and especially the three legal experts who advise that board.

repeatedly tried to eviscerate Dutch takeover protection. His goal was to render all protection mechanisms temporary so hostile takeovers would become possible in the Netherlands. All his initiatives to render protection temporary failed. This section summarizes the key episodes in Dutch takeover politics, while the remainder of the chapter explores the mechanisms that allowed managerial organizations to subvert these liberalizing initiatives.

I call the first episode the Takeover Compromise, which unfolded between 1994 and 1997. Upon coming to office, Zalm signaled his dissatisfaction with the compromise that had been agreed to by the VEUO and the stock exchange in 1991.[14] That agreement had meant that in practice a hostile acquirer could buy a majority of the shares of a listed company but still be unable to replace the managing board because the various antitakeover devices in place separated economic and voting power. Zalm first requested that the VEUO and Amsterdam Stock Exchange renegotiate their original deal, but in two rounds of discussions they failed to reach an agreement to avert government intervention. Zalm then negotiated directly with the Exchange, the VEUO, and the VNO-NCW; unions were not included in this negotiation process. The outcome of the negotiation reached in 1996 was extraordinarily mild: if a suitor had acquired more than seventy percent of the economic shares in a company, then after one year the continuation of existing protection mechanisms could be reviewed by the enterprise court.[15] However, Parliament refused to consider even this weak compromise bill, thus condemning it to Dutch legislative purgatory until 2005 when it was withdrawn in favor of the law implementing the EU takeover directive.[16] According to Minister Zalm, the bill was not considered because of a concentrated lobbying offensive of the VEUO.[17]

The outcome of the Takeover Compromise is not directly inconsistent with the corporatist compromise of Gourevitch and Shinn because at this time the Labor Party was indeed divided on Zalm's initiative. Together with the opposition Christian Democrats (CDA), they blocked the bill from being introduced into parliament. There was no union activity on this issue, but the veto points that exist in the Dutch political system – which are often considered part of the corporatist arrangement – played a role in the bill's demise. Unlike in parliamentary systems that concentrate agenda-setting power in the hands of the government vis-à-vis parliament, the Dutch system strictly separates the government from the parliament and delegates the power for the legislative agenda

---

[14] The VEUO and the Amsterdam stock exchange had agreed to add an appendix to listing rules spelling out that listing companies could adopt no more than two measures of takeover protection (e.g., they could have preference shares and certification, but not priority shares).

[15] Frentrop (2002: 463).

[16] The Netherlands is one of the few parliamentary systems where bills never die unless they are defeated by a vote. So all bills introduced to Parliament by the government, but never considered by Parliament, sit in a sort of purgatory where they cannot expire but will never be acted upon (Doering 1995: 242–243).

[17] Interview with Gerrit Zalm, former Finance Minister of the Netherlands, July 31, 2007.

entirely to the parliament.[18] Such a system, which is in many ways more akin to the legislative system of the United States than to a typical European parliamentary system, provides ample opportunities for lobbyists opposed to a bill to kill it.

Between 1998 and 2002, there was no major legislative movement in the Netherlands on the subject of hostile takeovers, as policymakers in the Hague waited for the European Takeover Directive before taking up the issue domestically. The next important issue in takeover politics was the development of the Committee on Corporate Governance in 2003.[19] Led by a neoliberal CEO, Morris Tabaksblat, whose name became the eponym for the committee, the Tabaksblat Committee united reformist managers and shareholders' representatives. Although the Tabaksblat Committee excluded any union representatives, its findings were nevertheless supported by the Labor Party in Parliament. And it was convened simultaneously with the outbreak of a big accounting scandal, which substantially increased the group's impact.

Weeks before the formal announcement of the Tabaksblat Committee's formation, the share prices in Ahold, a large supermarket chain, collapsed after it acknowledged overstating its U.S. profits by more than $500 million. Following closely on the accounting scandal of Enron in the United States, Ahold was widely described as the Dutch Enron. Jaap Peters of the Peters Committee argued, "just the way the Enron matter happened in the U.S., in the same way we needed such a shock as well, just to push us a bit further ahead. That shock was Ahold."[20] In part because it deliberated in the wake of the Ahold accounting scandal, the Tabaksblat Committee went well beyond its defined mission to suggest on a number of changes to practices in Dutch corporate governance, including a recommendation to make all takeover defenses temporary. This was an instance when elements of both the investor and transparency coalitions were firmly in favor of reforming the system of Dutch patient capital.

Despite the possibilities of the moment, however, the government failed to put forward any legislation to render all defense measures temporary in the year that followed the release of the Tabaksblat report. This outcome contradicts both the partisan and coalitional models of corporate governance reform. Both

---

[18] Among eighteen western European political systems, Doering found that the Dutch system delegated the highest level of agenda-setting control to the parliament (Doering 1995: 225–231). At the opposite end of the extreme were the United Kingdom and Ireland. See also Tsebelis (2002: 99–109).

[19] In December 2002, when the negotiations over the formation of the Committee on Corporate Governance began, Gerrit Zalm was leader of the VVD in Parliament, not the finance minister. This was the period of the short-lived government coalition that included the List Pim Fortuyn (LPF), a party led by a charismatic right-wing politician who was murdered days before the election in May 2002. His party quickly disintegrated after the election, and new elections were held in January 2003. Coalition negotiations lasted until May 2003, when Zalm again became finance minister and deputy prime minister for a right-wing coalition including his Liberal Party (VVD), the Christian Democrats (CDA), and D'66.

[20] Interview with Jaap Peters, chairman of the Peters Committee and former CEO of Aegon, August 21, 2006.

literatures assume that laws are only stable so long as the dominant party or coalition has sufficient political resources to obstruct attempts to change the law. There was, however, no attempt to change the law in 2004 when the resources of managers seemed to be at low ebb and their opponents were united. This is because, unlike scholars of corporate governance, governments do not always care most about reforming hostile takeover laws. Public attention in the Netherlands on the issue of hostile takeovers was very low in 2003 and 2004, in spite of the Ahold scandal. The issue did not gain enough salience with the general public to make legal change in this area a pressing priority for the government.

The final episode of the period is the attempt to use the implementation of the European Union Takeover Directive in 2005 and 2006 as an opportunity to make all Dutch protection measures temporary. After the defeat of Bolkestein's more radical EU-level proposal in 2003, the European directive on takeovers contained optional recommendations on the breakthrough clause and board neutrality. That is, states were free to adopt them or not, as discussed in Chapter 3. Zalm, Bolkestein's handpicked successor in the Liberal Party, chose to support a version that included both clauses using the breakthrough clause as his newest instrument of attack on Dutch takeover defenses. In 2005, Zalm still had the support of the opposition Labor Party for this reform. According to the partisan logic of Höpner and Cioffi, the left party should have been consistently opposed to these measures, which protected managers. Yet the left party in the Netherlands did not have a consistent position on this issue because takeover protection was viewed as a dry and technical matter. In March 2006, the Labor Party abruptly switched sides and helped defeat Zalm's proposal after managerial representatives succeeded in raising political concerns about the threat of foreign hostile takeovers in the Netherlands. But, as freely admitted by the Labor Party's representative on this issue, the switch was a matter of political convenience. Because takeover protection was a second order issue for all parties, and usually for the public, the ability of managers to frame the issue in the press as one of national protection consolidated the power conferred by their lobbying and informal advisory roles. In March 2006, opponents of the law implementing the takeover directive forced the government to eliminate a requirement making all takeover protections temporary. With this requirement the last challenge to Dutch takeover protections died.

Table 4.1 summarizes the expectations of the principal theoretical approaches in the politics of corporate governance and the overall outcomes of the three Dutch episodes. In all three cases, the law was not changed to make protection mechanisms temporary. In the Takeover Compromise, this is the expectation of all three theories, given the multiple veto points and divisions within the Labor Party on this issue. In the latter two episodes, though, the partisan and coalitional literatures both predict change in takeover protection laws. The coalitional literature predicts change because of the active emergence of an investor coalition of shareholders and renegade managers supported by

TABLE 4.1. *Summary of Theoretical Predictions in Dutch Takeover Politics,*
1994–2006

Predictions→	Quiet Politics	Coalition Theory	Partisanship	Outcome
Takeover Compromise (1994–1997)	Protection	Protection	Protection	Protection
Tabaksblat Committee (2002–2004)	Protection	Breakdown of Protection	Breakdown of Protection	Protection
Implementation of EU Directive (2005–2006)	Protection	Breakdown of Protection	Breakdown of Protection	Protection

the Labor Party. The partisan argument predicts change because of the commitment of the Labor Party to reform, with support from the government. Both these expectations turn out to be incorrect. In the first case, the bill was never considered in parliament; in the second case a bill was never proposed by the government because of other priorities; and in the third case the government was defeated in a straight up-or-down vote. Three political modalities, one outcome: managerial victory.

Existing theoretical approaches fail to anticipate the success of managers in takeover politics because they do not sufficiently recognize the dynamics of quiet politics. The low salience of corporate control increases the usefulness of three tools of managerial influence: lobbying capacity, deference to informal policy-making bodies, and the ability to influence the tenor of press coverage. The rest of this chapter examines in detail the functioning of these mechanisms in the policy-making process.

The Political Salience of Takeover Politics in the Netherlands

There are no public opinion data asking Dutch voters about their views of the relative importance of corporate control as a political issue. To assess those views, I conducted a search of all articles in the Dutch press dealing with hostile takeover protections between January 1, 1995 and December 31, 2006. A standard search protocol in LexisNexis identified all articles on this topic in the four most widely read newspapers in the Netherlands – *De Telegraaf, Algemeen Dagblad, De Volkskrant,* and *NRC Handelsblad,* as well as *Het Financieele Dagblad,* the business press equivalent of the *Financial Times* or the *Wall Street Journal.*[21] This is essentially the universe of the Dutch national

---

[21] Articles from *De Telegraaf* were only available through LexisNexis from 1999.

press.[22] These search terms initially yielded 2,727 articles, many of which were not relevant to the general issue of takeover protection in the Netherlands. Articles were classified as relevant if they made some mention of the existing Dutch rules on hostile takeover protection.[23] Roughly twenty-five percent of the articles (679 of the original 2,727) were relevant to the broader question of takeover rules in the Netherlands. All calculations in this chapter are made on the basis of this sample of 679 articles.

To compare the political salience of hostile takeover rules with that of other policy areas of Dutch politics during this time, I employed press searches over the same time period in three other domains of governance, as in Chapters 3 and 5: bargaining rules, the pension system, and vocational training.[24] Because we included as relevant only one-quarter of the articles found using our search terms for takeover protection, we also include in our comparative presentation only one-fourth of the articles retrieved by the other search terms. This probably underestimates the salience of the categories of pension system and vocational training rules, whose search terms appear to bring up a higher proportion of relevant articles than the takeover protection terms. The term "bargaining rules," like "takeover protection," brings up many articles about purely firm-specific rules rather than about the bargaining system more generally, so the twenty-five percent deflator may be more appropriate for that case. Even using this conservative procedure, it is clear from the data presented in Figure 4.1 that bargaining rules and the pension system are far more politically salient

---

[22] These are the four largest circulation newspapers and the leading business newspaper for a country with a population of 16.5 million people. By inexact analogy, one could compare this to a sample of articles for the New York metropolitan area in the United States – population 19 million – drawn from the *New York Times*, *New York Daily News*, *New York Post*, the *Newark Star-Ledger*, and the *Wall Street Journal*. This metric excludes free newspapers, which have only recently become an important press phenomenon in the Netherlands.

[23] Those articles eliminated as irrelevant to the Dutch takeover debate dealt either with entirely different subjects, with the takeover arrangements of one particular company without reference to the broader takeover rules in the Netherlands, or with takeover debates in other countries without making reference to Dutch takeover arrangements.

[24] In an attempt to create institutional categories that were as conceptually comparable as possible, the search relied on terms that would capture articles dealing with rules of governance in each issue area. The search terms used in LexisNexis were the following (Dutch original is followed by bracketed English translation):

Takeover Protection: "bescherming!" [protection*] AND (overname! [takeover*] OR bod [bid]).

Vocational Training: "Beroepsonderwijs" [vocational education] AND (leerbedrijf OR praktijkopleiding OR stageplaats OR werkend leren OR werkervaringsplaats! OR leerbanen OR leerbaan) [learning company OR practical training OR internship post OR work-learning OR work experience post* OR learning jobs OR learning job].

Bargaining Rules: "(CAO OR collectieve arbeidsovereenkomst!)" [collective labor agreement*, in either abbreviated or spelled-out form] AND (arbeids!) [labor*].

Pension System: "Pensioen!" [pension*] AND (systeem OR regeling) [system or regime].

The search and subsequent coding of articles were performed by a Dutch research assistant, David Vermijs, for whose help I am extremely grateful.

than takeover protection every year. Bargaining rules are especially widely covered, which is certainly consistent with the importance of bargaining between unions and employers through a variety of corporatist institutions in the Netherlands.

As in the previous chapter, we use the average level of press coverage of the pension system to provide a baseline (the Mendoza line) for the minimal amount of coverage we might expect a high salience issue to receive. Over this entire time period, there was not a single year when the number of articles published about the system of takeover protection reached the average annual number of articles about the pension system. Remember that this sample includes the articles from five newspapers; if there were only one article per month on takeover protection in each of the five papers searched, that would result in an annual figure of sixty articles. Any politically salient issue is going to get more coverage than one article per month, as we see every year for bargaining rules and the pension system. Even so, Figure 4.1 illustrates that there were only three years during which the media paid any attention at all to the issue of takeover protection: 1995, 1996, and 2006. During those three years, there was an average of 102 articles per year dealing with this topic. In all the other years, there was an average of only forty-one articles on the subject of takeover protection (the coverage of youth vocational training is of even lower salience than takeover politics in the Netherlands). Only in 2006 is the amount of press coverage of takeover protection remotely comparable to that received by the areas of bargaining rules and the pension system.

What was so special about those three years that caused the press to pay more attention to the issue of hostile takeover protection in Dutch companies? Interesting to note is that these points of relatively higher salience did not exactly correspond to the years when significant legislation was submitted to parliament on this issue.[25] If that had been the case, we would have expected peaks in 1997 (Takeover Compromise), 2003 (Tabaksblat Committee), and 2006 (EU Takeover Directive Implementation). Instead, there appear to be two different dynamics at work here. Zalm's initial political attack on protection mechanisms, which began in 1994 when his government first came to power, was big news. This was the first significant attempt by a politician to restrict protection mechanisms in the Netherlands, and it engendered a strong response from both supporters (representing shareholders) and opponents (representing management). It was in this sense newsworthy, and not only for the financial press.[26] In 2006, by contrast, the tenor of coverage did not center on the

[25] Nor does it correspond to the electoral years during the period when we might expect politicians to pay more attention to issues because voters will be evaluating their performance that year. For three of the major policy areas whose salience we measured, there was virtually no difference between election years and nonelection years. For bargaining rules, there were substantially more articles per year, on average, in nonelectoral years (288) than during years with national parliamentary elections (222).

[26] 1995 was the only year in which the business newspaper, *Het Financieele Dagblad*, provided as few as one-third of the articles in the total sample.

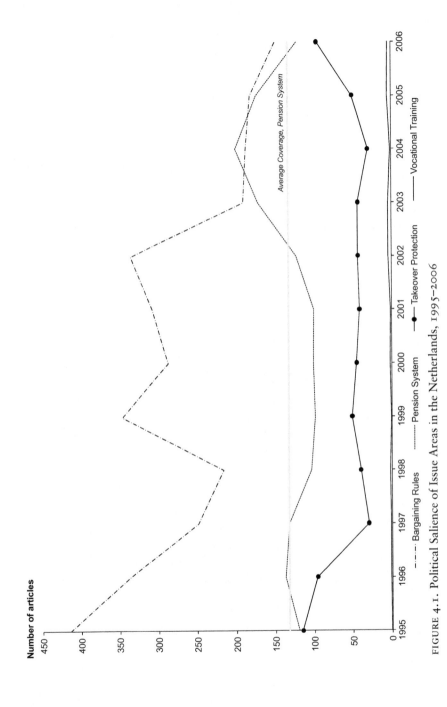

FIGURE 4.1. Political Salience of Issue Areas in the Netherlands, 1995–2006

political dispute between Zalm and the large companies, but instead on the situation of Dutch companies in international comparison: how easy are they for foreign companies to take over? Such a framing was helpful to managers; and as we shall see later in this chapter, managerial organizations influenced the tenor of this debate.

Political Parties, Unions, and Dutch Takeover Politics

Although political scientists often concentrate only on the politics of one issue, governments in the real world are engaged in multiple areas of policy making at any one time. This simple observation poses a challenge for partisan approaches that try to explain changes in corporate governance politics by reference to the same structural sort of regularities that lead us to expect parties of the right to oppose income redistribution and parties of the left to favor it. Tax policies, which directly affect redistribution, are much more politically salient than any policy having to do with corporate governance. Partisan theorists such as Cioffi and Höpner elide this difference when they anchor their claims about partisanship in the deep preferences of parties.[27]

In the real world, other political issues can take priority over issues like hostile takeovers and corporate governance. Indeed, even for Finance Minister Gerrit Zalm, the political protagonist of every Dutch reform effort between 1994 and 2006,

> the regulation of hostile takeovers was not an issue we expected to win or lose elections on. Of course, it was an important issue, but it never had a very high profile.... It was by far not my biggest issue.... I'm not even sure if this will be a subject in my memoirs, first because there are less interesting anecdotes [in this area]. It has been a subject where I consistently had a policy idea, but it was not one of my biggest issues.[28]

Zalm emphasized this issue more than any other politician in the Netherlands over the past two decades, and yet in his telling, this was a secondary issue.

It is possible that Zalm chose to downplay the subject not because it was of secondary importance, but because he repeatedly lost in trying to reform it.

←───

FIGURE 4.1. Political Salience of Issue Areas in the Netherlands, 1995–2006
Source: LexisNexis search of *Algemeen Dagblad, Het Financieele Dagblad, NRC Handelsblad, De Telegraaf,* and *De Volkskrant.* As noted in the text, this graph includes twenty-five percent of the articles found for each search term, which was the "noise deflator" originally developed for takeover protection. Definition of the search terms used for the issue areas is provided in footnote 24.
Note: The gray horizontal line shows the average number of articles per year published on the subject of the pension system, which is the less covered of the two high-salience issue areas depicted in this figure. This is one rough indicator of a minimal level of media coverage we might classify as being associated with an issue of high political salience.

[27] Cioffi and Höpner (2006: 464).
[28] Interview with Gerrit Zalm, July 31, 2007.

If that were the case, perhaps Zalm's opposite number at the Labor Party (PvdA) would tell a different story about the importance of the issue area. Kris Douma was the Labor Party's parliamentary spokesperson on corporate governance between 2002 and 2006. He led the party's position on this issue during both the Tabaksblat Committee and the EU Takeover Directive's implementation. I asked in an interview about his autonomy in setting party policy in this area:

> I was the spokesperson for the topic, and the majority of PvdA parliamentarians were just not interested. It was technical, it was complex, and it had to do with finance. [Their opinion was,] 'if you think you know what you have to do, be our guest.' I think there were only three people who were interested: [Frank Heemskerk and Fred Crone, the two other PvdA parliamentarians with financial briefs]. And the third of course was Wouter Bos [the party leader], who was interested in this issue. And he asked me a number of times to give him the highlights of what I was doing, and checking to see if this was in accordance with his own views. And that was about it.[29]

Like their counterparts in the Liberal Party, members of the Labor Party were not that interested in takeover protection. Contrary to the view of partisan theorists, corporate governance reform in the Netherlands was perceived as a specialist issue, rather than a central concern of the party.

There are at least two groups that *did* care a lot about the politics of corporate governance. One is the managers whose political organizations have already been discussed. The other is minority shareholders' organizations. The largest and most influential shareholder organization in the Netherlands is the VEB.[30] Peter Paul de Vries headed the VEB from 1995 to 2007, and he was a member of the Tabaksblat Committee. If Gerrit Zalm led the political charge against takeover protections, De Vries was the most visible interest group representative of the shareholders who opposed these protection mechanisms.[31] In response to a question about the interest of voters in corporate governance, De Vries answered

> Well, voters haven't cared. And it hasn't been an element in the elections.... We look in all programs of political parties for the words 'shares,' 'governance,' 'corporate governance,' and we find maybe one word or two words, and then sometimes 'share' means 'market-share' or something. That is really not an issue in any political battle.

What about unions, to whose influence Gourevitch and Shinn's work attributes much importance? In terms of their interests, by the late 1990s

---

[29] Interview with Kris Douma, July 30, 2007.

[30] VEB stands for Vereniging van Effectenbezitters, or Dutch Shareholders' Association. In addition to the VEB, the nonprofit group Eumedion has also been an active political voice for the rights of institutional shareholders in the Netherlands (Engelen et al. 2008).

[31] In an interview for this project, Tabaksblat named De Vries as one of the five most influential people in the debate about takeover protection in the Netherlands (Interview, October 11, 2006).

the pension funds of the unions had accumulated large investments in the market, leading them to behave mainly as institutional investors.[32] Gourevitch and Shinn argue that some of these funds have flowed abroad because of the inability of unions to exercise voice in the Dutch system. Even with their Dutch investments, however, there is no evidence that unions ever even tried to exercise such influence. Kris Douma, the Labor Party speaker on corporate governance, who in the 1990s was head of policy for the largest Dutch union, observed in an interview with the author that

> there's hardly any proof of unions using their stake in pension funds to really influence the policy of the pension funds.... If you ask the top executives of the unions, they would say that [corporate governance issues] are important, but the fact is that they don't pay much attention to that and they have specialized people to run pension funds.... There is a sort of schizophrenia between them: the pension fund experts do their own business and see that there is maximum profit on the assets, and they don't rely very much on what the unions have as a general policy.[33]

In politics, moreover, Dutch unions act mainly through the Social and Economic Council, which is the government's advisory body for economic and social policy.[34] Beyond this statutory role, there is no evidence that unions have attempted to exercise voice in the politics of takeover protection. In one limited sense, Cioffi and Höpner are correct in their critique of Gourevitch and Shinn: it is the party of the left, rather than the unions, which is the political voice of the left in Dutch takeover debates. Yet the amount of attention that party devotes to this issue is, as with other parties, limited. Takeover politics carries little resonance with the general public, most of the time, and Dutch political parties act accordingly.

Lobbying and Expertise

> It is not so hard anymore to lobby. Look, Zalm is not mindless, he just doesn't have any practical business experience. So you offer him your expertise there. Because they are not mindless, you can clarify it for them.... They don't understand anything in the Hague about how markets work in a company.
>
> Former Senior Official of the VEUO[35]

> These legislators don't know what happens in real life; they have very little industry experience. So we try to educate them a little by showing examples. We can show what they think might happen that does not happen and vice versa. A great

---

[32] Gourevitch and Shinn (2005: 179).

[33] Interview with Kris Douma, July 30, 2007.

[34] The Social and Economic Council (SER) is the central corporatist advisory body in the Netherlands with equal union and employer representation.

[35] Interview, September 4, 2006.

thing about the Dutch MPs is that they are very reasonable people.... Whether
you see things from the right or the left, it is the rational that counts.

Official of the VNO-NCW[36]

Managerial representatives in the Netherlands think of their great comparative
advantage as lying in information. Government proposals are typically trans-
mitted to the social partners for comment before being submitted to parliament.
Sometimes, as in 1995 and 1996, the government negotiates directly with the
VEUO or the VNO-NCW. Moreover, these organizations can directly lobby
parliamentarians over whom governments have limited control.[37] In this section, I use evidence from interviews with actors directly involved in the political
process to illuminate how the VEUO saw its own lobbying efforts, and how it
was seen by the major players in the Dutch politics of hostile takeovers. Few
people in politics like to admit that they changed their mind in response to
lobbying, and it is difficult to know exactly what might have happened in the
absence of the advocacy of the VEUO. A senior figure in the managerial lobbying group nicely summed up the social scientific problem of showing the causal
effect of lobbying: "Recently, a minister wanted to talk.... Well, we dropped
by, he listened well, and later it turned out that his speech contained a number
of elements that we brought up. These [elements] may also have been brought
up by others, as he spoke to a variety of people."[38] Where I can show that
positions changed after the lobbying in the direction intended by managerial
lobbyists, I take this as important evidence in favor of the proposition that
lobbying was indeed an important causal mechanism in determining political
outcomes in the Netherlands.

For the large member companies of the VEUO, as for one of its former
leaders interviewed for this book, the organization's goal was straightforward:
"Together with the three top lawyers, our main policy was keeping as many protection constructions intact as possible [...] The three lawyers knew the judicial language and had contact with the government officials. They knew where
we [member companies] stood, and others could let us know what they thought
they needed. It worked really well."[39] Another senior official of the VEUO
expanded on this statement of the importance of these three expert lawyers:

> Most of our work has to do with legislative processes.... That is why it is
> important that we as the VEUO have lawyers of name and fame. That the
> opinion we bring forth carries some authority. [When] Eisma, Maeijer, and

---

[36] Interview, two VNO-NCW officials with responsibility for corporate governance issues,
August 17, 2006.
[37] Recall that in the Netherlands members of government do not sit in parliament and cannot
pilot bills through parliament, as in many other parliamentary systems. So the two stage process
provides two discrete opportunities for lobbyists to influence the content of bills.
[38] Interview, October 11, 2006.
[39] Interview, September 1, 2006.

Raaijmakers had a certain opinion, then that carried a lot of weight. You have to stand strong in your shoes to disagree with them.[40]

Another VEUO leader described the legal process and the potential points of influence it presented to his organization in the following terms:

[after receiving a legal proposal] we have a legal committee, which consists of three persons, highly qualified jurists, to look at it.[41] This committee then writes a comment. I put my signature on the comment, although it is often too technical for me. This then goes to the Finance or Justice department.... But we also visit Members of Parliament.[42]

The way in which the VEUO construes lobbying as a two-stage process – of legal consultation (from the government) and then direct lobbying of potential allies (in parliament) – looks no different than does the lobbying strategy of any well-connected interest group in Washington, DC. Yet in working as a single-issue lobbying group, the VEUO stands outside the normal corporatist coalition to which coalitional theorists attribute causal primacy in Dutch politics.

The VEUO works closely with the more broad-based peak association of business (the VNO-NCW), but its raison d'être lies in defending protection constructions. The preference definition of managers of large firms is influenced by this organizational history. A former high official interviewed for this book underlined the clarity of the VEUO's goal: "The VEUO has principally concentrated itself on the protection constructions. That was also what it was designed to do. If we wouldn't have succeeded there, it would all have been finished."[43] In 1995–1996, representatives of the VEUO negotiated a compromise bill directly with Zalm and the stock exchange under which a shareholder that acquired seventy percent of shares could, after one year, go to court to override the existing protection mechanisms.[44] Whereas the VNO-NCW's broader policy interests and repeated interactions with the government may have given it more incentive to hold to an agreement negotiated with the finance minister, the single purpose of the VEUO leaves it free to fight in a no-holds-barred manner that hardly resembles a corporatist compromise. Finance Minister Zalm summarized the bargain and its political aftermath in the following terms:

[the representatives of the government and of the VEUO] sat at the table and they agreed more or less to this compromise, but I suppose at the same time they were lobbying in the parliament because [the proposed law] was

---

[40] Interview, September 4, 2006.
[41] In 2005, when the VEUO elected a new chairman, the three experts on the legal committee also stepped down. They were replaced by Harm Jan de Kluiver, Sven Dumoulin, and Mick den Boogert.
[42] Interview, October 11, 2006.
[43] Interview, September 1, 2006.
[44] Verbraeken (1996).

too far-reaching. In that sense, they were not very loyal partners in making deals.... Probably with the VNO-NCW we could have done business more easily, because they are used to compromise and sticking to compromise.[45]

For the VEUO's former high official, who does not consider the organization a corporatist group, all means are fair game in lobbying: "If you start wrestling, then you also get punches under the belt. That is how it goes."[46]

I observed in an earlier section that the corporatist compromise might account for the failure of the Takeover Compromise in 1997 because corporatism depends on the existence of many institutional veto points to induce moderate compromise from competing actors. Yet, in practice, there was only one side actively lobbying against the bill – managers – and they were lobbying against the same compromise they had struck with the government. This is how many bills die in Washington, DC, but it is not a legislative trajectory that is typical of a corporatist compromise.

In the case of the European Takeover Directive in 2005 and 2006, Zalm proposed maintaining the breakthrough rule, which would have rendered all mechanisms temporary. The VEUO's initial lobbying failed to remove this provision from the government's draft of the law implementing the directive in 2005. This is where the second stage of lobbying began, with members of parliament. According to a VEUO leader, "we visited the VVD, CDA, and PvdA, and they did not like the sound of our story. But CDA and PvdA have picked up something, and went on to do something with it, and this helped remove elements in the takeover directive that we did not like."[47]

This is a vague account from an interlocutor who might be interested in overstating the effect of his organization's lobbying. To understand what this meant in detail, I spoke to someone with no interest in showing the effect of lobbying: Kris Douma, the spokesperson of the Labor Party (PvdA) for issues of takeover protection. Douma had come out clearly in favor of using the EU takeover directive to make all protection mechanisms temporary in June 2004, even as a member of the opposition. Yet he and the PvdA switched sides in March 2006, defeating the government's bill in a parliamentary vote. Douma justified his party's vote in terms that resonated with the theme of the foreign takeover threat but also in light of new information. The PvdA had been in favor of dismantling protection, but reversed its position because "other countries do nothing [about protection] either. And I have been persuaded by experts that current law and jurisprudence work well enough."[48] In an interview with Douma, I asked about his source of expert legal advice:

> During the period that I was in parliament there was a group of about ten experts with sympathies for the PvdA that I consulted on a number of

---

[45] Interview with Gerrit Zalm, July 31, 2007.
[46] Interview, September 4, 2006.
[47] Interview, October 11, 2006.
[48] FD (3/30/06).

issues.... There were a couple of lawyers, like Harm Jan de Kluiver who is a real expert on corporate law in the Netherlands. And he was one of the people in this group of ten that I consulted.... But I rely most on Harm Jan de Kluiver.[49]

Harm Jan de Kluiver was also one of the three expert lawyers on the VEUO's Legal Committee. This evidence, while indirect, does suggest that Douma, who set the Labor Party's position on this issue, was exposed to the legal point of view stressed by the VEUO in its lobbying campaign, which was the same legal reasoning cited in his justification before parliament of the *volte-face* of the PvdA.

There is no evidence to demonstrate conclusively that the PvdA switched its vote on the takeover directive as a direct result of the VEUO's lobbying campaign.[50] Yet the existence of the lobbying campaign and the fact that the press was focusing on the threat of foreign takeovers raised by managerial heavyweight Aad Jacobs are demonstrable, as we will see. Of course, politicians are likely to frame their decisions in ways that are politically useful, but that very fact suggests the improbability of the mechanisms emphasized by the coalitional literature. If the real reason for the PvdA's decision were to protect employment and the role of labor stakeholders as a member of a corporatist coalition, a statement emphasizing these aspects of takeover protection would be a more likely vote-winner for a Labor Party politician. Moreover, if the party had the deep antipathy to ownership protection attributed to it by partisan theorists, the party's turnaround on this issue would make no sense at all. The most parsimonious explanation that is consistent with the historical record links the intense interest of the VEUO in defeating this proposal with its assiduous lobbying capacity and its close ties to the country's best legal expertise.

Managers and Informal Bodies of Policy Making

The most important argument to do it yourself instead of through a legislative track is, it does not have to take years like legislation does. [Also], we prefer to participate in steering, rather than letting someone else, the lawmakers, determine what is going to happen. We think that we have a good feel for what is going on in real life, while the civil servants are in a sort of ivory tower.

Official of the VNO-NCW[51]

---

[49] Interview with Kris Douma, July 30, 2007.

[50] Following my interview with Kris Douma, I emailed a clarifying question about the reasons behind the PvdA's change of position in 2006. He explained the legal reasoning that had been presented to him at length, and then said, "This is the technical/juridical information that made me change my mind, though I must admit that two other factors influenced me in making this change. One was the fact that for me it became clearer and clearer how many protection mechanisms are used in the United States and there would be no level playing field. Second, public opinion already became more protective, elections were coming nearer and (since I was in the opposition) there was a chance to defeat the coalition, which caused a slight change towards a more opportunistic approach."

[51] Interview, August 17, 2006.

Managers in the Netherlands rely on legal protections, not informal arrangements among owners, to defend their companies from hostile takeovers. Yet Dutch managers, like their counterparts elsewhere, also use their positions in informal advisory bodies as a means of shaping or delaying government intervention in the field of corporate governance. In both 1996–1997 and 2005–2006, Zalm's attempted policy reforms were undermined after lobbying by the VEUO. In both instances, legislative action was only one regulatory track pursued by the government. The second was the convening of informal groups, dominated by management representatives, whose mandate was to draw up new codes of corporate governance. However, the connection of these groups to the dominant political line of the VEUO was very different. The Peters Committee, assembled in 1996, fell directly in line with the political strategies of the VEUO and had no effect on the corporate governance practices of companies.[52] The Tabaksblat Committee, whose formation was announced days after the outbreak of the Ahold scandal in 2003, would pose serious challenges to the protection mechanisms of VEUO members. How did these two committees come to have such different outcomes?

The Peters Committee, chaired by the former CEO of Aegon, Jaap Peters, comprised representatives of the VEUO, the Amsterdam Stock Exchange, and pension funds.[53] There was no union representation. The committee's brief was to establish a voluntary code of best practice in corporate governance, along the lines of the earlier Cadbury Report in the United Kingdom.[54] Like the Cadbury Report, the goal of the Peters Committee was self-regulation, although Finance Minister Zalm raised the possibility of legislative response if companies ignored the committee's recommendations. Yet the explicit goal of self-regulation was to allow market forces as the mechanism of generating compliance.[55] The Peters Committee released its list of forty propositions for good corporate governance in June 1997. Studies have found no observable impact of the Peters Committee on corporate governance practice, and that the Dutch market actors were skeptical that the committee would have any effect.[56] The committee's own monitoring report, published in December 2002, confirmed a widespread failure of Dutch firms to comply with the recommendations of the Peters Committee.

---

[52] De Jong et al. (2005).

[53] De Jong et al. (2005: 474). The initial compromise between the VEUO and Zalm and the formation of the Peters Committee were both announced in February 1996. According to Jaap Peters, the Committee "grew out of a conversation between Zalm and the VNO-NCW and that conversation dealt with protection constructions. And the result was that they would establish us [the committee]" (interview, August 21, 2006). According to Gerrit Zalm, the law on protection constructions and the Peters Committee were not directly related. The Peters Committee "came from the same attitude, you could say. Both intended to give more influence for shareholders at the cost of management" (interview, October 11, 2006).

[54] Groenewald (2005: 300).

[55] De Jong et al. (2005: 474–475).

[56] Akkermans et al. (2007), De Jong et al. (2005).

Scholars of corporate finance point to the Peters Committee as a text-book example of the failures of self-regulation of business without any legal enforcement.[57] Yet from the viewpoint of the managerial interests that dominated the committee, its results were consistent with their highest political priority: to defend protection mechanisms. In general terms, the VEUO is able to influence the likely findings of such informal committees not only by selecting the managerial representatives, but also by influencing the "independent scholars" who participate. According to a former leader of the VEUO, "What they also always want is a number of scholarly gentlemen, so the key was, how would they think? [...] The scholars were on that side, entrepreneurs were clearly on that side. We did the same thing with the Peters Committee."[58]

After the finding of widespread noncompliance with the Peters Committee recommendations in 2002, the government reiterated the threat of legally binding regulation, calling for the formation of another committee to put together a more effective code on corporate governance.[59] As with the case of the Peters Committee, the VEUO exercised important input on the constitution of the new informal group. However, Zalm and the Finance Ministry under Minister Hans Hoogervorst also took a prominent role in negotiating the composition of the group, and particularly its chair.[60] According to Zalm, "There were problems of who should be in and who should be out. So we had to use some force sometimes against the VNO-NCW, stating that: 'if you don't agree that on we do it like that, we'll do it on our own.'"[61] Using the leverage of a potentially government-constituted committee, Zalm and Hoogervorst convinced the VNO-NCW and the VEUO to nominate the former CEO of Unilever, Morris Tabaksblat, to head the new committee.[62]

Although the VEUO and the VNO-NCW failed to control the leadership nomination process, they attempted to constrain the new group by sharply restricting its mandate. For the former high official of the VEUO, the most important issue of the Tabaksblat Committee was "Protection walls [against hostile takeovers], so that American situations would certainly not emerge."[63] A VNO-NCW official echoed this emphasis: "look, eventually what matters

[57] De Jong et al. (2005).

[58] Interview, September 1, 2006.

[59] Groenewald (2005: 301).

[60] The formation of the Tabaksblat Committee coincided with the time when Zalm was the parliamentary delegation leader of the Liberal Party, while his colleague Hans Hoogervorst was Finance Minister. The two worked closely together on this issue.

[61] Interview with Morris Tabaksblat, October 11, 2006.

[62] Asked why the VEUO would nominate someone like Tabaksblat, who was a known maverick in the business community, a VEUO leader said in interview, "That was mainly the Ministry of Finance.... It was also by the initiative of Zalm, or the government, that it became a committee; that had not been the case with the Peters Committee" (interview, September 1, 2006). Tabaksblat, asked in an interview why managerial organizations would accept his nomination, said, "Because I was known as reasonably independent. They knew I knew a lot about the subject" (interview, October 11, 2006).

[63] Interview, September 1, 2006.

is, what task do you set for the committee? Some parties, especially the VEB [the shareholders' organization], specifically wanted the committee to make direct recommendations for adjustments of the law, including guidelines for takeovers. We thought, 'No way!' You should only self-regulate where there is no law, and we can only give advice as to how to make laws which facilitate self-regulation."[64] Thus, the formal charge of the committee was indeed to take existing laws as given; it was forbidden to propose new laws.

The choice of Tabaksblat as chairman of the committee would prove to be important and extremely threatening to the legal protections against hostile takeover favored by the VEUO and VNO-NCW. This outcome was not foreseeable as of early 2003 when the group's composition was being negotiated. In many respects the composition of the committee (with thirteen members) was led by the VEUO and VNO-NCW, who ensured strong representation for their interests: executive board members of both organizations were named to the committee, including Rob Pieterse, who would become chairman of the VEUO in 2005. The committee also included Jan Kalff, former chairman of the board of ABN Amro, who had led the defense against Zalm's first attack on protection mechanisms during the Takeover Compromise.[65] There were no union representatives on the committee. Indeed, other than the fact of the government's greater involvement in selecting the chair of the committee, there is nothing about the composition of the committee that should have raised alarm bells at VEUO headquarters in December 2002. What changed the effect of the committee was the timing of the committee's first announcement and an initiative of Tabaksblat.

The composition of the Tabaksblat Committee was formally announced on March 10, 2003, just after the Ahold scandal became public. Tabaksblat himself credits Ahold with changing the nature of the discussion:

> It started with Ahold. . . . People started to see that a number of Dutch companies were on the wrong track. And then it became clear that also in the Netherlands we have our [governance] problems. So at that moment, I was asked to lead that committee. When we started out the extent of the problems weren't that clear yet. But by the time we finished the Royal Oil Company [Shell] was the exemplar of a Dutch company with problems. And all of this led to the acceptance of the code. I think that acceptance of the code would have been difficult in a different time, when the economy would have been rising, when the mutual feeling would have been that all was fine in the Netherlands.[66]

In the opinion of the Labor Party's spokesman, too, Ahold gave corporate governance broader resonance: "Ahold was the thing that really got the thing moving here in the Netherlands and made it into a public issue."[67]

---

[64] Interview, two VNO-NCW officials with responsibility for corporate governance issues, August 17, 2006.

[65] Frentrop (2002).

[66] Interview with Morris Tabaksblat, October 11, 2006.

[67] Interview with Kris Douma, July 30, 2007.

The Ahold scandal may have influenced public opinion, but it did little to change the opposition of leading managerial organizations to limiting the protections of Dutch companies, and several of their prominent representatives sat on the committee. Yet once the group met, Tabaksblat deliberately broke with the normal practice of widespread consultation characteristic of Dutch corporatism:

> We made a deal [amongst members of the committee] that nobody was to speak to his supporters.... I said that if we wanted to complete the work within half a year, everyone had to take responsibility [without consulting their supporters] and decide what we thought was acceptable for the Netherlands. In the end this worked very well. But it is a very unusual way to do things because normally everyone is just a representative. The way we did it was also better than working with a committee with only independent people because then nobody would feel committed to the recommendations. Now at least all the participating organizations had to say that they got the best possible result for them. The VEUO for example was very angry with Pieterse, because they were not content with the result but had to accept it because Pieterse had participated as their spokesman.[68]

Both the VEUO and VNO-NCW reacted strongly against the initial recommendations of the committee, although they had themselves been complicit in its formation, and their members sat on it. Asked about why these two organizations allowed this to happen, Tabaksblat said,

> There was no way back for them. They never expected what happened in the summer of 2003. They insisted that we should make a draft to hand out to interested parties. We did this, and put it on the internet, so that everybody stepped in. We got 256 reactions. For comparison, Higgs in the UK, where a much more heated debate took place, did not get more than 100 [reactions]. That [number of reactions] surprised everyone. It was summer and there was not much going on in the Netherlands. So every news report, every news channel, paid attention. The newspaper, *Het Financieele Dagblad*, used this code as the saving piece of their summer. They really kept the attention going.[69]

As we will see in the next section of this chapter, however, the prominent coverage in the business newspaper did not spill over into the general press. Its low priority on the government's legislative agenda allowed the moment to pass without any legislation being proposed. The Tabaksblat Code succeeded in adopting the "comply or explain" principle in several issues of corporate governance dealing with board composition and financial accounting.[70] Yet in the area of takeover protections, it was the great nonevent of Dutch politics, as the VEUO's opponents did not convert their tactical advantages into legislative

---

[68] Interview with Morris Tabaksblat, October 11, 2006.
[69] Ibid.
[70] Akkermans et al. (2007).

accomplishments.[71] In the view of Morris Tabaksblat, this was an opportunity missed: "we had a window of opportunity [to make takeover defenses temporary] and if Zalm had acted a bit faster, it could have been dealt with by now."[72]

Instead of using the political momentum of the Tabaksblat report to push immediately for a law making all protection measures temporary, the Finance Ministry concentrated first on passing unrelated laws that unified the system of financial supervision. When asked about the reasons for the delay, Zalm responded,

> First . . . we had a lot of legislation going on at the time, because there was a lot of legislation on supervision of the financial sectors[, and] it was a very large operation. So there were more parts of the legislation which came into some kind of delay. Also, a second issue is that – and that's a more political one and probably they are intertwined – we foresaw more difficulties [with passing a law regulating takeover protections]. . . . Although I cannot imagine for myself that seeing political problems would be a motive for delay, but maybe in the cabinet it took longer.

Faced with the likelihood of stiff managerial opposition to any attack on takeover protections, the government preferred to take on an easier issue: that of financial supervision. This, despite the fact that the new government was still early in its term, had support on the issue from the opposition Labor Party, and faced an elite and public discourse after Ahold and Tabaksblat that was favorable to reform.

The significance of the Tabaksblat episode lies in the limits it reveals in the capacity of managerial organizations to impose their preferred outcomes in politics. It highlights two potential weaknesses in the façade of managerial power: intramanagerial political difference and the possibilities that scandals undermine business claims to expertise. The figure of Morris Tabaksblat, former CEO of Unilever – which is listed on both the London and Amsterdam stock exchanges – is emblematic of a minority of managerial activists in the Netherlands who favored the limitation of protection mechanisms. Gerrit Zalm was only able to impose Tabaksblat as the leader of the committee after the

---

[71] A law reforming supervisory board structure and appointments – the so-called structure regime – took effect in 2004, but its legal passage in 2003 predated the Tabaksblat Code, and it did not directly affect takeover protection. The law allowed works councils to propose one-third of the members of supervisory boards in Dutch companies, while workers simultaneously lost the right to object to other appointments to the board (Groenewald 2005: 299–300). Asked in an interview about the possibility of using appointment powers to the supervisory board as a shareholder disciplining mechanism, Peter Paul de Vries of the VEB said "in practice [a shareholders' representative] will never have the chance to come up with a proposal of a supervisory board member" (interview, July 30, 2007). The sentiment of de Vries is consistent with that of scholars who judge the reform of the structure regime a minor event, one in which works councils gained more than shareholders (Schnyder forthcoming).

[72] Interview with Morris Tabaksblat, chairman of the 2003 Corporate Governance Committee, October 11, 2006.

failure of the Peters Committee to induce any change in corporate behavior. And the committee itself was only able to make such sweeping recommendations because the Ahold scandal created an environment in which managers were on the defensive. Managers benefit from the deference of politicians and the press to their superior knowledge of how things work in the economy. An accounting scandal such as Enron or Ahold directly undercuts such claims of expertise and the deference associated with it. This constellation of interests and events turned the normal managerial advantage of self-regulation into a potential source of weakness for the VEUO.

The Framing of Hostile Takeover Politics in the Dutch Press

Managerial lobbying groups benefit by keeping low salience issues off the radar of most citizens, so as to maximize the effect of their influence through lobbying and participation in informal bodies of policy making. Every representative of the VEUO interviewed for this book made this point in some form or other:

> The discussion in the papers focuses on who is right and who is not. I don't think that is really relevant. What we focus on is transparency. [This is] a neutral subject, which keeps the discussion away from the good-bad discussion. But traditionally our preference is to work behind the scenes, and it still happens that way for a minimum of seventy percent. Sometimes publicity may help creating a certain atmosphere, but you have to be careful with that.[73]

Another VEUO leader noted that proinvestor interest groups such as the VEB of Peter Paul de Vries "are very visible; they like to get attention from the press. We do this to a lesser extent, [since] our members have very different backgrounds.... We are much more from the background of silent diplomacy. We think you can exert more influence like that than by being on the front page of *Het Financieele Dagblad* every day."[74]

Managers cannot control whether or not issues become politically salient. They can, though, attempt to influence the character of coverage on the occasions when the press and public opinion do pay attention to the topic of corporate control. To gauge the tenor of press coverage in the Netherlands and its variation over time, I used the sample of press articles discussed earlier in this chapter to analyze the dominant rhetorical frames of articles that appeared on the subject of corporate control. As in the French press analysis discussed in the previous chapter, different rhetorical "frames" were associated with the arguments of different interest groups. The notable difference between the two countries was that the framing pursued by managerial organizations in the Netherlands was diametrically opposed to the one pursued by their counterparts in France. Dutch managers employed a "foreign threat" frame, which linked their interest in takeover protection to national interests

---

[73] Interview, September 4, 2006.
[74] Interview, October 11, 2006.

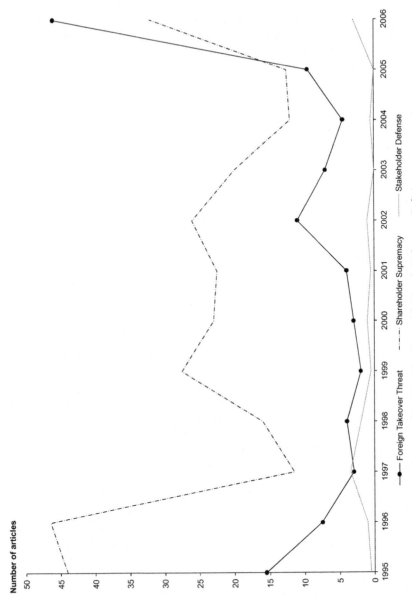

FIGURE 4.2. Dominant Frames of Articles Dealing with Dutch Takeover Politics, 1995–2006

in keeping Dutch companies under Dutch control.[75] Articles with this frame emphasize one of two features of takeover regulation. The first feature is the claim that a relaxation of protection would make national firms vulnerable to acquisition by foreign predators. The second feature is the claim that market rules in other countries make takeovers more difficult there than in the Netherlands (defending takeover protections as necessary to ensure a level-playing field). The other two frames used in the Netherlands were similar to those used in France. Members of the investor coalition, such as institutional investors and members of the Liberal Party (VVD), tended to argue in terms of shareholder supremacy. The "shareholder supremacy" frame emphasizes market efficiency, minority shareholder rights, shareholder value, and transparency.[76] Dutch unions and Christian Democrats tended to frame arguments in terms of

---

FIGURE 4.2. Dominant Frames of Articles Dealing with Dutch Takeover Politics, 1995–2006

Note: The LexisNexis search of articles in the area of takeover protection yielded 679 relevant articles between 1995 and 2006 from *Algemeen Dagblad, Het Financieele Dagblad, NRC Handelsblad, De Telegraaf*, and *De Volkskrant*. A Dutch research assistant coded all those articles based on one of three frames, or assigned them to the category "no dominant frame" (many articles were short factual accounts). The three frames were Foreign Takeover Threat (or level playing field), Shareholder Supremacy, and Stakeholder Defense. Articles could be coded as having a maximum of two dominant frames. Where we coded an article as having two frames, each frame counts as 0.5 of an article. The headline and first three paragraphs of the article, as well as the last paragraph, were given priority in assigning frames to the articles, although the whole article was analyzed. We coded 293.5 articles as Shareholder Supremacy; 117 as Foreign Takeover Threat; and 13.5 as Stakeholder Defense (the coding protocol for this exercise is included as an appendix). The remaining articles were coded as having no dominant frame. We coded as Foreign Takeover Threat any article that characterized takeovers as a threat for Dutch firms, as indicated by the use of negative phrases such as predator (to describe foreign firms) or prey (to describe Dutch firms), or any article that referred to the need for maintaining takeover protections to maintain a "level playing field" between the Netherlands and other countries. We coded as Shareholder Supremacy any article that referred to the stakes in takeovers as affecting shareholder value, shareholder rights, one-share one-vote, market functioning, transparency as a value for shareholders, or a high share price as its own best defense. We coded as Stakeholder Defense any quotation that characterized takeovers affecting a broader group than just shareholders, including employees, unions, long-term owners, customers, and local communities. See the appendix to this chapter for a longer discussion of the procedure used to identify article frames.

---

[75] Frentrop (2002).

[76] In the Dutch political context, the argument that a high share price was the best defense was employed mainly by opponents of takeover defenses, and we coded it as falling under shareholder supremacy. This was different from the French case, where managers used the idea of share price as their best defense in order to advocate largely neoliberal rules of transposition of the takeover directive.

stakeholder defense. The "stakeholder defense" frame highlights the importance of the broader community of stakeholders in a firm, as opposed to the narrow community of shareholders, or the potential employment losses associated with the possibility of liberalizing takeover rules. I identified a number of typical keywords associated with the given frame. The headline and first three paragraphs of each of the 679 articles in the sample, as well as the last paragraph, were given priority in assigning frames to the articles, though the whole article was analyzed (this coding procedure is discussed at greater length in the appendix to this chapter).

Between 1995 and 2005, the dominant framing of articles about hostile takeover defenses in the Netherlands was that of "shareholder supremacy." This was true of both left-wing and right-wing papers, and of the financial as well as the general press. The two figures below demonstrate this latter point by showing how the framing of articles in the financial paper, *Het Financieele Dagblad* (FD), was fundamentally similar to the framing in the nonfinancial press. As we would expect on a financial subject like hostile takeovers, the FD ran more stories per year on this topic than did the other four newspapers combined. Of the total of 679 articles in my sample, slightly more than half (353) appeared in the FD. As illustrated by the two figures below, the financial newspaper and the nonfinancial press followed similar trends in coverage.[77] Moreover, and perhaps more surprising, the general press showed the same "shareholder supremacy" dominance in framing as did the FD, even though we would expect the business press to be somewhat politically more predisposed to the shareholder supremacy view (Figure 4.3). Indeed, in its coverage of hostile takeovers, the FD turned to a "foreign takeover threat" frame one year *earlier* (2005) than the general press (Figure 4.4). By 2006, both the financial and the nonfinancial press had moved to a "foreign takeover threat" framing. By way of contrast, this coding of articles showed very little reliance on the employment and worker defense tropes associated with the "stakeholder defense" frame in either the general or the business press.

If these indicators accurately reflect both the salience and the ideological tenor of press coverage of hostile takeovers in the Netherlands, then Gerrit Zalm's real window of opportunity may not have been at the end of 2003, as suggested by Tabaksblat, but instead in 1996. In the second half of 2003, many of the articles in *Het Financieele Dagblad* about protection were about the Tabaksblat Committee, and they were conducted in language that was propitious to reformers. However, the general press failed to pick up any of these articles. The FD ran thirty-two articles in 2003 that dealt with hostile takeovers; the rest of the press ran only nine articles, the least of any year between 1995 and 2006. While the Ahold scandal generated outrage and corresponding press coverage about accounting systems and executive pay in the Netherlands, the general press never linked the Ahold scandal to the issue of takeover defenses.

---

77 The correlation coefficient between the number of articles on hostile takeovers per year in the in *Het Financieele Dagblad* and in the nonfinancial press is 0.54.

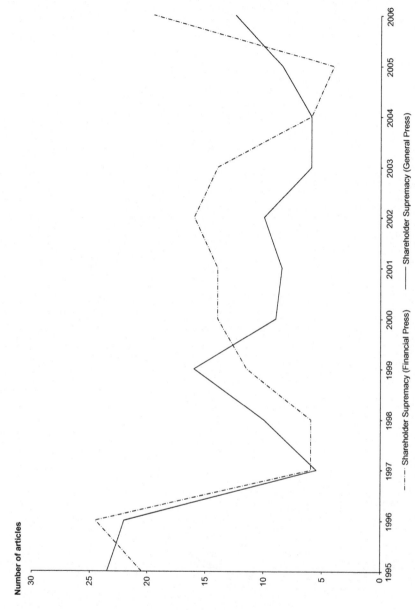

FIGURE 4.3. Financial Press vs. General Press, Use of Shareholder Supremacy Frames, 1995–2006. See Figure 4.2 for sources and explanation of coding procedure.

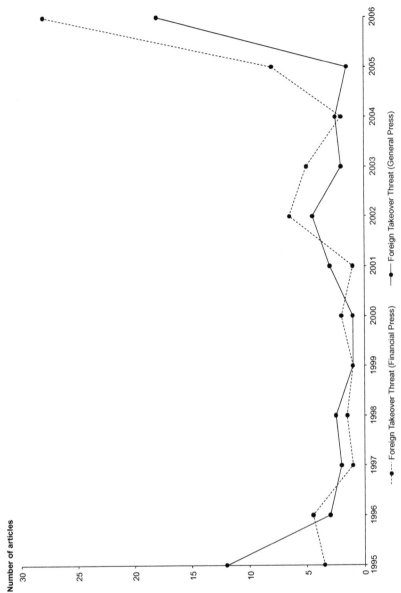

FIGURE 4.4. Financial Press vs. General Press, Use of Foreign Takeover Threat Frames, 1995–2006. See Figure 4.2 for sources and explanation of coding procedure.

The Tabaksblat Committee did deal with both issues, but the focus on protection never captured general media attention. In contrast, both the financial and the general press had been paying attention to the issue of hostile takeover protection in 1996, and the overwhelming majority of that coverage was conducted on terms favorable to reformers: shareholder rights, transparency, and efficiency were the watchwords of the debate. Representatives of managerial organizations, which in 1994 and 1995 had experienced at least some success in injecting notions of the potential threat of foreign takeovers into the debate in the popular press, found that these frames picked up very little traction in press coverage in 1996.

Gerrit Zalm and the VVD's final assault on Dutch takeover protection followed the adoption of the EU takeover directive at the end of 2003. Zalm, who was by now both finance minister and deputy prime minister in the Netherlands, favored a law implementing the EU directive which would include the breakthrough rule (article 11). The breakthrough rule, as legally interpreted in the Netherlands, would in case of a hostile takeover bid in which the acquirer passed an ownership threshold, have cancelled all protective mechanisms after a period of six months. The breakthrough rule had its political origins in the same reformist coalition that supported the Tabaksblat Committee. Jaap Winter, a member of the Tabaksblat Committee, chaired the Expert Group that had proposed the rule during the EU deliberations over takeover reform in January 2002, and Frits Bolkestein, who had preceded Zalm as the leader of the Liberal VVD Party in the Netherlands, had fought against the compromise version of the EU directive that made the breakthrough rule optional.

The Dutch law transposing the EU takeover directive was presented to the social partners for consultation at the beginning of 2005. The VEUO and the VNO-NCW led the opposition to the bill, focusing their fire on the breakthrough article. As Figure 4.2 shows, there was a sharp increase in the press usage of idiom related to the foreign takeover threat in 2006. This upsurge of articles actually began in late 2005 in *Het Financieele Dagblad*, shortly before the bill was formally presented to parliament in December, and it was later picked up by other newspapers.[78] On February 15, 2006, an article in the FD quoted Aad Jacobs, the former chairman of the board of Royal Dutch Shell, warning that Dutch companies would all become branches of foreign companies if the government's proposal passed.[79] Of the seven articles that appeared on the subject of takeover protections between that date and the parliament's ultimate rejection of the draft law at the end of March, four of them mentioned Jacobs by name and three reprinted his reference to the likely "branchification" of Dutch companies. The VEUO was successful in dominating the news cycle

---

[78] Thus, articles under the following three headlines appeared in December in the FD: "Dutch Listed Companies are Wild Takeover Prey" (12/6), "The Hunters and Dutch Prey" (12/6), "A Qadafi can take over Schiphol" (12/15) [Schiphol is Amsterdam's airport].

[79] Shell is the largest company in the Netherlands and one of the largest in the world by revenue. Aad Jacobs was one of the most well-known Dutch executives, and he had been a prominent defender of Dutch takeover protections since the early 1990s.

in 2006. According to an official of the VEUO at the time, "the outcome [of the Takeover Directive episode] was not clear from the start. We as VEUO did think, [when] there were voices in the newspaper from prominent Dutch people like Aad Jacobs and Kalff,[80] that our chances were greater.... You sense in politics and the media that there is a tipping point, and then it is a good moment to see if you can benefit from that."[81] It is impossible to demonstrate a conclusive causal link between the press coverage of takeover protection and the decision of the PvdA to switch sides and vote the bill down. But the ability of managerial representatives to influence Dutch press coverage of takeover protections at this time cannot have hurt them politically.

Conclusion

At the end of 2006, the VVD was voted out of office after twelve straight years of serving in the governing coalition. Fewer Dutch companies have multiple protection mechanisms than they did in 1993, but those protections they do enjoy have not been limited in duration. And as a former leader of the VEUO was quick to point out in an interview, when it comes to protection mechanisms, "you only need one, one is enough."[82] As we saw in Chapter 2, a majority of Dutch companies had preference shares in 1993, and a majority of companies still maintained those protections in 2007. The legislative onslaught led by Gerrit Zalm and the Liberal Party, which aimed to make these legal protections automatically expire after six months in the event of a hostile takeover, failed. The takeover compromise of 1997 was subverted following an intensive lobbying campaign by the VEUO, because parliament refused to consider it. The Tabaksblat Committee's recommendations on making all protection temporary were not converted into law in 2004, even though the opposition Labor Party and the governing Liberals strongly supported these recommendations. In 2005–2006, when the government finally did attempt to implement the EU Takeover Directive, including the optional breakthrough clause, it was defeated in parliament. The Labor Party, which had supported such a change in 2004 and 2005, reversed its position, again in the wake of a strong lobbying campaign of the VEUO.

By tracing the perceptions of the central political actors involved in this process as well as the press coverage of it, this chapter has illustrated how the low salience of corporate control converts the expertise of managers into a powerful political weapon. Dutch managers in the VEUO are keenly interested

---

[80] Jan Kalff, the former chairman of ABN Amro and a highly visible executive in the Netherlands, had led the challenge to Zalm's first reform effort, beginning 1994. "I am concerned about Minister Zalm's [proposals to limit the mechanisms] companies use to protect themselves from undesirable takeovers.... I consider it extremely important that the market should come up with balanced measures in this regard, so that legislation is not required." Such measures, he added, risked creating an "unlevel playing field" in which "attractive Dutch companies" could be sold to foreigners (Frentrop 2002: 375).

[81] Interview with senior VEUO official, September 4, 2006.

[82] Interview, September 1, 2006.

in preserving the protection mechanisms that serve them so well. Dutch political parties and unions, by contrast, have much less of a clear material interest in the issue. Zalm pursued these reforms as part of his party's program of liberalizing regulation the Netherlands. But for him, it was never an issue of overriding importance: "I would never make a cabinet crisis on a corporate governance issue. I *would* make a cabinet crisis on budgetary policy or social insurance or tax reforms." The Labor Party shifted position on this issue – it was split in 1997, and favored making protection temporary between 2003 and 2006, until its sudden reversal of position in the parliamentary vote of March 2006. This shifting position makes sense only in the context of an issue in which the party did not have a strong view which its voters monitored.

The defining political feature of the Dutch regime of corporate control is not its defense by a corporatist coalition of managers and unions, but its low political salience. Both coalitional and partisan theories are anchored in views of the world in which voters and parties have a clear understanding of the way in which the politics of corporate control relates to their own material interests, and that this view is important in determining their political priorities. This perspective is a serious distortion of the political reality of Dutch corporate control. Most of the time, most voters do not care about corporate governance or hostile takeovers. They care about salient material issues such as taxes and salient symbolic issues such as immigration. Only when an issue achieves high visibility do voters begin to pay attention to how politicians act on it. When issues are of low salience, the lobbying capacity of managers and the deference to their expertise by politicians and the press are important assets. These assets best explain the surprising durability of the institutions of takeover protection in the Netherlands.

Appendix 4.1: Coding Scheme for Dutch Newspapers, 1995–2006

There are three potential codes, as well as "none of the above":

> Foreign Takeover Threat
> Shareholder Supremacy
> Stakeholder Defense

Coding Protocol

Foreign Takeover Threat: any article that characterized takeovers as a threat to Dutch firms, as indicated by the use of words such as predator (to describe foreign firms) or prey (to describe Dutch firms), or any article that referred to the need for maintaining takeover protections to maintain a "level playing field" between the Netherlands and other countries.

> Examples:
> "We should guard against becoming a country of branches. The Netherlands does not want to become like Belgium where all companies were bought up and their headquarters moved abroad."

"The Netherlands should not want to be the teacher's pet. It is unwise to force companies to break down protection where other countries leave the protection of their companies untouched."

"The predators are coming and Dutch companies are easy prey for them."

Shareholder Supremacy: any article that referred to the stakes in takeovers as affecting shareholder value, shareholder rights, one-share one-vote, market functioning, transparency as a value for shareholders, or a high share price as its own best defense.

Examples:
"In the end the 'Dutch Discount' is bad for the attractiveness of the Dutch economy to investors."

"Such measures contribute neither to transparency of the company nor to the beneficial input by shareholders and capital markets."

"A higher price/profit ratio contributes to better financing terms and is thus a competitive advantage. It is also a market-conforming way to protect firms from takeovers."

Stakeholder Defense: any quotation that characterized takeovers affecting a broader group than just shareholders, including employees, unions, long-term owners of the firm, and local communities.

Examples:
"A firm belongs not just to its shareholders, but also to its workers."

"There is a group of owners who have demonstrated a commitment to the long-term strategy of the firm. We should give them proportionally more voting rights."

"The major criteria for evaluating the effect of a takeover must include the potential unemployment effects of a merger, which can have major ramifications for local communities."

Examples of quotations that fit none of the above:

"The Tabaksblat Code is an attempt to bring companies to good corporate governance through self-regulation."

"Legally, remuneration and stock options are subject to approval by the shareholders' meeting."

"This law is a minor question. We must stay focused on the major problems of the economy, not technical details."

"When one says the directive is neoliberal inspiration, this ignores the fact that the United Kingdom and the United States, both neoliberal countries, have very different rules for takeovers."

5

Managers, Bureaucrats, and Institutional Change in Japan

Studying corporate control in Japan is like landing in the middle of a murder mystery. There is indisputably a corpse: in this case, the takeover protection once provided by long-term shareholders was killed between 1996 and 2005, as shown in Chapter 2. How the corpse died and especially what threat the killer poses to other institutions of the Japanese political economy are hotly contested questions. Some adduce the collapse of cross-shareholdings as a sign of the thoroughgoing liberalization of the market for corporate control, in which western institutional investors now call many of the shots in Japanese companies.[1] Others claim, contrariwise, that the limited number of takeovers to date is proof positive that the Japanese market for corporate control remains closed even without cross-shareholding, and that entrenched managers can protect themselves from any unwanted advances.[2] A third group of scholars sees a new organizational diversity in Japan: some firms play by the rules of an active market for corporate control, while others have tried to rebuild interfirm alliances as a form of protection.[3] As this book goes to press, it is not entirely clear how active the market for Japanese corporate control is in international comparison. While hostile takeovers have rarely succeeded in recent years in Japan, the increasing number of attempted takeovers suggests that the character of market monitoring of managers is higher than it was before the death of the cross-shareholding regime.

What is much clearer is that the governance of Japanese takeovers has shifted away from the informal arena of stable shareholding to the formal institutional arena of courts. It is in this formal venue that the future of the Japanese market for corporate control will be determined. This is a significant institutional change. How it happened is the subject of this chapter.

[1] Schaede (2008), Ahmadjian (2007).
[2] Gilson (2004), Witt (2006).
[3] Vogel (2006), Jackson and Miyajima (2007).

The overwhelming problem for Japanese business in the 1990s was how to move beyond the economic stagnation of the decade after 1993, retrospectively called the "lost decade" by most Japanese. The economic crisis drove many Japanese large companies to change their competitive strategies at the end of the 1990s as they began to focus on their core business and to spin-off unrelated subsidiaries.[4] Like their counterparts in France, managers of large companies in Japan were able to restructure aggressively because of the weakness of labor representation at the company level. Japanese firm-based employee organizations lack the legally-mandated rights enjoyed by Dutch and German works councils. As Gregory Jackson has argued, this weaker institutionalization of labor at the level of the firm has made it much easier for Japanese firms to introduce measures aimed at increasing shareholder value, even when labor organizations might be opposed to such measures.[5] The competitive strategies chosen by Japanese business led many to seek out foreign institutional investors, and those foreign investors in turn pushed managers further in the direction of maximizing shareholder value,[6] Firms with higher levels of foreign investment during this period were more likely to downsize employment or to reorganize by selling off parts of the company.[7] The political consequence of this firm-level change was the focus by the peak association of managers, the Keidanren, on reforming corporate law so as to facilitate this process of restructuring.[8]

The destruction of stable shareholding in Japan took place against this same backdrop of an economy in crisis. As share prices collapsed in the late 1990s, banks with large cross-shareholdings had to sell those shares to meet the capital requirements of the Bank for International Settlements (known as the Basel II requirements). Many banks were perceived by nonfinancial corporations to be increasingly risky investments. As one company involved in cross-shareholding with another sold its shares, the other company was likely to respond in kind.[9] The unraveling of cross-shareholding was not driven primarily by views about takeover protection, but by the short-term challenges posed by the economic crisis. It was not an intentional decision, on the part of either companies or government officials.[10] The death of Japanese patient capital was really a case of manslaughter, not of murder.

---

[4] Schaede (2008).

[5] Jackson (2003, 2007).

[6] Tiberghien (2007).

[7] Ahmadjian and Robins (2005), Ahmadjian (2007).

[8] Vogel (2006), Gilson and Milhaupt (2004). The Keidanren (the Japan Business Federation) has historically been the political defender of large corporations in Japan (Hamada 2010). In 2002, the Keidanren merged with the Nikkeiren, a formerly separate organization of employers' associations responsible for social and employment-related issues (Vogel 2006: 56–57). Large firms are well-represented at the Keidanren. Its first postmerger chairman was Hiroshi Okuda, president of Toyota Motor Corporation. Fujio Mitarai, chairman of Canon, succeeded Okuda in 2005.

[9] Miyajima and Kuroki (2007).

[10] The Basel II capital adequacy requirements were the product of an international regulatory action, but they were not aimed at eliminating cross-shareholding in Japan or elsewhere.

The breakdown of shareholding networks as takeover protection was accompanied by the emergence of isolated hostile takeover bids in Japan after 1999. However, these bids were all for small companies. No large Japanese company was the subject of a hostile attack prior to 2004. For managers acting through the Keidanren, there was no apparent cost to donning the mantle of economic reformers in terms of autonomy lost to other market players or threats to internal work organization.

That changed with the onset of two events in 2004 and 2005: the UFJ/Sumitomo battle and the attempted hostile takeover of Nippon Broadcasting (NBS) and the broadcasting giant, Fuji TV. The prospect of a hanging concentrates the mind, and these two episodes brought home to managers of Japanese large companies that the changes in the market for corporate control were not only of concern to small company managers. Japanese large companies are generally more reliant on firm-level cooperation with their workforce than are the smaller companies involved in earlier takeover bids.[11] As a result, the majority of large companies in Japan opposed the introduction of rules that could make these companies themselves the object of hostile takeover bids.

From a focus on the flexibility of law as a tool for reorganizing companies in the early part of the decade, the Keidanren moved toward a much more aggressive use of the political system to regulate hostile takeovers.[12] Having abandoned long-term shareholding with other companies, Japanese managers were fortunate in that some bureaucrats had already begun thinking at this time about what sort of measures of takeover protection might be helpful to Japanese business. The most important set of guidelines governing hostile takeovers would not come in the form of laws or regulations, but from an informal advisory group convened by the Ministry of the Economy, Trade, and Industry (METI) and the Ministry of Justice (MoJ). This Corporate Value Study Group (CVSG) developed a new set of institutional rules for "fair and reasonable" takeovers and the defenses firm management could deploy against them.[13] The group was an initiative of the bureaucracy, not of organized managers. Yet the position of organized managers in its informal deliberations allowed them to have a significant influence on the final rules the group produced, even though it was an issue about which most large company managers had been unconcerned at the beginning of 2004.

In 2005, the attempt by a maverick internet company, Livedoor, to acquire a corporate giant generated widespread public interest in the subject of hostile takeovers in Japan. After this event, corporate control became an issue of high political salience in Japan. Under these conditions, the Keidanren would encounter difficulties achieving its political objectives in trying to derail a new

---

[11] I am indebted to an anonymous reviewer for emphasizing this point.

[12] Vogel (2006).

[13] Thanks to Curtis Milhaupt for suggesting this phrasing of the new METI standard for acceptable hostile takeovers.

style of merger known as the triangular merger. Japanese business is still an important interest group under conditions of high salience, but it was unable to dominate other actors in the governance space when the public and political parties were paying close attention to the policy domain. The triangular merger episode is the only one in the book where we can say that organized managers failed in their objectives for a regime of corporate control, and it took place in a time when corporate control had achieved a high level of political salience. I argue that the tools of managers, which had allowed them to be so influential in earlier episodes of reform, worked less well under the conditions of sustained political salience.

The Political Narrative of Japanese Corporate Control, 1997–2007

Between 1997 and 2004, the liberalization of Japanese corporate governance was overdetermined. Every actor that we would expect to matter in affecting the outcome of deregulatory battles favored liberalization. Managerial organizations all pushed for liberalizing regulations, as did foreign and domestic institutional shareholders and reformers within the ruling party. The general pattern of reform, as described by Steven Vogel, was one in which business and government jointly pushed for regulatory changes that gave Japanese companies more options.[14] The rise of shareholdings by foreign investors, and the more aggressive pursuit of shareholder value by domestic institutional investors was plainly in evidence in Japan in the early part of the century.[15] At the same time, entrepreneurial actors in the ruling LDP and the bureaucracy teamed up to support an aggressive program of reform of corporate law.[16] This was a project of reform that the Keidanren actively endorsed and partially initiated.[17] However, studying the consensual aspects of corporate law reform can tell us little about the relative power of these actors in the political sphere.

This chapter examines how these actors fared in three important and non-consensual episodes affecting the Japanese regime of corporate control. These actors are the most relevant ones to investigate because they represent the most plausible operationalization of the different theoretical approaches compared in this book. In coalitional theory, the rise of powerful institutional investors, both foreign and domestic, can swing the balance of power in institutional reforms that move away from stakeholder protection toward shareholder rights.[18] Theories of partisanship expect change to be pushed by political parties. The theory of quiet politics predicts that managerial organizations will prevail under conditions of low political salience because of their capacity for lobbying and their

---

[14] Vogel (2006).

[15] Ahmadjian (2007), Schaede (2008).

[16] Tiberghien (2007).

[17] Shishido (2007), Vogel (2006).

[18] Gourevitch and Shinn (2005). The other potential coalitional actor – unions – played almost no role in discussions of Japanese corporate law reform (Vogel 2006: 94).

ability to wield influence through informal groups where they are included because of their expertise.

The first episode of interest conflict was not directly over an issue of corporate control. It was, though, regarded by observers as the key conflict over whether the Japanese system of corporate governance would converge on the American system.[19] The Ministry of Justice (MoJ) and the Ministry of the Economy, Trade, and Industry (METI) in 2001 both favored a legal reform that would require all Japanese large companies to have at least one director appointed from outside the company.[20] This was known as "U.S.-style" board reform. The mandatory appointment of independent board members is characteristic demand of stakeholder activists who argue that such directors provide a better check on management than those with direct ties to the company. The Keidanren, lobbying through parliament, was able to convince legislators instead to adopt a rival commercial law proposal that made the choice of board structure optional. That is, firms could choose to have independent directors or they could remain instead with the traditional Japanese system of statutory auditors. The Diet (the Japanese Parliament) adopted this rival proposal in 2002. The vast majority of listed companies did not opt for independent boards. Most of the companies that did opt for this American-style corporate structure were perceived as having extremely internationally oriented senior managers, as in the case of Sony.[21] In the most significant battle that divided the reforming coalition prior to 2005, the Keidanren view prevailed.

The most important change to the rules governing Japanese takeovers did not take place through the adoption of a new law, but through the promulgation of an informal code in 2005. METI and the MoJ had jointly convened the Corporate Value Study Group as a forum to develop guidelines about the legality of takeover defenses in Japan while the issue was not on the public radar. A major question debated by this group was whether to permit the use of poison pill takeover defenses, as allowed under Delaware law in the United States, or instead to adopt the strict board neutrality requirement in the City of London of the United Kingdom, which was the basis for the EU takeover directive.[22] In the choice between the UK- and U.S.-style takeover guidelines, the investor coalition and neoliberal reformers should both favor the UK-style City Code, which is less protective of managers and more concerned with the problem of shareholder value. The Delaware model, by contrast, provides more protection to management by allowing barriers to hostile takeovers.

The final episode of the battle over corporate control in Japan took place in the formal arena under conditions of high salience. These are conditions

[19] Gilson and Milhaupt (2004).
[20] Tiberghien (2007).
[21] Gilson and Milhaupt (2004).
[22] Milhaupt (2005); interview with Hideki Kanda, Chair, Corporate Value Study Group, and Professor of Law at the University of Tokyo, June 5, 2007.

TABLE 5.1. *Summary of Theoretical Predictions in Japanese Corporate Politics, 1997–2007*

Predictions →	Quiet Politics [Manager-Led]	Coalitional Theory [Investor-Led]	Partisanship [Party-Led]	Outcome
Law on Board Structure (2001–2002): Low salience	Independent board optional	Independent board mandatory	Independent board mandatory	Independent board optional
Corporate Value Study Group (2004–5): Low salience at outset	Poison pills allowed	Poison pills banned	Poison pills banned	Poison pills allowed
Triangular Merger Law (2005–2006): High salience	Liberal bill implemented	Liberal bill implemented	Liberal bill implemented	Liberal bill implemented

under which we expect the positioning of political parties and public opinion to be the decisive variables, as predicted by coalitional theorists. This episode involved a legal amendment enabling the use of triangular mergers. Triangular mergers allow potential acquirers to establish a subsidiary company in Japan, and then use stock of the parent company as consideration in a merger with another company in Japan. One goal of the reform was to promote foreign direct investment in Japan by making it easier for foreign firms to acquire domestic ones. This device was applicable only for friendly mergers – where both boards of directors approved – but it became embroiled in the general debate about hostile takeovers in light of concerns of Japanese companies from 2004 that they might face a threat from potential acquiring firms located elsewhere. And the battle directly opposed the organization of large business, the Keidanren, and interest groups and partisan actors favoring neoliberal reforms. Under these circumstances, the liberal coalition prevailed, although the Keidanren managed to extract an amendment delaying the implementation of the measure. Organized business is a strong actor even under high salience, but the decisive conflicts are likely to happen within political parties once an issue attains durable salience, which militates against the business dominance we have observed elsewhere in the domain of corporate control.

Table 5.1 presents the theoretical expectations of the different approaches in the current literature on the politics of corporate control, as well as the actual outcome of these episodes. The quiet politics approach anticipates that when salience is low and preferences over laws or informal rules diverge within the reformist coalition, the preferences of organized managers are likely to

prevail. The coalitional approach focuses on the rising role of foreign inve
in Japanese companies and the concomitant political power these groups ex.
cise in the Japanese polity.[23] If coalitional politics were the driver of change in
the market for corporate control in Japan, we would expect foreign investors
to team with liberal managers and/or liberal politicians to impose the most
shareholder-friendly outcomes on recalcitrant managers. In Japan, the battle over neoliberal reforms never involved the parties of the left, suggesting
that Cioffi and Höpner's stress on the left as the ineluctable force for reform
in corporate governance is falsified for Japan.[24] However, one can expand
the partisan theoretical approach to include all work focused on parties and
their leadership as the agents of change. Such an approach stresses instead the
causally important role of the maverick prime minister, Junichiro Koizumi,
and the reformers whom he promoted in the ruling Liberal Democratic Party
(LDP), such as Yasuhisa Shiozaki.[25] This version of the partisan approach is
the one assessed in the following discussion.

The remainder of this chapter shows how and why managers were able
to achieve their preferred outcome over the objections of politically powerful
opponents. Hostile takeovers and the market for corporate control were low
salience issues from 1997–2004, which enabled the Keidanren to achieve many
of its objectives during this period through its direct lobbying in parliament
or through cooperation with the bureaucracy. As I show in the next two sections, the events that galvanized the Keidanren to adopt more conservative
positions on reform, at the end of 2004 and beginning of 2005, also brought
the issue of hostile takeovers to general attention and higher salience. This
increased the leverage of reformers in the LDP because the initial wave of
coverage of the Livedoor takeover bid painted Livedoor in a positive light.[26]
Yet the issue was not debated in parliament, but in an informal working group
whose members had been determined before the rise in political salience of
hostile takeovers. In this group, managerial interests were well represented and
managerial opponents were not. Thus, the informality of the Corporate Value
Study Group guidelines preserved managerial influence even in a high salience
atmosphere.[27] The final section explores the lobbying efforts of the various
actors in the implementation of the triangular merger law.

Japanese Managerial Preferences

Between 1997 and 2004, the overriding concern of managerial organizations
and of political reformers in the LDP was to restructure companies in order to

---

[23] Schaede (2008), Ahmadjian (2007).
[24] Cioffi and Höpner (2007).
[25] Tiberghien (2007).
[26] Whittaker and Hayakawa (2007).
[27] Livedoor's positive image proved short-lived, as its charismatic CEO, Takafumi Horie, was
arrested on charges of financial malfeasance in early 2006.

nic crisis. The sharp fall in long-term shareholding, which
vided hostile takeover protection for many Japanese com-
lle any significant concern among managers of large firms.
gers were at the forefront of pushing for legislation that
tools to enable corporate reorganization.[28] Three-quarters
of the 472 largest companies in Japan reported undertaking some form of corporate reorganization between 2000 and 2006.[29] These measures of restructuring were facilitated by a host of legal changes made at the end of the 1990s
with active managerial support.

During this period of economic crisis, the political organizations of Japanese
managers were not proponents of a more active market for corporate control,
but neither were they opposed to it. The fall in stable shareholdings that came
about during this period went hand-in-hand with the beginnings of activity
in the previously quiescent hostile takeover market. The companies involved
were small. There was no political concern about this trend among managers of
large firms, nor was this phenomenon of interest to the wider Japanese public.
These takeovers were seen as signs of the restructuring that the Keidanren had
been advocating. Japanese managers of large firms only began to be concerned
in the summer of 2004, when the UFJ merger deal made it clear that the rules
of the game had also changed for large companies. The attempt by Livedoor to
acquire the media giant Fuji TV catalyzed this rising managerial concern and
also caught the interest of the public.

The Beginnings of an Active Market for Corporate Control
The first successful hostile takeover in Japan occurred in 1999 when the British
firm Cable & Wireless took over International Digital Communications (IDC),
a small telecommunications company. Two takeover attempts took place the
following year, including the first ever hostile takeover bid launched by one
Japanese company against another. M&A Consulting (MAC), a company led
by former METI high-flyer Yoshiaki Murakami, launched a bid against Shoei
after failing to convince the company's management to change its strategy. The
MAC bid was seen by the press and some scholars as the end of the norm against
hostile takeovers in Japan.[30] Both Murakami and the firm that financed his bid,
the financial services group Orix, were considered outsiders by the Japanese
managerial establishment.[31] The extent to which such outsiders could change
mainstream managerial norms about takeovers is questionable.[32] In the two
years after the deal, the only unsolicited bids in Japan were launched by Japan
Steel Partners (JSP), an American fund. MAC and JSP were involved in a variety

---

[28] Vogel (2006).

[29] Schaede (2008: 11).

[30] Milhaupt (2001).

[31] Commenting on Orix's backing of the MAC bid for Shoei, a Japanese banker interviewed by
Milhaupt (2001: 2114) said, "That's the type of thing Orix would do. Big Japanese banks
wouldn't dare – they worry too much about what others would think."

[32] Culpepper (2005).

TABLE 5.2. *Unsolicited Deals in Japan, 2000–2004*

Target Firm	Hostile Acquirer	Month/ Year	Transaction Value ($ million, year 2000)	Takeover Successful?
SS Pharmaceutical	Boehringer Ingelheim	1/2000	207.1	Yes
Shoei Co.	M&A Consulting	1/2000	133.4	No
Yushiro Chemical	Steel Partners Japan	12/2003	135.0	No
Sotoh	Steel Partners Japan	12/2003	192.9	No
Kintetsu Buffaloes	Livedoor Co.	6/2004	16.3	No
Miyairi Valve	Banners Co.	6/2004	71.3	No
UFJ Holdings	Sumitomo	7/2004	29,674.6	No

Source: RECOF; information on corporate valuation from T1B database, except for Kintetsu (from public sources) and Miyairi (from McKinsey Tokyo).

of shareholder activism cases, in the years between 2001 and 2004, but the perception of much of corporate Japan was that these companies were acting as "greenmailers," using takeover bids against smaller companies to convince management to raise dividends paid to shareholders. When asked about the impact of the Shoei case on general managerial perceptions of takeovers, one senior M&A lawyer I interviewed observed that "Shoei is maybe not a good case. It was conducted by Murakami, and Murakami and Steel Partners were considered greenmailers."[33] As Table 5.2 shows, these two companies were the only ones active in the takeover market prior to 2004, and their targets were exclusively small companies, as indicated by the column in Table 5.2 on transaction value.

Politically, there was no pressure from leading managers in the Keidanren to intervene in the area of hostile takeover regulation at this time because they favored corporate restructuring and because Murakami's bid was not perceived as a threat. A senior Keidanren official whom I interviewed summarized the organization's view toward the Shoei takeover in the following terms:

> At first we were not concerned, because [Murakami] was an ex-MITI bureaucrat running a fund. This was quite an anomalous actor.... Our business attitude was, wait and see.... From the viewpoint of the Japanese business

[33] Interview, mergers and acquisitions lawyer, Mori Hamada & Matsumoto Law Firm, April 25, 2007. Curtis Milhaupt argues that MAC's takeover attempt was primarily an attempt to change the norm against hostile takeovers. This interpretation of Murakami's intent is consistent with what I was told by a former high-level bureaucrat from METI: "Murakami is a former METI guy; I know him well. He came to me when he left METI and said, 'METI changed the rules but unless management feels that they have to change, these new rules won't mean anything. So I'd like to start a fund to push managers to be active in using the assets given them by shareholders.' He started a small fund – did Shoei and Tokyo Style [another small company for against whose management Murakami led a proxy fight]. These [companies] were small, but [Murakami's] mouth was big." (Interview, former METI official, April 20, 2007).

community, Shoei is a miniscule company. Its takeover did not attract much attention from big companies.... In 2001 and 2002, the top agenda item was how to deal with non-performing loans and restructuring. We thought funds, like Murakami and others, were going to play a role in the buying and selling of these assets.... If Murakami had gone after key companies in the Keidanren, this might have caused concern.[34]

Between 1997 and 2003, the legislative attention of the Keidanren was fixed squarely on the problem of reforming corporate law to enable them to reorganize, not on the issue of corporate control. As summarized by legal scholar Zenichi Shishido, the reform of corporate law,

> such as deregulation of share purchases, stock options, and reorganization schemes, were demand-pull reforms. In other words, business sectors demanded these deregulations of what had been prohibited by Japanese corporate law, which has many more mandatory restrictions compared with American corporate law. Japanese management wanted to do what American management could do.[35]

The consistent line of Japanese business was that liberalization should provide more options for business, and the Keidanren's political priorities clearly reflected this line between 1997 and 2003.[36]

What political resources did the Keidanren use to pursue its political preferences for liberalization? Structurally, the business organization has a seat on the Legislative Council of the Ministry of Justice (MoJ), which is the central administrative authority for reforming corporate law. This allows it to review and influence proposed legal reforms. The organization also maintains representation in the deliberative councils (*shingikai*) set up by major ministries with interests in corporate and economic reform, including METI and the FSA.[37] The Keidanren maintains close ties to legislators in the ruling LDP, as well as in other political parties. A Keidanren lobbyist I interviewed in 2008 told me that the best tactics for lobbying depend on the political context.

> Right now, politicians are losing power – populism is on the rise, and the mass media and the bureaucracy are gaining power. When Koizumi was in office [2001–2006], politicians had a lot of power, and our lobbying was focused on the LDP, because they had the chance to make the difference.[38]

In the reform of corporate law, the Keidanren's direct ties with legislators would prove instrumental in getting around bureaucratic opposition to reforms of corporate governance.

---

34 Interview, senior official of economic policy directorate, Keidanren, April 18, 2007.
35 Shishido (2007: 322).
36 Vogel (2006).
37 Yoshimatsu (2000), Estevez-Abe (2008). The FSA is the Financial Services Agency, which is responsible for securities law.
38 Interview, lobbyist for Keidanren, April 10, 2008.

Legal scholars describe the changes in Japanese corporate law between 1997 and 2003 as a sea change representing the "most sweeping and fast-paced changes to corporate law" in a century.[39] The vast majority of these changes were supported aggressively by the Keidanren.[40] The MoJ is often considered conservative in the area of reform and in the late 1990s the Keidanren and reformers within the LDP joined forces to bypass the MoJ. In passing a law that legalized stock options and simplified merger procedures, the employers' organization used a parliamentary maneuver, a member's bill, to circumvent the MoJ and some conservative LDP-members.[41] The procedural device of the member's bill, heretofore rarely used in the domain of corporate law, was employed five times between 1997 and 2003 by members of this reforming coalition who wanted to go around conservative opposition.[42] By all accounts, lobbyists of the Keidanren and the reformist wing of the LDP worked together as close allies in this reform process.[43]

Because the LDP was divided between a reformist and a traditionalist faction, as were the bureaucracies involved in reform, the Keidanren occupied a pivotal position in the corporate reform process. It was able to rely on a reformer in the LDP to present member's bills when it wanted to overcome traditionalist opposition, as in the stock options case. Yet many reformist politicians also looked to the Keidanren in making judgments about the desirability of new reforms. The battle in 2001–2002 was the first significant division within the reformist alliance. According to Yves Tiberghien, "Keidanren was suspicious of METI because of its international openness agenda, an agenda pursued since the 1960s and because of the close personal links between METI and foreign investors (or the U.S. Chamber of Commerce)."[44] When the alliance between METI and foreign investors attempted to impose a METI plan on recalcitrant managers, the Keidanren convinced Seiichi Ota, chair of the LDP subcommittee on commercial law and author of the original (pro-reform, pro-Keidanren) member's bill in 1997, to propose another member's bill making the choice of independent directors optional.[45] The government ultimately adopted this formulation in its compromise legislation in 2002. In one of the few clear moments of opposition between the different members of the

---

[39] Milhaupt (2003: 5).
[40] Tiberghien (2007), Shishido (2007).
[41] Vogel (2006: 92–93).
[42] Tiberghien (2007: 148–154). The head of the Economic Law Bureau of the Keidanren during this epoch noted that the Keidanren also established a think tank in 1997. The 21st Century Public Policy Institute was established to provide a source of expertise for legislators who wanted to propose member's bills. "Some politicians started to indicate interests in making laws by their way of thinking, such as [Yasuhisa Shiozaki, a prominent reformer]; we call them the new generation. So, I think this institute, in my personal opinion, would have been able to help the new generation to make laws by Diet members, not bureaucrats" (interview, April 15, 2008).
[43] Vogel (2006), Tiberghien (2007), Shishido (2007).
[44] Tiberghien (2007: 153).
[45] Vogel (2006: 92); Gilson and Milhaupt (2004).

reformist coalition, the ability of the Keidanren to rely on key supporters in parliament allowed it to get the legislation it preferred.

The Keidanren Turns Against Takeovers

Organized managers in Japan only turned against the liberalizing agenda in corporate law in 2004. From the perspective of the Keidanren, though, this was not a large change. Its consistent line in the rapid reforms between 1997 and 2003 had been to use corporate law to create more options for managers to reorganize their firms.[46] The existence of funds like MAC, for example, were perceived as helpful resources for reorganization; threats to small firms, yes, but not to the managers of large firms. The battle between the giant banks Sumitomo and Mitsubishi for control of a third large bank, UFJ Holdings, shifted the terms of the conversation about hostile takeovers in Japan. As Table 5.2 makes clear, Sumitomo's hostile bid for UFJ was an order of magnitude larger than any of the bids that had taken place previously. It was, moreover, a battle between two large banks that sat at the center of Japanese business networks. Whereas the previous bids had come either from foreign firms or domestic outsiders (like Murakami), the bid from Sumitomo came from the heart of the Japanese business network.[47] As such, it was more likely to capture the attention of large business elites than were earlier bids for small companies from corporate outsiders.[48]

The UFJ case received so much attention not only because of the size and identity of the participants in the takeover battle, but also because of the tactics used, which broke with accepted business practice in Japan.[49] In May 2004, UFJ agreed to sell its trust bank to Sumitomo. The contract included a provision preventing either bank from negotiating with third parties in a manner that could obstruct the deal. Yet in July 2004, UFJ agreed to merge with the Mitsubishi Group (MTFG) in a deal that would result in the largest bank in the world, based on assets, at that time. Sumitomo sued to invalidate the transaction, which was initially stopped by the court, but that ruling was then reversed in a high court decision in August, after which the boards of UFJ and MTFG approved the merger. Sumitomo then attempted to pressure the UFJ board by publicly launching its own hostile offer for UFJ Holdings (a tactic called a "bear hug" in mergers and acquisitions).[50] Following the upholding of the UFJ/MTFG deal by the supreme court, UFJ issued preferred shares to MTFG to help protect it from Sumitomo's ultimately unsuccessful bid (ibid). In legal terms, the case was noteworthy both for the fact that UFJ reneged on its original deal with Sumitomo, and for the aggressive response pursued by Sumitomo through the courts.[51] Even the American financial press claimed that the outcome of the

---

[46] Vogel (2006).

[47] Scott Jones, a practicing M&A lawyer in Tokyo, described Sumitomo as the first of the "domestic old-boy raiders" (Jones 2007).

[48] Cf. Culpepper (2005).

[49] This paragraph relies on the account of the UFJ/Sumitomo fight presented in Milhaupt (2005).

[50] Milhaupt (2005).

[51] Milhaupt (2005).

UFJ case "represents a paradigm change on the legal side. It shows a more legally aware business mind-set in commercial dealings. The days of unspoken understandings underpinned by personal relationships are fading away."[52]

The UFJ deal itself was not of direct concern to the Keidanren, which took no position on it. The legal questions it raised, though, were of central import to the managerial organization. On November 16, 2004, the Keidanren issued a policy paper in which it announced a new concern about hostile takeovers. The policy statement began by noting that the organization had promoted several changes in company law over the past years, and that these changes had led to a desirable increase in foreign direct investment. It then sounded a new note of caution:

> However, over the last few years we have seen the unwinding of cross-shareholding and a decline in the aggregate value of listed stocks caused by a slumping stock market. These negative factors, together with the lack of reasonable defense mechanisms, have led to growing fears of takeovers that would harm corporate value.[53]

This was the organization's first public expression of concern about the threat of hostile takeovers in Japan since the reform process of 1997 had begun. The document then went on to suggest that triangular mergers were one tool that posed a threat to the Japanese model of stakeholder capitalism. This was a reversal of position on the desirability of triangular mergers, as a Keidanren lobbyist explained to me: "On the triangular merger law, for example, we changed our mind. Keidanren initially proposed it in 2002. We proposed it as a way to get more foreign investment, which we thought would be good for Japan. And then later we decided it was dangerous."[54] The change of position was striking enough to warrant commentary in an *Asahi Shimbun* editorial on December 9: "This sort of foreign capital phobia has even spilled over to the pro-deregulation Keidanren camp.... Up until now they had been saying exactly the opposite [on the desirability of triangular mergers]." The position paper of November 16 foreshadowed the two important episodes of reform in the market for corporate control: the discussion of hostile takeover defenses and the implementation of the triangular merger law.

Political Salience and Livedoor

Until 2004, hostile takeovers were not an issue of great importance for the Keidanren. And if a *managerial* organization cares little about hostile takeovers, it is likely that the issue will have low political salience with the wider public. In fact, as we shall see in this section, the Japanese public paid very little

[52] Fackler and Sender (2004).
[53] Keidanren (2004), "Reasonable Defense Measures against Takeovers Detrimental to Corporate Value are Needed" (available at http://www.keidanren.or.jp/english/policy/2004/085.html; downloaded 1/12/09).
[54] Interview, lobbyist for Keidanren, April 10, 2008.

attention to the issue of hostile takeovers between 1997 and 2004. That situation would change dramatically in January 2005, when the internet firm Livedoor launched a takeover bid for Nippon Broadcasting (NBS), the parent company of Fuji TV.[55] The CEO of Livedoor was Takafumi Horie, a brash young entrepreneur who was rarely seen in a tie but often seen in a sports car. He styled himself the enemy of old corporate Japan. In his initial bid for NBS, public sentiment largely viewed Horie in a positive light.[56] Within the Keidanren and its LDP allies, however, the reception to Horie's bid was one of alarm. As a manager at a large financial holding group told me, "Fuji TV is huge, and so the big companies thought, 'oh, it could happen to us too.'"[57] The Livedoor takeover attempt galvanized managerial concern about the risk of takeovers even as it brought the issue to broad public attention.

To assess the political salience of hostile takeovers in Japan, I relied on a review of press coverage of five major Japanese newspapers.[58] These five national papers cover most of the most political spectrum in Japan. With the help of two Japanese-speaking research assistants, I used the Nikkei Telecom21 database to compare the salience of hostile takeover politics with three other technical domains of economic policy: bargaining rules (over wages and working conditions); the pension system; and youth vocational training.[59] Tracking

---

[55] Fuji TV was the fiftieth largest company in Japan by market capitalization in the year 2000.

[56] Whittaker and Hayakawa (2007); Nakamoto (2005). One survey by an Asahi news program found that even older people – sixty percent of those in their 50s and 60s – supported Horie (Nakamoto 2005). One business reporter for the *Yomiuri Shimbun* whom I interviewed disagreed with the assertion that press coverage of Horie and Livedoor was sympathetic: "NBS is a broadcast company. Every major newspaper has its own broadcast network. There was a worry that if Horie succeeded, we [journalists] could be vulnerable to attack. We tried to protect NBS. We were not neutral in [our] coverage." (Interview with staff writer, *Yomiuri Shimbun*, May 2, 2008).

[57] Interview, senior executive at Millea Holdings, April 15, 2007.

[58] The newspapers included were the *Yomiuri Shimbun*, the *Asahi Shimbun*, the *Mainichi Shimbun*, the *Nihon Keizai Shimbun (Nikkei)*, and the *Sankei Shimbun*. Of the seven newspapers with the highest circulation in the world six are Japanese. As of 2007, the *Yomiuri Shimbun* had the highest circulation in the world, with ten million subscribers; the *Asahi Shimbun* was second, with eight million; the *Mainichi Shimbun* had almost four million subscribers; the *Nihon Keizai Shimbun*, the business newspaper of record, had three million; and the *Sankei Shimbun* had two million (see http://adv.yomiuri.co.jp/m-data/english/2008_2010/newspaper1.html and http://www.wan-press.org/article2825.html; downloaded 1/12/09).

[59] These searches were performed by Tomohiro Hamawaka and Nathan Cisneros, for whose assistance I am grateful. To create institutional categories that were as conceptually comparable as possible, the search relied on terms that would capture articles dealing with rules of governance in each issue area. The search terms used were the following (English translation is followed by bracketed Japanese original):

Takeover Protection: "(takeover or merger) and (protection or bid) and (hostile)" [(買収 or 合併) and (防衛 or 買い付け) and (敵対的 or 非友好)].
Vocational Training: "(youth or youth) and workplace training" [(若者 or 少年) and 職業訓練].
Bargaining Rules: "spring wage offensive" [春闘].
Pension System: "pension system" [年金制度].

the newspaper coverage over time in these areas gives a useful estimate of the relative political salience of these different policy issues over time.

Between 1997 and 2004, there were very few articles in the Japanese press on the subject of hostile takeovers. As in Chapters 3 and 4, Figure 5.1 sets the Mendoza line of political salience at the average annual number of articles on the least well-covered high salience issue measured. In Japan, this issue is bargaining rules. The average number of articles per year on bargaining rules in the Japanese press was 985. By contrast, the average number of articles per year on takeover protection was fifty-seven, which means that fewer than *one article per month* in each newspaper made any mention of hostile takeovers.[60] However, Livedoor's attempt to take over Fuji TV brought immediate public attention to the area of hostile takeovers. In 2005, the average number of articles per paper per month was twenty-five, surpassed only by the almost thirty-eight articles per paper per month in the area of the pension system, and well above our Mendoza line based on the coverage of bargaining rules. While that number declined in 2006, the coverage of hostile takeovers stayed above the Mendoza line and only dipped slightly below it in 2007. In contrast to our other cases, takeover protection was a high salience issue in Japan in 2005 and 2006.

In interviews with actors involved in this policy subsystem, as well as in academic accounts of them, one perception was consistently reported: that coverage of hostile takeovers in the Japanese press was tinged with nationalist reactions against the possibility of foreign takeovers. The main lobbying group for European business, the European Business Council Japan (EBC), released a position paper on foreign direct investment in May 2005, in which it observed "The current debate in Japan gives the impression that foreigners are eager to engage in 'hostile' take-overs of Japanese companies.'"[61] With two research assistants, I attempted to gauge the framing of press articles in this domain, as in the research on France and the Netherlands. We were unable to find any consistent set of frames in the Japanese coverage of hostile takeovers, including one that emphasized the threat of foreign takeovers. Compared with the Dutch and the French press, news articles tended to make little use of metaphors and evocative quotations from leading businessmen. This was all the more surprising because a Keidanren lobbyist I interviewed said that the managerial organization had adopted a new press strategy from 2003 on. "We wanted to get our point of view out in the public domain by talking

---

[60] This compares with an average of more than eighteen articles per paper per month on the subject of wage negotiation and thirty articles on the pension system (coverage of which spiked in 2003 and 2004).

[61] EBC (2005b) (Position Paper on FDI, http://www.ebc-jp.com/news/2005%20EBC% 20Position%20Paper%20on%20FDI%202005%20(English)-May.pdf), downloaded 1/13/09. The American Chamber of Commerce in Japan (ACCJ 2005) observed the same tendency: "Groundless and emotional assertions about an impending "foreign threat" unfairly taint the image of foreign direct investment (FDI) within Japan," (http://www.accj.or.jp/doclib/pc/ 050516toMETI_E.pdf), downloaded 1/13/09.

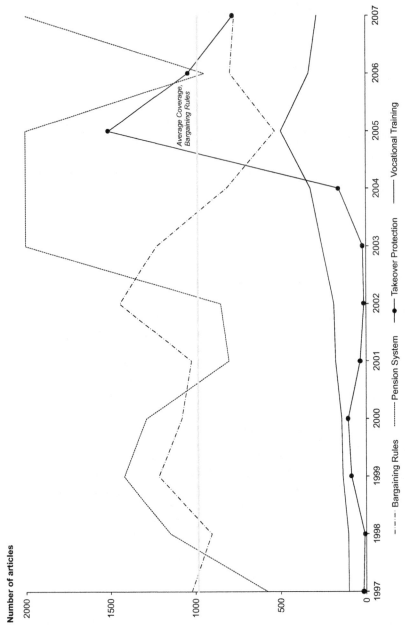

FIGURE 5.1. Political Salience of Issue Areas in Japan, 1997–2007

- - - Bargaining Rules   .... Pension System   —•— Takeover Protection   —— Vocational Training

Number of articles

Average Coverage,
Bargaining Rules

to the writers who write about the big issues. [This strategy] was a response to Koizumi, who was a master of using the media."[62] It is possible that the Keidanren succeeded in affecting press coverage in a way that our attempted content analysis was unable to measure, but which actors on the ground, such as the EBC and ACCJ, perceived. Using similar protocols to those we attempted in the European countries, though, it appears that Japanese press coverage of hostile takeovers was more neutral than in the other countries studied.[63]

The theory of quiet politics predicts that a rise in issue salience will blunt the effectiveness of managerial tools of influence, such as direct lobbying of politicians, because those politicians have incentive to respond to voters on the issues voters care about. In 2005, hostile takeovers reached a high level of political salience in Japan as a result of the Livedoor takeover. And indeed, no major reform of hostile takeovers did pass the Diet in 2005. Yet the key reform of Japanese corporate control was never *debated* in parliament. The new rules of corporate control would be elaborated instead by an informal group with no legal standing, a group that had been assembled before the

---

FIGURE 5.1. Political Salience of Issue Areas in Japan, 1997–2007
Source: Nikkei Telecom21 Database. See footnote 58 for a discussion of search terms.
Note: This graph only shows an annual total for the number of articles appearing on a given subject up to a threshold of 2,000 articles. It therefore understates a spike in the coverage of articles about the pension system between 2003 and 2005 (there were 2,912 articles dealing with the pension system in 2003, 5,571 articles in 2004, and 2,262 articles in 2005). The increased coverage of an already high-salience issue during this period was a product of a major pension reform as well as a scandal related to politicians failing to contribute to their system (Japanese politicians are part of a pension system that requires self-payment as opposed to automatic employer deduction). Even in the peak year of coverage of hostile takeovers in the Japanese press (2005), when the issue was unquestionably of high political salience, there were still more than 750 articles dealing with the pension system than with hostile takeovers. The gray horizontal line shows the average number of articles per year published on the subject of bargaining rules, which is the less covered of the two high-salience issue areas depicted in this figure. This is one rough indicator of a minimal level of media coverage we might classify as being associated with an issue of high political salience.

---

[62] Interview, lobbyist for Keidanren, April 10, 2008.

[63] The Japanese press corps has been labeled an "information cartel" by one scholar (Freeman 2000). Most government ministries, as well as the Keidanren, have their own press clubs in which reporters from major news organizations have offices in the ministries (or association) with the expenses paid by the ministry (McCargo 1996). Freeman argues that the existence of such clubs leads to a homogenization of news coming out of them, since each reporter gets the same information and all are discouraged from seeking outside scoops. Moreover, she argues that the high circulation of most Japanese newspapers has led editors to avoid alienating readers by taking political positions: "they have largely avoided independent pursuit of scandals involving the elite of Japanese society and have also refrained editorially from taking partisan political stances" (Freeman 2000: 19).

Livedoor affair brought takeovers to public attention. Such informal councils, known as *shingikai*, are often used by bureaucracies in Japan to strengthen their position vis-à-vis the legislature and each other.[64] These groups are composed in a way that favors managerial input and excludes some of their political opponents, including notably institutional investors. Thanks to the initiative of an entrepreneurial civil servant, managers in Japan were able to benefit from this mechanism of quiet politics even in turbulent political conditions.

Informal Influence and the Corporate Value Study Group

The group that developed the key reform of Japanese hostile takeover rules was conceived in the spring of 2004 before the LDP or the Keidanren or the general public paid much attention to hostile takeovers. It was a product of METI's reforming agenda, and particularly of one senior bureaucrat, Satoshi Kusakabe, who had headed the team at METI charged with reforming corporate law. The process through which the corporate value report was developed reveals the structural advantages afforded business in Japanese policy making. The group comprised three types of representatives: managerial interests of non-financial firms; professionals in mergers and acquisitions as well as investment bankers; and legal experts (see Appendix 5.1 for a roster of the group). What is glaring in this list is who was absent. There were no representatives of institutional investors and there were no representatives of labor unions. As an informal advisory group, its composition was not mandated by law, but left up to its organizer. The question debated was not a political one, such as, "What are the competing interests involved in hostile takeover protections?" It was instead, "Given the possibility of hostile takeovers, what rules would be consistent with managerial interests and the practice of corporate law in Japan?" As one investment banker on the group told me,

> it was consensual. Everybody there was interested in poison pills, but no one knew how to introduce them safely (i.e., so that they would stand up in court). And companies were concerned about being taken over. It was like brainstorming: the experts talked alot, and the people from industry tended to do more listening.[65]

Managers were not responsible for the formation of the group. Its very composition, though, reflected the view that rule making was primarily a technical issue to be decided by experts and managers, rather than a distributional one to be decided by a broader set of stakeholders.

Political scientists are often skeptical of arguments that attribute important causal power to decisions made by bureaucrats, unless those arguments have a foundation in the interests of bureaucrats themselves. Some claim bureaucrats

---

[64] Estevez-Abe (2008).
[65] Interview, member of Corporate Value Study Group, May 16, 2007.

are agents, controlled by political parties, their principals.[66] Others assume bureaucracies are captured by economic interest groups. There is no evidence that either the LDP or any particular set of economic interests directly drove the decision of Kusakabe to constitute the CVSG. Instead, it appears that METI had a bureaucratic rationale for forming the group, and that the continued low salience of the area gave the organization the possibility of taking a lead role in rule making.

Whereas MoJ is responsible for any change to corporate law, and the FSA is responsible for securities regulation and takeover bids, METI has no legally mandated responsibility for a body of law. Its bureaucratic power derives largely from its convening power. By staking a claim to a role in the discussion of hostile takeovers, before the issue had been discussed in parliament or by other agencies, "METI deftly ensured that it would be at the center of future developments in this important area of economic policy."[67] A senior bureaucrat at the FSA, which is widely considered to have a competitive relationship with METI, summarized Kusakabe's motivations in these terms:

> While our financial councils are written in law, [Kusakabe] created an informal group of key players. His leadership and strategy was central to its function. METI has good officials, but they do not control the law. So they are always looking for the next subject.[68]

When I asked Kusakabe himself why METI led the formation of the group, rather than MoJ, he answered,

> MoJ had other things to do. And METI has close relations with the front lines of economic industry. So it's easier for us to take up these activities.... It is customary in reforms in Japan for METI to make the preparation first; then other agencies will follow the lead of METI.[69]

With MoJ active in finishing its reform of corporate law, and both the Keidanren and the LDP unconcerned about hostile takeovers in early 2004, the political space was open for METI to play an agenda-setting role.[70]

The self-described mission of the Corporate Value Study Group was "to change the business community from one without rules [about hostile takeover

---

[66] Ramseyer and Rosenbluth (1993).

[67] Milhaupt and Pistor (2008: 104).

[68] Interview, official at FSA, April 17, 2007.

[69] Interview with Satoshi Kusakabe, METI (convenor of the Corporate Value Study Group), June 26, 2007.

[70] Cf. Tiberghien (2007). In recruiting participants for the panel from industry in early 2004, Kusakabe reported having difficulty finding managerial representatives who were interested. The two exceptions he reported were from Toyota, whose management had been interested in the issue of hostile takeovers since a celebrated but failed hostile bid for one of its suppliers in 1989; and Yamanouchi, a pharmaceuticals company which was in the process of merging with another company to form Astellas (interview with Satoshi Kusakabe, METI convenor of the Corporate Value Study Group, June 26, 2007).

protections] to one governed by fair rules applicable to all."[71] In September 2004, just after the Sumitomo/UFJ battle, the group oriented its second session around defining the perceptions of Japanese business. A METI survey of listed firms found that eighty-five percent of the companies surveyed "felt threatened" by hostile takeovers. Yet a majority of respondents said they would not adopt measures to prevent such a takeover: one-third because they were uncertain if the measures were legal, and one-third because they worried about the reaction of the markets to the adoption of takeover defenses.[72] The goal of the group was therefore to determine if, and under what conditions, takeover protections could be legal in Japan.

The name of the group, chosen by Kusakabe and the chair of the committee, the eminent legal scholar Hideki Kanda, was itself illustrative of how that question would be answered. According to Kusakabe, "I discussed [the name of the group] many times with Professor Kanda. We considered 'anti-takeover defense measure study group,' but this was too straightforward. It ultimately came from Kanda's philosophy: whether a takeover is good or not depends on its effect on corporate value."[73] Kanda added in his comments to me that,

> We thought about 'shareholder value group,' but we thought [shareholder value] was only part of the question.... We wanted to allow takeovers that would improve 'corporate value' and stop those that did not – corporate value for the shareholder, but also for society at large. [Some people on the group were] arguing strongly in favor of protecting shareholder value. But the name of the group meant some of this issue had already been decided.

As stated in the report itself, the group's goal was to produce "fair" rules for takeover defense, which satisfied the considerations of both corporate value and those of global standards, that is, "on a par with those adopted in the United States and European countries."[74]

The group reviewed the legal arrangements surrounding takeover protection in other countries, including the United States and the European Union (particularly the United Kingdom, Germany, and France). A central problem for the group was whether or not takeover defenses would be consistent with the principle of shareholder equality enshrined in Japanese company law.[75] The report ultimately determined they were, and then made a series of recommendations enumerating the features of rights plans (poison pills) that could be allowed under Japanese law. This choice essentially adopted the Delaware

---

[71] METI (2005: 8).

[72] METI (2005: 21–23, 108). METI polled forty large institutional investors (twenty from the United States and twenty from the United Kingdom) about their potential reactions to adopting takeover protections as a way to find out the "market" response to takeover protections.

[73] Interview with Satoshi Kusakabe, METI (convenor of the Corporate Value Study Group), June 26, 2007.

[74] METI (2005: 25). The report also enunciated principles of nondiscrimination between foreign and domestic companies and increasing options for shareholders and investors.

[75] METI (2005: 79).

standard from the United States, rejecting the strict neutrality of boards required by UK law (and incorporated into the EU takeover directive, as discussed in Chapter 3). This is not because of the obvious superiority of Delaware law nor for its better fit with Japanese legal traditions. As Milhaupt observes,

> the City Code [arguably] represents a more attractive candidate for transplant into Japan than Delaware takeover law. Its relatively straightforward rules are much simpler to replicate and easier to enforce than a complex body of foreign judicial doctrine. And the quasi-administrative role of the Takeover Panel is more consistent with traditional Japanese approaches to economic regulation than is Delaware's court-centric approach.[76]

The attraction of the Delaware standard was not that it was the most easily reconcilable with the Japanese principle of shareholder equality nor that it represents the unique global standard. The UK City Code is plausibly more attractive on both these dimensions.

Instead, the choice of the Delaware standard appears to have been a product of both familiarity with the lawyers on the panel and an appeal to the interests of METI, lawyers, and managers – the three interests represented in the study group. One member of the Study Group noted the bureaucratic incentive for METI to favor the Delaware standard. "The UK style is reasonable, but to do it that way would have required a change in [takeover bid] rules, and that is the jurisdiction of the FSA. The FSA and METI, they are competitive."[77] Curtis Milhaupt claims that Delaware corporate law is more familiar to many Japanese lawyers: "For elite Japanese corporate lawyers as well, most of whom received graduate legal education in the United States and are members of the New York or California bars, the transplantation of Delaware takeover law, particularly the need to adapt the poison pill to the domestic legal regime, represents a substantial new business opportunity."[78] Finally, Japanese managerial interests were well represented on the group, and Delaware law favors managers far more than the UK City Code. "Thus, Delaware takeover law provided the METI and Ministry of Justice planners with the best of all possible worlds: a familiar and politically attainable 'global standard' that is somewhat protective of management."[79]

One group that was unhappy with the outcome of the Corporate Value Report was the institutional investors identified in coalitional theory as the likely leaders of reform. The most important political representatives of foreign institutional investors in Japan are the American Chamber of Commerce in Japan (ACCJ) and the European Business Council Japan (EBC). We might have expected the Americans to rejoice over the triumph of Delaware law, while the Europeans bemoaned it. But that is not what happened. Both lobbying groups

---

[76] Milhaupt (2005: p. 49).
[77] Interview, member of the Corporate Value Study Group, May 16, 2007.
[78] Milhaupt (2005: 51–52), Osugi (2008).
[79] Milhaupt (2005: 50).

launched identical warnings, that adopting Delaware law without Delaware legal infrastructure favored managerial entrenchment.

> [T]he ACCJ is concerned that the sudden and hurried enabling of a broad menu of new takeover defenses, occurring without simultaneous strengthening of legal requirements for corporate governance practices that provide an essential counterbalance, may . . . threaten the equal protection of shareholders, lead to abuse of discretion by 'insider' boards, and result in disputes regarding the ultimate legality of various 'defense' mechanisms.[80]

On release of the report, the EBC urged the government not to "give in to pressure to include comprehensive defensive measures of the Delaware type to prevent greenmailing. Within the Japanese context, these measures would risk a virtual stranglehold on the M&A market and, therefore, on FDI."[81]

The ACCJ and the EBC are lobbying groups used to fighting in legal forums and defending their interests there. And the post-Livedoor boost in political salience had given the release of the report a very high profile, which might have helped their cause. As Hideki Kanda, the group's chair, told me,

> When Livedoor happened we went from being a quiet study group, producing something like a research report, a dissertation, to being very well known, even famous. Livedoor was an unfortunate case for us: at that time, Livedoor was considered the good guy. What Nippon Broadcasting did to defend itself was bad. We were designing takeover defenses, but not of the sort they were using.[82]

The EBC in its statement called on the Japanese government not to adopt the suggestions of the Corporate Value Study Group. The government never did adopt the report, but it did not have to *adopt* the report. Simultaneously with the final release of the group's report in May 2005, METI and MoJ released a set of guidelines over appropriate takeover defenses in the Japanese context.[83] These guidelines spelled out the legal understandings of acceptable takeovers that flowed from the Corporate Value Report. The guidelines spelled out by METI and MoJ did not have the force of law, as they had neither been decided by a court nor adopted by a legislature:

> The Guidelines are not legally binding and should not be read to require that all legitimate takeover measures must conform to the Guidelines. But, if the Guidelines are shared and respected by interested parties including

---

[80] ACCJ (2005: 2–3). The ACCJ, in its detailed public commentary on the first draft of the report, prefaced its statement with a critique of the "excessively tight and narrow time frame between publication of the 130-page . . . report on April 22 and the announced deadline for public comments on May 11 [2005]." (ACCJ 2005: 1)

[81] EBC (2005b: 2).

[82] Interview with Hideki Kanda, Chair, Corporate Value Study Group, and Professor of Law at the University of Tokyo, June 5, 2007.

[83] Osugi (2008).

corporate managers, shareholders, investors, stock exchanges, lawyers, and financial advisors, they will facilitate a major change in the Japanese business community and lead to the enhancement of corporate value.[84]

The guidelines based on the report simply became the uniquely accepted standard about what the Japanese would permit in defending against hostile takeovers. Four months after releasing the report and the guidelines, METI surveyed Japanese corporations about their familiarity with and plans to use the guidelines. Top executives in ninety-six percent of the corporations surveyed said they would use the guidelines if they were planning to adopt hostile takeover defenses. Between the report's release in May 2005 and April 2008, 410 listed companies adopted takeover defenses of the sort discussed in the Corporate Value Report and the METI/MoJ guidelines.[85] One member of the Corporate Value Study Group, whom I interviewed two years after the release of the report, explained the impact of the report and the associated METI guidelines this way:

> In the U.S., I know companies think that anything that is not prohibited is allowed. Japanese companies are the reverse – they think anything not allowed explicitly is prohibited.... [Now] it is a standard. This is only one standard; it is not the same as the Tokyo Stock Exchange's standards, or others. But it is the observed standard. Companies like to say in their press release, they are adopting the METI standards.[86]

The standard by which hostile takeovers would be adjudicated thus emerged from a group in which the most important coalitional opponents of protection, institutional investors, were absent.[87]

---

[84] METI/MoJ 2005: 2.

[85] Osugi (2008); interview, Director of Corporate System Division, METI, April 25, 2008. This constitutes slightly more than ten percent of all listed firms in Japan. More than three-quarters of these defenses were "advance warning" rights plans, which dilute the power of a potentially hostile acquirer when triggered. The advance warning plan follows the central line of the corporate value report by forcing a would-be acquirer to reveal its postmerger business plan (Osugi 2008). This is the information used by independent committees or boards to determine whether an acquisition plan will contribute to building corporate value.

[86] Interview, member, Corporate Value Study Group, May 16, 2007. The head of a corporate strategy at a large financial holding company, when asked about the importance of the Corporate Value Report for designing takeover protection, told me "this is like the Bible.... I have a copy on my desk." (Interview, senior executive at Millea Holdings, April 15, 2007).

[87] The protests of the institutional investors were eventually acknowledged by the formation of a second "Corporate Value Study Group," with expanded membership (plus all the original members), in September 2005. This group added several financial sector representatives, including notably Tomomi Yano, head of the most important and activist pension fund in Japan, the Pension Fund Association (PFA). Yano has worked closely with activist American funds like CalPERS to bring the principle of shareholder primacy to Japan, and in this light he criticized the original task of the CVSG (Jacoby 2007; interview with Satoshi Kusakabe, METI, convenor of the Corporate Value Study Group, June 26, 2007). The second group published its findings, which dealt mainly with the principles for disclosure of hostile takeover regulations and shareholder/management relations, in March 2006.

The METI guidelines, together with the Corporate Value Report, rapidly established common knowledge among players in the market for corporate control about the new rules of the game.[88] In the process of institutional change, the emergence of common knowledge is an important sign of institutional consolidation because it creates shared understandings about what moves are fair and what moves are not.[89] Once players agree on the rules, they can go back to playing the game and take the rules as given. Once established, common knowledge is sticky; it cannot be unilaterally changed.[90] By creating common knowledge about the new rules of the Japanese hostile takeovers in the absence of institutional investors, the Corporate Value Working Group locked in a set of rules that paid more heed to the concerns of the Keidanren than to those of institutional investors. It enshrined the standard for acceptable takeovers as those that are "fair and reasonable" – that is, those takeovers built on the strategic logic of restructuring firms rather than the market logic of maximizing shareholder value. This was a logic that was consistent with the changes that the managerial organization had favored in corporate law earlier in the decade, in terms of using the takeover market to give firms more tools to reorganize themselves.[91] But it also established the principle that not all takeovers were to be allowed in the new regime of corporate control.

The Corporate Value Report was neither a creation nor an initiative of the managerial lobby. Its members included some of the most prominent experts dealing with corporate law in Japan alongside substantial managerial representation. As an informal group convened by METI, though, it provided a favorable venue for takeover protections to be developed that took account of managerial interests. It was a forum that could exclude institutional investors and other shareholders' representatives because there were no legal requirements of which societal interests must be included. The fact that managers, and the Keidanren itself, were well represented in the group, allowed them to present their views and may indeed have changed the way that other, nonmanagerial representatives presented their own opinions to the group.[92] Even when opponents such as the ACCJ and the EBC mobilized, they were able to have little impact on the takeover guidelines, because the guidelines did not have to be passed in parliament to have an effect. In the vacuum of existing jurisprudence on hostile takeovers, the administrative guidelines of METI quickly became the established rules of the game. These were rules of the game which coalitional actors outside the CVSG were unable to influence.

---

[88] Culpepper (2008).

[89] Aoki (2001).

[90] Culpepper (2008).

[91] Vogel (2006), Schaede (2008).

[92] One expert nonmanagerial representative told me, "It was important for me to present myself as one of the professionals, not as a representative of [my company]. [My company] is a big company in the Keidanren, and I did not want to present some view and then have the other members of business take it to the chairman of [my company]" (interview, member, Corporate Value Study Group, May 16, 2007),

Formal Governance under High Salience: Triangular Mergers

The struggle between the Keidanren and the representatives of foreign investors, the EBC and the ACCJ, was simultaneously taking place on two fronts in 2005. The second front in this conflict was the formal arena, over the law governing triangular mergers. The liberalizing coalition included the institutional investors and one of the most high-ranking and outspoken proponents of increasing FDI in the LDP, Yasuhisa Shiozaki.[93] In this high salience struggle, the managerial lobby lost: the Keidanren obtained a one-year delay in its implementation, but failed to stop the amendment's ultimate adoption. Business actors were unable to compel politicians and bureaucrats adopt their ideal legislation. However, the strong position of the business lobby within the ruling party, the LDP, enabled it to extract some concessions from the reformist coalition. This legal struggle unfolded within a political party and within the formal consultative groups of the bureaucracy. Business lobbying is still an important asset in such venues. But business domination is unlikely because political parties are more interested in responding to the public when the public actually cares about an issue.

Triangular mergers are operations by which a corporation creates a subsidiary, which then merges with a third company. The subsidiary corporation could use shares of the parent company as consideration in the merger. Their essential purpose was to create a legal structure by which foreign companies could use stock swaps, rather than cash, to acquire interested Japanese companies. This was a provision of the corporate law reform which had initially been favored by the Keidanren as a useful tool for company restructuring. Following the UFJ/Sumitomo conflict in 2004, when the Keidanren came out in favor of defenses against hostile takeovers, it also turned against triangular mergers as a potential threat to Japanese companies from foreign predators:

> Through such triangular mergers, a company could acquire a target company with a corporate culture totally different from that of the acquiring company by making a subsidiary merge with the target company. By providing the target company's shareholders with the acquiring company's stocks, instead of the merging company's stocks, the acquiring company can obtain 100 percent of the target company's stocks without paying any cash. Under the above mentioned situation, it cannot be denied that there is a growing risk that buyers who make no long-term commitment to corporate operations would pursue short-term profit for themselves, thereby harming corporate value and causing detriment to shareholders, employees, local communities, and other stakeholders.[94]

It was in this document that the Keidanren first linked the question of triangular mergers and hostile takeovers.

---

[93] Tiberghien (2007).
[94] Keidanren (2004).

The link between hostile takeovers and the triangular merger was also made explicitly in the Corporate Value Report in 2005. Technically, a triangular merger requires board approval and so cannot be undertaken against the vote of the board of the company to be acquired. However, the Corporate Value Report underlined that the triangular merger could be used in combination with a tender offer and a proxy fight, as a proxy fight allows an acquiring company to change the composition of management or the board of directors:

> In such cases, the hostile acquirer first buys up shares through TOB (tender offer) and replaces top management, and then conducts the merger, exchange of shares, triangular merger, capital tie-up, or transfer of business. For instance, in the case where the hostile acquirer makes the target a wholly owned subsidiary, it conducts TOB in the first stage and after that, it uses the system of exchange of shares (for M&A among Japanese companies) or the system of triangular merger (in the case where a foreign company makes a Japanese enterprise a wholly owned subsidiary).[95]

By this circuitous route the Keidanren was able to link triangular mergers to hostile takeovers. In response, the EBC and the ACCJ both explicitly pointed out that the triangular merger could only be used in friendly transactions, and that the ballyhooed "wave" of foreign hostile takeovers would simply not appear.[96] Nevertheless, the legislature approved a one-year delay in the implementation of the triangular merger law, from May 2006 to May 2007.

There were two issues at stake on triangular mergers. First, the Keidanren favored extraordinary measures to secure approval from stakeholders of a triangular merger. These extraordinary measures, if passed, would have made approval of triangular mergers effectively impossible.[97] On this issue, the MoJ sided with the institutional investors against the Keidanren, in using the same standard of shareholder approval required by domestic mergers.[98] The second issue involved the ability to secure tax deferral on shares exchanged through a triangular merger.[99] In Japanese law, tax deferral is granted on the condition that a merger creates synergies between the target company and the acquiring company. In its original draft, submitted to the Ministry of Finance (MoF)

95 METI (2005: 31).
96 ACCJ (2005); EBC (2005a and b).
97 The battle turned on the seemingly technical difference is between a *tokusu ketsugi* and *tokubetsu ketsugi* form of shareholder approval. The former measure, favored by the Keidanren for the case of triangular mergers, requires approval of fifty percent of all shareholders (by head, not by voting share), and also by two-thirds of the outstanding shares. The latter form of shareholder approval, which is the one applied in domestic mergers, requires the much less demanding standard of two-thirds of the shares voted at a meeting with at least fifty percent of all shareholders present (Benes and Katsuyama 2006).
98 Interview, senior official involved in triangular merger negotiations, June 8, 2007; interview, ACCJ representative, June 22, 2007.
99 If taxes on capital gains are levied during a share swap – i.e., as though the shares had been converted to cash – this would limit the appeal of the stock swap merger for shareholders. Thus the ACCJ and the EBC lobbied consistently to ensure tax deferral (EBC 2005b: 5).

by METI, those synergies could be considered between an acquiring company (based abroad) and the Japanese company being acquired. Lobbying through the LDP committee that oversees METI, the Keidanren was able to convince lawmakers to submit to MoF a revised version of the law under which the synergies could only take place between a Japanese subsidiary of the acquiring company (if based abroad) and the Japanese target company.[100] The EBC and ACCJ both denounced the change, saying that "new investors in Japan's market effectively would not be able to use the scheme."[101] At least partly in response to these claims, the MoF released a clarifying ordinance in April 2007, applying a nondiscriminatory framework for application between foreign and domestic companies.

In the triangular merger case, which was contested under conditions of high salience, organized managers were unable to block the adoption of the law on triangular mergers on the terms favored by the reformist coalition, which would allow foreign companies to use the measure. Unlike in the CVSG case, the ultimate decisions were taken by lobbying the ruling party directly. Under high salience, parties have more incentive to intervene, and the Keidanren has allies in the conservative wing of the LDP. Relying on these allies, managers achieved a procedural victory by having the party change the terms of tax treatment under the law. This small victory on tax treatment was largely viti-ated by the MoF's interpretive framework, which was supported by Shiozaki and the reformist group within the LDP and made the measure accessible to non-Japanese companies. Even under high salience, the close alliance between organized business and the ruling party were important in extracting conces-sions from liberal reformers. The important point is that under such conditions of sustained high salience, which the issue of hostile takeovers achieved in Japan following the Livedoor attempted takeover, business needs allies to win. It is under these conditions a powerful interest group, but it is still just an interest group.

Conclusion

Driven by the restructuring imperatives facing many large Japanese companies in the depths of the lost decade, organized managers were a powerful force behind the reform of Japanese corporate law from 1997 to 2004.[102] To push through these reforms, they allied with both foreign institutional investors and neoliberal reformers in the ruling LDP and the bureaucracy.[103] This was a powerful coalition for reform, to be sure. As a causal matter, though, this alliance of convenience obscures the relative influence of the three groups over

---

[100] EBC (2006); interview, senior official involved in triangular merger negotiations, June 8, 2007.
[101] EBC (2006). The Keidanren fired back, warning that "allowing foreign interests to meddle in the revision of our country's tax system should be cause for alarm" (ACCJ 2006).
[102] Vogel (2006), Shishido (2007), Schaede (2008).
[103] Gilson and Milhaupt (2004), Tiberghien (2007), Ahmadjian (2007).

the institutions of corporate governance. And for most of the period, organized managers were the dominant players in this coalition. When they broke with other members of the coalition, as in the 2002 reform of corporate structure, they succeeded in imposing their preferred outcome on the other members of the reformist coalition.

To understand why Japanese managers acquiesced in the breakdown of cross-shareholdings in an earlier period, but then later mobilized to adopt a system of hostile takeover protections in 2005, it is necessary to understand variations in their perception of the threat posed by an active market for corporate control. The Keidanren is an organization dominated by large firms. Those large firms aggressively reorganized in order to focus on their core business at the end of the 1990s.[104] The weakness of Japanese firm-level employee representation meant that workers were in no position to halt such reorganizations. The possibility of hostile takeovers is one that these managers were willing to accept in their attempt to return to economic growth after the lost decade, and indeed they viewed a more active market for corporate control as a potentially beneficial tool of reorganization. Beneficial reorganization looks especially helpful when it happens to someone else, and the attempted hostile takeovers that took place prior to 2004 affected only small companies, not large ones. The battle over UFJ, for which Sumitomo launched an ultimately failed hostile bid, was the first instance in which large firms at the center of the Japanese economy seemed to be at risk of hostile takeover. Livedoor's unconventional bid for Fuji TV, through its attack on NBS, triggered even more widespread concern about the threat of hostile takeovers. After 2005, the reformist coalition, which had previously included LDP reformers, institutional investors, and organized managers, ceased to exist. It was replaced by a series of battles pitting these former allies directly against one another.

The deliberations of the Corporate Value Study Group (CVSG) established a set of rules to govern the newly active Japanese market for corporate control. The managerial community had been uninterested in the CVSG when it was first convened by a METI bureaucrat in the spring and summer of 2004. The group was not a Keidanren initiative, but its composition favored managers and disadvantaged managerial opponents, notably excluding any institutional investors or labor representatives. When the Livedoor event occurred, bringing concentrated public attention to the issue of corporate control, the group was already in place and moving toward publication of its final report. The CVSG allowed managers and experts to deliberate in an informal group without legislative oversight or public scrutiny. The group's findings, which were published simultaneously with METI/MoJ guidelines for hostile takeovers, created a new standard for acceptable hostile takeover protections without ever needing to be passed into law. By creating common knowledge among Japanese companies of the new acceptable practices of takeover protection, this informal group

---

[104] Schaede (2008).

set the new rules of corporate control for Japanese companies, which would henceforth be adjudicated in the formal arena of courts. The arrangements adopted resembled those of the American state of Delaware, and like those of Delaware, they were highly protective of managerial prerogatives.[105]

Managers fared less well in the battle over the triangular merger amendment because it was decided in the formal political arena after hostile takeovers had acquired high political salience with the general public. The Keidanren attempted to impose onerous conditions of shareholder approval and tax deferral, conditions that would effectively have eliminated the ability of foreign companies to use triangular mergers in Japan. The Keidanren was defeated on this issue. The managerial organization scored a limited victory on taxation within the committees of the ruling party, which is where high salience battles are likely to be decided. However, its victory on taxation was heavily diluted by an ordinance drafted by MoF and supported by the reformists within the LDP to render the clause nondiscriminatory between Japanese and foreign firms.

The Japanese political system remains favorable to the protection of managerial interests, given the long and close ties among business, the bureaucracy, and the Liberal Democratic Party.[106] Thus, even on high salience issues, it would be surprising if Japanese managers were unable to exercise important political influence. The theory of quiet politics leads us to expect that the effectiveness of different tools of business influence varies according to political salience. The Corporate Value Study Group, which was constituted before hostile takeovers reached general public attention in Japan, provided a forum for rule making that was congenial to managerial interests. Such informal groups, or *shingikai*, have long been used by Japanese bureaucrats for the purpose of evading legislative oversight. Because the group had already been established by the time of the Livedoor event, it was able to lay down the new rules of the game without throwing the issue into the formal arena of the Diet. The triangular merger law, in contrary fashion, was decided by politicians through a battle between conflicting factions of the LDP. The sustained high salience of the issue meant that political party actors were much keener to intervene on it in defense of their respective constituencies. It was only in such a public battle, with close allies in the ruling party, that institutional investors were able to score points against organized managers in political battles over Japanese corporate control. The future functioning of the new rules of corporate control in Japan, which provide an important role for oversight of takeover activity by courts, will likely depend on whether the issue continues to be one of high salience. If it does not, the dynamics of quiet politics will reassert themselves and these dynamics do not favor interest groups that oppose the managers of large companies.

---

[105] Milhaupt (2005), Osugi (2008).
[106] Vogel 2006, Hamada (2010).

Appendix 5.1: Roster of the Corporate Value Study Group (2004–2005)

Chairman

Hideki KANDA Professor, University of Tokyo Graduate Schools for Law and Politics

Toshio ADACHI Corporate Director, Group General Manager, Tokyo Branch, Sharp Corporation

Gaku ISHIWATA Attorney at Law, Mori Hamada & Matsumoto

Takeki UMEMOTO Executive Officer, Director, Information Planning Department, RECOF Corporation

Toshio OSAWA Corporate Officer, Corporate Administration Division Head, Astellas Pharma Inc.

Kenichi OSUGI Professor, Chuo Law School

Masakazu KUBOTA Director, Economic Policy Bureau, Japan Business Federation Nippon

Nobuo SAYAMA Professor, Graduate School of International Corporate Strategy, Hitotsubashi University, CEO, GCA CO., LTD.

Kazufumi SHIBATA Professor, Hosei University Law School

Kazuhiro TAKEI Attorney at Law, Nishimura & Partners

Shirou TERASHITA Executive Officer, IR Japan, Inc.

Motoyoshi NISHIKAWA Chief Legal Counsel, Nippon Steel Corporation

Takashi HATA Managing Officer, Finance & Accounting Group, Toyota Motor Corporation

Nobuo HATTA Member of the Board, Director, Administrative Headquarters, ROHM Co. Ltd.

Takashi HATCHOJI Senior Vice President and Executive Officer, Hitachi, Ltd.

Kenichi FUJINAWA Attorney at Law, Nagashima, Ohno & Tsunematsu

Keisuke HORII Senior Vice President, Global Hub Compliance Office, Sony Corporation

Nami MATSUKO Director, Investment Banking Consulting Dept, Nomura Securities Co., Ltd.

Eizo MATSUDA Editorial Writer, Yomiuri Shimbun

Toshikazu MURATA Division Counselor, Planning and Research Division, Nippon Life Insurance Company

Division Counselor, Planning and Research

Noriyuki YANAGAWA Associate Professor, Graduate School of Economics, Faculty of Economics, The University of Tokyo

(Observer)

Tetsu AIZAWA Secretary, Civil Affairs Bureau, Ministry of Justice

6

The Noisy Politics of Executive Pay

Throughout this book, I have argued that managerial organizations are likely to dominate the politics of corporate control. This prediction flows from the fact that the rules governing regimes of corporate control are typically of low political salience. In contrast with work that emphasizes the centrality of political parties to corporate governance reform, I argue that political parties have few incentives to invest in the development of expertise and the promotion of reforms, so long as these questions are of low political salience. Neither voters nor the media care, which means it is not rational for politicians to thwart the political initiatives of managers. Politicians do not generally have the stomach for a fight that will generate little in the way of electoral rewards. We expect political parties of left and right defer to managerial lobbies in the area of corporate control, so long as voters are not attuned to it.

The findings of the previous chapters add to the accumulating evidence that political parties do not hold consistent positions on corporate governance.[1] Social Democrats are not in favor of reforming corporate governance across the industrialized democracies, *pace* the argument of John Cioffi and Martin Höpner. In the Netherlands, in Sweden, and in France, as well as in the German case that is central to their argument, Social Democratic parties readily switch their positions on corporate governance. Neither is it true, as implied by Mark Roe's empirical work, that Social Democratic parties are the upholders of patient capital. Where reformist neoliberal parties do try to overturn the status quo favored by managerial organizations, they are not likely to succeed. Given its low political salience, the story of corporate governance politics is not generally one in which political parties play a leading role.

What happens when the policy salience of a corporate governance issue becomes high and stays high? In such a situation, we expect that the role of political parties, and the differences between parties of the left and the right, will once again become important. Organized managers become a lobbying group

[1] Schnyder (forthcoming), Callaghan (2009).

like any other.[2] They will continue to have influence, as they do in other areas of contested high salience politics, such as taxes or pensions. Yet the outcome of reform efforts will depend primarily on the partisan composition of the government, political or policy entrepreneurs, or interest group activity – just as partisan and coalitional theories suggest. Business does not necessarily lose under high political salience; indeed, it remains a powerful interest group, even under those conditions. Where it is able to build coalitions with other interest groups, or where parties of the right are in power, business will continue to exercise significant influence over policy even under high political salience. What managerial groups will *not* do is exercise disproportionate influence due to their expertise and the deference politicians pay to it. These weapons of quiet politics work best in the shadows, not under the bright spotlight of sustained public attention.

In this chapter, I show how increased salience transformed the politics of executive pay first in the United States and then later in France. In both countries, the political salience of executive pay increased over time. Yet the change in the United States took place earlier than in France: after the scandal at Enron at the end of 2001, executive pay became a highly salient issue and remained so for the rest of the decade. The financial crisis of 2008 refocused public attention on executive pay, but it was Enron that had fundamentally changed the political landscape in the United States. In France, there has also been a steady increase in the press coverage of executive pay, partly stimulated by Enron, but the issue really caught the attention of the voting public only in 2007 and 2008. French managers have, as a result, been much more successful in forestalling reforms of executive pay regulation than is the case in the United States. French managers benefited politically from facing a lower salience environment for longer than their American counterparts. Moreover, even as the political salience of executive pay began to rise in France, French managers had the powerful ally of a president and parliament of the political right, which is generally sympathetic to business demands for self-regulation. As a political issue moves from low to high salience, this partisan advantage becomes much more important in protecting the political interests of managers.

The setting of executive pay, like the issue of corporate control, is an important part of corporate governance. Yet issues of executive pay are somewhat less abstruse to the average voter than are other issues of corporate governance regulation. In the next section of this chapter, I explore these differences, as well as the sort of cognitive bias that can influence how the press covers executive pay. The remainder of the chapter examines the rising salience of executive remuneration in the United States and France between the go-go years of the late 1990s, when executive remuneration was rarely discussed in the press, to the near collapse of the global financial system in 2008, when it was a politically hot topic in both countries. In the United States, media coverage of the issue spiked in 2002 in the wake of the Enron scandal. As coverage of the

[2] Vogel (1987).

issue intensified, it became an issue of regular partisan contestation between Republicans and Democrats. The degree of public intervention in executive pay setting rose in tandem with these conflicts.

In France, meanwhile, Enron did not have the same transformative effect on public interest in the issue. The French electorate only became interested in executive pay in the latter part of the 2000s, as pay scandals erupted in France. However, because of the weakness of the Socialist Party in France, the only real contestation has taken place between business and the Gaullist Party, which tends to favor business self-regulation rather than government intervention. Higher salience creates political incentives for parties to intervene in this formerly unregulated policy area, but some political parties have greater capacity for, and interest in, intervention than do others.

Scandals, Executive Pay, and the Media

How does executive pay ever become politically salient? If issues of corporate control are boring and technical, as I have claimed repeatedly in this book, what is it about the related issue of executive pay that enables it to get into the headlines and stay there? Among issues of corporate governance, what is distinctive about executive pay is that it is rarely discussed in abstract terms, but rather in concrete individual cases. It is much easier to grasp a $165 million individual annual compensation package than it is to understand the implications of hostile takeover rules, even if the latter may have greater overall distributive consequences than any one executive's payday. In both cases, however, the issue of framing remains important. If the $165 million pay is discussed as an example of the well-earned return of a virtuoso executive, this framing has very different political implications than if the discussion is one of the bloated salaries of the executives of failing companies. But the particularly obvious distributive ramifications of executive pay mean it does not really suffer from the problem of complexity that makes the reform of corporate control illegible to many voters. Corporate pay has clear winners: the recipients of large executive salaries.

As long as the focus of pay is on its celebrity-creation power, this still does not guarantee it becomes a high salience issue. Just as "Lifestyles of the Rich and Famous" attracts television viewers without making wealth a political issue in the United States, so do articles about high executive pay titillate newspaper readers who make a lot less money. This is as true of French readers as it is of American readers. But when the issue of corporate pay is paired with systematic abuse of the system in an easily summarized scandal, then it can become as hot a political topic as that of tax increases.

This is most likely a product of the cognitive bias known as the "availability heuristic."[3] People use the availability heuristic when they "estimate frequency

---

[3] Tversky and Kahneman (1973). I am indebted to Richard Zeckhauser for suggesting to me the relevance of the availability heuristic in this context.

or probability by the ease with which instances or associations could be brought to mind."[4] For example, if American Airlines damages my baby's stroller in transit, I am much more likely to judge the baggage-handling performance of American Airlines based on this event – which springs readily to mind – rather than by looking up statistics on damaged baggage maintained by the Federal Aviation Administration. In their dramatic experiment documenting this cognitive phenomenon, Amos Tversky and Daniel Kahneman started from the fact that K is one of eight consonants more likely to appear as the third rather than the first letter of English words. For most people, it is nevertheless much easier to think of words that begin with K than words in which K is the third letter. "King" occurs more quickly to most people than "cake." The experimenters asked subjects whether, in a randomly chosen English-language text, the letter K is more likely to appear as the first letter of the word or the third letter of the word.[5] As expected under the availability heuristic, the respondents guessed the letter should fall in the first position by a ratio of about two-to-one, even though that is the wrong answer.

The availability heuristic is relevant to scandals such as Enron because such events create a high-profile point of reference linking high executive pay with accounting fraud. "Pay for performance" lay at the heart of the Enron scandal because the incentives for false reporting went up as executive pay was linked to stock price increases, and the stock price responded to regular earnings reports. The relationship among these factors is complex and often uninteresting to people who are not compensation consultants or chief executives. Enron cut through all that complexity and laid bare the stark distributive issues involved in accounting scandals. Enron workers holding company shares in their pension plans lost everything after the scandal, while the company's leading executives were already rich from their inflated "performance-based" pay. The Enron case became a story ripe for journalistic coverage, and thereby created its own effect, through the availability heuristic: a cognitive bias on the part of readers that outsized executive pay might well be related to accounting fraud. Through this effect, Enron changed the tenor of commentary on pay: CEOs moved from a presumption of innocence to a presumption of guilt when they had a big payday. Every big payout became a potential scandal, and thereby much more newsworthy. This change caught the attention of politicians in the United States and created an incentive for them to respond to the preferences of the public rather than of managerial organizations on executive pay.

The Political Salience of Executive Compensation

As a political issue, the history of executive compensation in the United States cleaves neatly into a pre- and post-Enron phase. Prior to the 2001–2002 accounting scandals that brought down the companies Enron and Worldcom,

---

[4] Tversky and Kahneman (1973: 164).
[5] The experiment used five of the eight consonants for which this is true: K, L, N, R, and V.

interest in executive pay was essentially flat, even as soaring global equity markets carried executive compensation into the stratosphere. Many of the news stories at this time dealt with the ways in which executive pay could be more closely aligned with the interests of shareholders. The primary instrument for achieving this alignment of shareholder and executive interests was the stock option, which gave managers incentives to increase stock prices of their companies over the short term. As the market expanded rapidly in the late 1990s, led by the stocks of dot.com companies, executive pay ballooned. This rise, in itself, did not generate a correspondingly large jump in press coverage. CEO pay packages were going way up, but press coverage of them did not, as shown in Figure 6.1.

Figure 6.1 compares the evolution of press coverage of executive pay in France and the United States between 1996 and 2008. In order to make the figures directly comparable across the two countries, this graph presents the coverage of executive pay as a proportion of all articles that appeared in the leading general newspaper and the leading business newspaper in each country. For France, the coverage refers to *Le Monde* and *Les Échos*; for the United States, the coverage refers to the *New York Times* and the *Wall Street Journal*.[6] Executive pay only gained public attention in both countries after accounting scandals revealed the problems of using stock price to align pay with performance. The accounting scandals at Enron and Worldcom were deeply embroiled with issues of pay because the incentive of executives to fudge the books increased as their

[6] Articles in the *New York Times*, *Le Monde*, and *Les Échos* were searched using the LexisNexis Academic database. LexisNexis does not include the *Wall Street Journal*, which was searched using the Factiva database. The search terms used for the American newspapers were "executive compensation" OR "executive remuneration" OR "executive pay"; the corresponding terms for the French newspapers were "rémunération des dirigeants" OR "rémunération des patrons" OR "salaire des dirigeants" OR "salaire des patrons."

The total number of articles published (which is the denominator of the proportion shown in figure in 6.1) was directly available for only the *Wall Street Journal*. LexisNexis Academic does not return the number of articles published in a given newspaper in a given year beyond a threshold of three thousand articles, and all of these newspapers publish more than three thousand articles per year. To establish the denominator of the total articles published yearly for the *New York Times*, *Le Monde*, and *Les Échos*, I therefore used the following estimation procedure. I chose the number of articles published in a given week (February 8–February 14) as a basis and multiplied by fifty-two. This week in February was chosen because it is fairly representative of a regular week for a newspaper in terms of number of articles published: I could find no potential bias that would drive the numbers of articles upward or downward (e.g., no major elections). When a significant change in the number of articles published compared with previous years was noticed in the newspapers, another search was performed using a week in September (September 19–September 25). In case of a change in a newspaper's format (hence modifying the number of articles published per year), the number used in the analysis is the average of the number of articles published in the week February 8–14 and the week September 19–25 (i.e., before and after the format change). I observed such a change in *Le Monde* in mid-2004, when that paper significantly reduced the number of articles it published per year, and for *Les Échos* from 1999, when that paper significantly increased the number of articles it published per year.

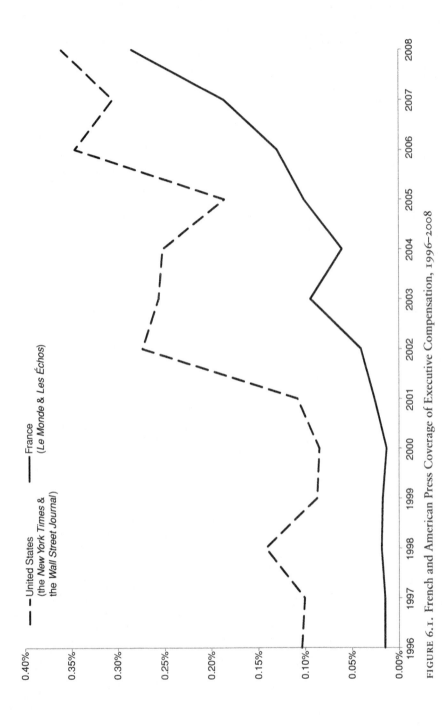

FIGURE 6.1. French and American Press Coverage of Executive Compensation, 1996–2008

pay was tied ever more tightly to short-term movements in the stock price. Thus, as summarized by Curtis Milhaupt and Katharina Pistor,

> executive compensation arrangements and market expectations created a single-minded focus on stock price at exactly the time when the incentives of market actors to exercise vigilance in ensuring that financial results were accurately reported to investors were being degraded. In several major cases, including Enron, the high-powered incentives to engineer fictitious financial results simply overwhelmed the enfeebled watchdogs.[7]

The discovery of these scandals shifted the level of press coverage of executive compensation in the United States to a substantially higher plane than in the period prior to 2002. In three leading American newspapers – the *New York Times*, the *Washington Post*, and the *Wall Street Journal* – there was an average of 184 articles per year on this topic between 1996 and 2000. Between 2002 and 2008, that number jumped to 545 articles per year. This means that in the first period there was only about one article per week dealing with executive pay in each newspaper. In the post-Enron period, each of these newspapers ran an article on executive pay *every other day*, on average. Coverage in the French press also increased, though with a lag and from a lower base.

How did regulatory involvement in executive pay setting respond to the increasing political salience of the issue? To answer this question, I developed a scale for each of the three dimensions on which governments intervene in executive compensation: transparency, shareholders' rights, and legal rules limiting pay. Transparency refers to the extent to which governments require the salaries of leading executives in listed companies to be made public. At the low end of regulation, there may be no such requirement at all. At the high end, all forms of compensation, including free use of the company jet, must be made public in a standardized format (known in the United States as a "plain English" requirement). In between these extremes, there are intermediate points in which compensation must be disclosed, but not in a standardized format; or in which some compensation, but not necessarily family use of the company

---

FIGURE 6.1. French and American Press Coverage of Executive Compensation, 1996–2008

Note: The *y*-axis refers to the number of articles per year on the subject of executive pay as a proportion of all articles appearing in these four newspapers.

Source: The *New York Times*, *Le Monde*, and *Les Échos* were searched using the LexisNexis Academic database; the *Wall Street Journal* was searched using the Factiva database. The search terms used for the American newspapers were "executive compensation" OR "executive remuneration" OR "executive pay"; the corresponding terms for the French newspapers were "rémunération des dirigeants" OR "rémunération des patrons" OR "salaire des dirigeants" OR "salaire des patrons." Between 1996 and 2008, there were 3,494 articles dealing with executive pay in the United States and 1,394 in France.

---

[7] Milhaupt and Pistor (2008: 55).

jet, must be disclosed. This creates a scale from zero to three, in which a score of zero refers to no transparency requirement at all, and a score of three refers to the most demanding standard of transparency.

The other two dimensions have similar scales that range from zero to three. The second dimension is that of shareholders' rights, which refers to the required input of general shareholders over executive pay. A score of zero means there is no shareholder input at all, which was not the case in either France or the United States throughout this period. A score of one refers to indirect shareholder control through the legal requirement that a compensation committee, which presumably represents the shareholders' interests, sets chief executive salaries. A score of two denotes the existence of legislative "claw-back" provisions, which give shareholders claims over "performance-based" executive compensation when that performance is later discovered to have been specious. A score of three means shareholders have the right to vote on CEO salaries at general shareholder meetings; this is known as a "say on pay" provision.

The final dimension is the most direct intervention by governments in the practices of listed companies – namely, legal rules constraining executive pay. A score of zero on this scale entails no government intervention at all. A score of one refers to limits on the extent to which companies can deduct executive pay from tax obligations. Neither measure intervenes directly in pay setting of leading executives, but each tries to exercise indirect influence over them. A score of two refers to direct restrictions on the size of bonuses or golden parachutes for CEOs in some companies. A score of three refers to similar restrictions on bonuses or golden parachutes of a broader set of top executives in a listed company, not only the chief executive.[8]

These scales are summarized in Table 6.1. Pictorial representations of the evolution of American and French law along these three dimensions of executive compensation regulation are shown in Figures 6.2 and 6.3.

Figures 6.2 and 6.3 illustrate that the United States and France moved in similar directions – toward greater regulation – but from different levels. Just as the political salience of executive compensation in France has been consistently lower than in the United States, so, too, has the degree of state intervention been correspondingly lower. These graphs omit the degree of *failed* legislation on this issue, which has also been higher in the United States where attempts by Democratic lawmakers to rein in executive pay were rebuffed in 2005 and 2007 before being enacted in strengthened form after the financial crisis of 2008. Moreover, an SEC rule change in 2006 took place under pressure from

---

[8] For reasons of simplicity, this scale excludes an important aspect of government intervention, which is the character of enforcement. Thus, in 2009 the United States and France both moved to level 3 in terms of the legal rules governing pay-setting (in companies that received government bailout money). Yet the American pay czar, Kenneth Feinberg, was given much stronger enforcement powers over excessive pay packages than his French counterpart, Michel Camdessus, who was only given the authority to make nonbinding recommendations.

TABLE 6.1. *Dimension and Extent of Government Intervention in Executive Pay Setting*

Transparency	Legal Requirements
0	No requirement.
1	Disclosure requirement, no standardized format.
2	Disclosure of top executives' direct compensation in a standardized format.
3	Disclosure of top executives' total compensation in a standardized format, which must be written in "plain English."
Shareholders' Rights	
0	No formal control.
1	Indirect control through compensation committee.
2	Expost facto clawback provision.
3	Direct voice through "say on pay."
Legal Rules on Pay	
0	No formal rules.
1	Limitation of tax deduction for executive compensation.
2	Restriction on bonuses and golden parachutes to CEO.
3	Restriction on bonuses and golden parachutes to CEO and other leading executives.

Source: Tax Executives Institute (1994), SEC (1996), Cooley et al. (2002), GovTrack (2002), Gov-Track (2008), Glazier (2007), Cioppa (2006), Michel (2009), *Revue Fiduciaire* (2005), Ministère de l'Économie (2008), Guélaud (2009).

the political discussion around the 2005 law and responded to some of its perceived shortcomings. From the moment the scandal broke at Enron, executive compensation has been on the radar of American politicians, and it has been propelled by the identification of this issue by policy entrepreneurs in the Democratic Party.[9]

The political salience of executive pay also rose in France in response to Enron, and to a set of infamous paydays of French CEOs in 2003. But France has been ruled by a party of the right since 2002, and the French left has not seized on the issue of executive compensation to the same degree as activists in the American Democratic Party. The only big change in French regulation did not take place until 2005, but the working group developing governmental reform first began to fashion the reform in 2003 at the time of growing popular cries for more regulation. It was enacted in 2005 as part of a broader reform package of neoliberal Finance Minister Thierry Breton. Whereas the major conflicts in the United States took place in Congress between Democrats and

---

[9] As we shall see below, policy entrepreneurs on the left also helped initiate the previous round of regulatory innovation in the United States in 1992. Yet 1992 did not provide the sustained change in salience that Enron did. In the absence of sustained political salience, the issue quickly returned to being one dominated by managerial organizations until the Enron scandal occurred ten years later.

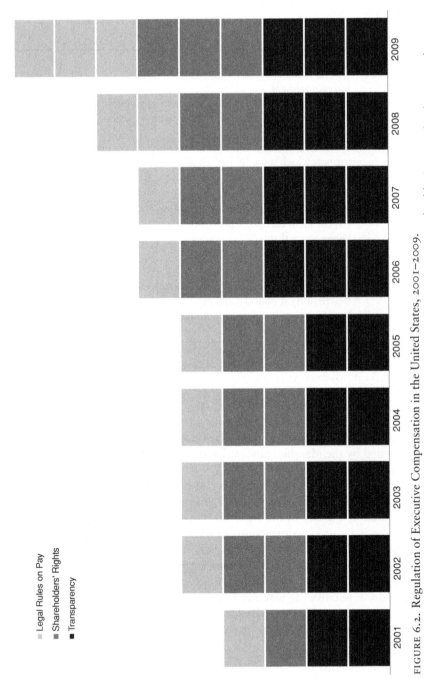

FIGURE 6.2. Regulation of Executive Compensation in the United States, 2001–2009.
Note: See text for a discussion of the scales of measurement for each of the dimensions of public intervention in pay setting.
Source: See Table 6.1.

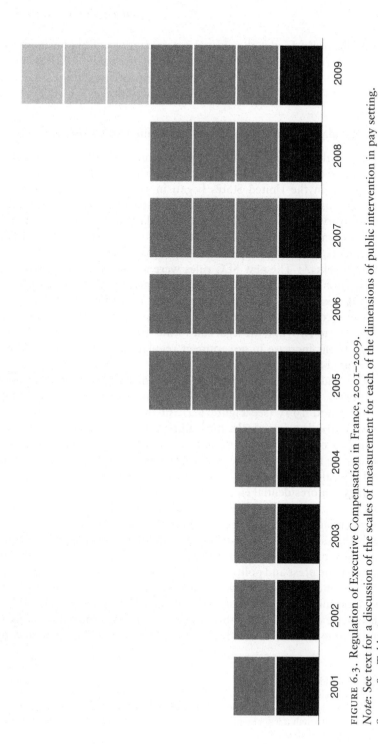

■ Legal Rules on Pay
■ Shareholders' Rights
■ Transparency

FIGURE 6.3. Regulation of Executive Compensation in France, 2001–2009.
Note: See text for a discussion of the scales of measurement for each of the dimensions of public intervention in pay setting.
Source: See Table 6.1.

Republicans, in France they pitted representatives of big business (who advocated informal regulation) against those of the ruling UMP (Gaullist) party. Only when public pressure in France got very intense did the UMP impose new regulations on its allies in the business community.

The Regulation of Executive Pay in the United States, I: 1992

Although the Securities and Exchange Commission (SEC) first required disclosure of executive pay in 1938, the modern history of executive compensation regulation in the United States began in 1992. That year, the SEC adopted new disclosure rules that required companies to publish more detailed and straightforward information about the salaries of senior executives.[10] These rules expanded the types of compensation that must be included in company statements, notably incorporating the terms of severance packages and retirement benefits.[11] The new SEC rules were accompanied the following year by a provision in President Bill Clinton's budget, which for the first time tried to use the tax code to limit the compensation of leading executives.[12] These two measures combined resulted in a one point jump on both the transparency scale (from one to two) and the legal rules scale (from zero to one), and they reflected a significant increase in government regulation of executive remuneration in the United States.

This sudden burst of regulatory enthusiasm was a direct response to the temporary spike in public attention to the issue of executive compensation in 1992 and 1993 (see Figure 6.4). In the *New York Times* and the *Wall Street Journal* – respectively, the leading general and business newspaper in the country – coverage during these two years was more than twice as intense as during the remainder of the period between 1985 and 1995 for a subject that had typically received about one article per newspaper per week on average. 1992 was a presidential election year in the United States, of course. However, given the generally weak level of public interest in executive compensation, presidential election years from 1985 to the present have not been characterized by higher average levels of press coverage than nonelection years. The rise of executive pay to political prominence in 1992 had its origin in the interaction between the press and politicians. In May 1991, two leading business magazines (*Forbes* and *Business Week*) each carried cover stories asking, "Are CEOs paid too much?"[13] The *Business Week* article correctly observed that the SEC classified executive compensation as being "ordinary business" of the company, and therefore a subject on which shareholders were not entitled to vote. Senator

---

[10] Vafeas and Afxentiou (1998).

[11] Dew-Becker (2008).

[12] This law gave companies no tax deduction on executive salaries of more than one million dollars, although it left a loophole in that companies could use "performance-related pay" and not lose the deduction.

[13] Byrne (1991), Linden and Contavespi (1991).

Carl Levin – who had previously exhibited no interest in the area of executive pay – responded by convening hearings of his Senate subcommittee to consider forcing the SEC to change its ruling.[14] In June of 1991, he introduced legislation to require stockholder votes on, and wider disclosure of, executive pay.

Levin's bill did not cause any increase in press coverage of the issue over the remainder of the year. Neither did Bill Clinton's proposal to limit the tax deductibility of executive pay, which was buried in a campaign speech on economic policy the future president gave at Georgetown University in October 1991. Both the Levin bill and the Clinton proposal were low-profile moves to seize a political issue, and as such created little attention on their own.[15] What actually catalyzed press interest in executive pay was President George H.W. Bush's decision to take "a retinue of highly paid executives on his [January 1992] trip to Japan, where company chiefs are paid far less [than in the United States]."[16] *The Washington Post*, for example, ran eighteen articles on executive pay during the entire year of 1991; it ran seventeen articles on executive pay in the first two months alone of 1992. The fact that Levin had taken up the issue in committee the previous year created immediate pressure on the SEC when the explosion of press interest in executive pay took place in 2002. His subcommittee convened a meeting on January 31 to discuss the issue. In an article on the meeting, Senator David Pryor of Arkansas was quoted as throwing down the gauntlet: "This is a classic example of one of those issues that Congress does not want to touch. We do not feel we have the expertise. However, this issue is leaving us no options. We are going to be involved."[17] The SEC got the message. In mid-February, it announced plans to require greater disclosure of the compensation of senior managers. Only when the SEC finally passed the new rules, in October 1992, did Senator Levin agree that legislation would no longer be required.[18]

Public attention to executive pay swiftly abated after 1992. Executive pay did not become politically salient again until a decade later with the outbreak of scandals at Enron and Worldcom. It is worth noting here that it is just not the

---

[14] Wildstrom (1991), Doyle (1991).

[15] The Clinton campaign proposal to limit the deductibility of executive compensation from corporate taxes to salaries of one million dollars was virtually ignored in the press. According to LexisNexis, Clinton's campaign promise that "there should be no more deductibility for irresponsibility" was mentioned only twice in the print media between the day he gave the speech in October 1991 and the election in November 1992. One article was in the *Washington Post*, the day after he gave the speech at Georgetown; the other was in a March 1992 article in *USA Today* entitled "Little Debate on CEO Pay" (Osborn 1992).

[16] Lohr (1992).

[17] Cowan (1992).

[18] Labaton (1992). The one area where Levin did say he was still considering legislation was on the issue of requiring accounting changes that would treat stock options as a liability. The issue was not taken up by the standards body of accounting, the FASB, until mid-1993. By this time, press attention to executive pay was declining, and managers remobilized against the initiative (Cioffi forthcoming). As the issue no longer retained political salience, business groups were able to prevail easily and the FASB rule change on stock options was withdrawn.

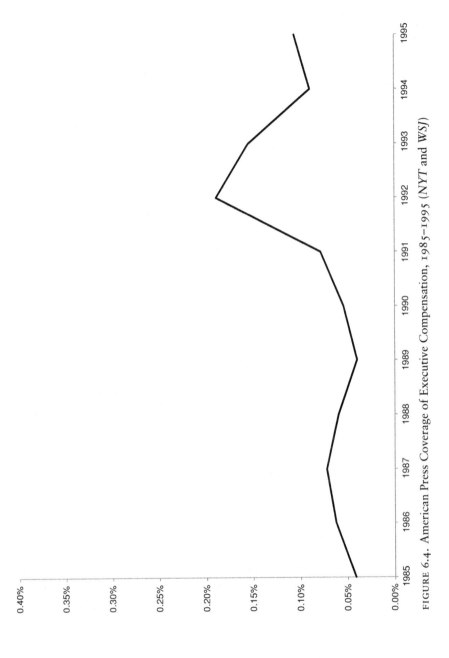

FIGURE 6.4. American Press Coverage of Executive Compensation, 1985–1995 (*NYT* and *WSJ*)

level of pay that drives its political salience in the United States. As illustrated in Figure 6.5, the most vertiginous rise in American CEO compensation took place between 1996 and 2000, when average CEO pay moved from 100 to almost 300 times the pay of the average worker. Yet press coverage of this issue changed only slightly in this period. In 2002, when Enron ignited a new wave of public interest in the issue of executive pay, the level of average pay was well down from its year 2000 heights as a result of a bear market. It is likely that high executive pay levels, relative to that of average workers, are a necessary condition for executive compensation to become politically salient. But high pay levels alone are not sufficient to kindle public outrage unless joined with some catalyzing event. The Enron and Worldcom scandals together would constitute such an event.

The Regulation of Executive Pay in the United States, II: Enron and the High Salience Era

The passage of the Sarbanes-Oxley law is typically seen as the watershed event of American corporate governance regulation. Yet the passage of Sarbanes-Oxley was only possible because the Enron scandal, followed by the Worldcom scandal a few months later, forced a reluctant Congress to act. Sarbanes-Oxley changed the law, but Enron fundamentally changed the political rules of corporate pay regulation. The scandal caught public attention and ignited public anger. This had an immediate effect in stimulating legislative passage of new rules of corporate governance, but the rise of Enron as an informational shortcut for corporate excess had its own discursive importance. It made a class of scandals easier to explain to the wider public. And if the availability heuristic is an accurate representation of cognition, the prominence of the scandal raised the probability that average voters would associate extremely high executive pay with potential fraud.

Enron was an accounting scandal driven by an executive incentive structure that tied salaries to short-term share price performance. The compensation of the 200 highest paid employees at Enron in the year 2000 was $1.4 billion, and three-quarters of that money was made up of stock options and

---

←

FIGURE 6.4. American Press Coverage of Executive Compensation, 1985–1995 (*NYT* and *WSJ*)

Note: The *y*-axis refers to the proportion of all articles appearing in the *New York Times* and the *Wall Street Journal* that dealt with executive pay during this period.

Source: The *New York Times* was searched using the LexisNexis Academic database, while the *Wall Street Journal* was searched using the Factiva database. The search terms used were "executive compensation" OR "executive remuneration" OR "executive pay." There were 868 articles dealing with executive pay in the *New York Times* and 469 in the *Wall Street Journal* during this period.

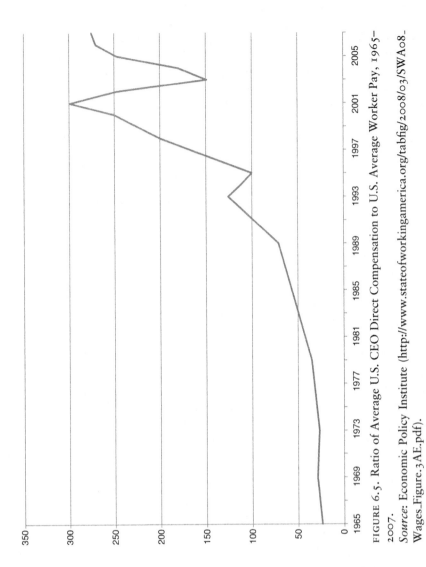

FIGURE 6.5. Ratio of Average U.S. CEO Direct Compensation to U.S. Average Worker Pay, 1965–2007.

Source: Economic Policy Institute (http://www.stateofworkingamerica.org/tabfig/2008/03/SWA08_Wages_Figure.3AE.pdf).

bonuses (i.e., remuneration related directly to the company's share price).[19] After the bankruptcy of Enron in December 2001, Republicans (who controlled the House of Representatives) and Democrats (who controlled the Senate) developed alternative legislative responses to the collapse. The Republican proposal, championed by Representative Michael Oxley and supported by President George W. Bush, included no new proposals and deferred to the SEC.[20] The Democratic proposal, backed by Senator Paul Sarbanes, pushed for strict accounting reforms and included clawback provisions to allow shareholders to recoup performance-based bonuses that were later revealed to be based on illusory performance. The institutional configuration, with Republicans controlling the House and the White House, favored the Republican bill. According to press reports from the time,

> few people [in May 2002] gave Sarbanes much chance of bringing his bill to the Senate floor, much less passing it into law. It had been months since Enron Corp.'s sudden collapse focused attention on long-standing problems of the nation's financial system, and the reformist zeal had faded.[21]

What Senate Democrats needed to have any hope of passing their bill was another business scandal. And they got it. On June 26, "front pages of newspapers across the country relayed reports that WorldCom had misstated billions of dollars of expenses."[22] Able to capitalize on the renewed public outrage, Sarbanes and the Democrats refused any substantive negotiations with Oxley and the Republicans, imposing their more stringent reforms in the Sarbanes-Oxley bill, which passed the Senate on July 15 by a vote of 97–0.

As John Cioffi observes in his analysis of this case, the passage of Sarbanes-Oxley was a contingent event, made possible by the occurrence of two prominent business scandals, which effectively refocused public attention on the case and disempowered business interest groups. Sarbanes-Oxley placed significant new limitations on company accounting, but it only introduced minor changes in the regulation of executive pay, which was the major source of the incentive structure behind the accounting scandal at Enron.[23] The importance of that scandal, from the perspective of the political salience of executive compensation, is that it became the embodiment of that distorted incentive system. Corporate scandals acquired a new watchword: thus Parmalat was called the "Enron of Italy," Ahold was the "Enron of the Netherlands," and even the American utility company Westar became the "Enron of Kansas."[24] Enron

---

[19] Milhaupt and Pistor (2008: 50).
[20] Cioffi (forthcoming).
[21] Hilzenrath et al. (2002).
[22] Hilzenrath et al. (2002).
[23] Milhaupt and Pistor (2008).
[24] Johnson (2004). The Ahold and Parmalat scandals were both covered as the "Enron of Europe." Web references to the various scandals can be found at the following sites:

Parmalat (http://marketplace.publicradio.org/display/web/2008/05/05/parmalot_lawsuits/);
Ahold (http://marketplace.publicradio.org/display/web/2007/10/26/upscaling_supermarkets/);
Westar (http://www.nytimes.com/2007/01/12/business/12westar.html?pagewanted=print).

gave journalists an easy way to communicate the central narrative line of otherwise boring stories involving accountants and falsified earnings records.

Enron, the Press, and Political Entrepreneurship

The Enron scandal broke out at the end of 2001. For all of 2001, a LexisNexis search of the entire database of American news sources retrieves only thirteen articles featuring the word Enron and the phrase "executive pay." Over the next five years, the same search never retrieved fewer than eighty articles per year. Five years after the scandal, in fact, the joint search terms still retrieved 184 articles.

To evaluate the role of scandals in the framing of press coverage pre- and post-Enron, I compared the composition of articles on executive remuneration in the two time periods (Figure 6.6). I examined two years that featured no obvious national financial scandal: 1999 and 2000 from the pre-Enron period, and 2005 and 2006 from the post-Enron period. The search returned all articles using the terms "executive compensation" or "executive remuneration" or "executive pay" in the *New York Times*, a total of 466 articles. Articles were coded as having one of four primary frames; nonclassified articles were coded as "other." "Scandal" refers to articles that were principally about some sort of pay-related scandal; "legal commentary" captures articles dealing primarily with ongoing legislation related to executive pay; "social commentary" refers to articles that mainly discuss the social phenomenon of executive pay without linking it to a particular episode of malfeasance; and "specific company" refers to articles dealing solely with the pay policies of individual companies, without reference to either scandals or broader trends in pay patterns.[25]

As shown in Figure 6.6, hardly any of the articles published in 1999 and 2000 referred to a scandal in executive pay, even though the year 2000 was the period when executive salaries reached their peak in comparison to the salary of average workers (see Figure 6.5). The vast majority of articles from this early period dealt with either individual companies or social commentary on executive pay. By way of contrast, in 2005 and 2006, almost thirty percent of the articles published in this area dealt with scandal. Moreover, even the tone of articles dealing with individual companies during the latter period was different, as many of these articles focused attention on the very high payouts of CEOs as they left their company. Not only was *coverage* of executive pay much higher in the latter two years, but its *composition* had changed, with forty percent of articles devoted to executive pay scandals or the development of laws to regulate executive pay scandals. Public outrage over pay scandals is the phenomenon that most distinguishes the press coverage of 2005–2006 from 1999–2000.

This figure also drives home a point already made implicitly in the discussion of the previous political episodes: newspaper coverage is not primarily a

---

[25] These articles were retrieved using LexisNexis academic. For this coding, I only included articles; letters to the editors, business briefs, business digests, and obituaries were excluded.

Number of articles

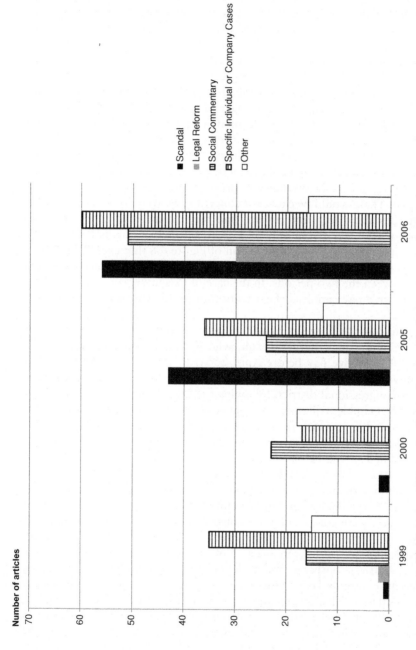

FIGURE 6.6. The Framing of Executive Pay in the *New York Times* Pre- and Post-Enron

Note: N = 466. All articles retrieved using Lexis-Nexis using the search terms "executive remuneration" OR "executive pay." OR "executive compensation" OR "executive pay." See text for explanation of coding. The vertical axis shows the number of articles that correspond to the given frame.

product of legal proposals, but causally prior to them. Some readers of this book may have wondered, reasonably, whether using press coverage as a measure of political salience raises what social scientists call a problem of endogeneity. Simply put, this sort of problem occurs when the value of the explanatory variable (political salience measured as press coverage) is in some way a result of the value of the dependent variable (regulation of executive pay), rather than being a cause of it. In this case, the endogeneity problem would be that newspapers sometimes cover issues debated in legislatures just because they are debated in legislatures. So what I have been arguing is an increase in salience that *caused* an increase in legislative activity in the United States might be only a *product* of that increase in legislative activity. It is certainly true that activity in a legislature almost always increases press coverage of an issue, other things being equal. There would be cause for concern if we were to remove the additional articles about legal reform and find that the increase I am attributing to salience was in fact driven only by a greater degree of law-making activity. However, it is apparent from observation of Figure 6.6 that excluding all articles on legal reform would not significantly change the observation of increased salience between the two periods. In the case of executive pay, public concern about executive pay captured the attention of politicians, not the other way around.

One politician who appears to have responded to this change in public concern was Congressman Barney Frank, who had never been associated with the topic of executive pay before April 2005. In January of 2005, the issue of executive pay had suddenly become highly salient in Frank's own Massachusetts congressional district, following the sale of the Boston firm Gillette to Procter & Gamble. Gillette's CEO, James Kilts, received a payout from the deal of $165 million, which provoked a storm of criticism in the local media. Massachusetts Secretary of State William Galvin investigated the case, and Kilts complained in a speech before the Boston Chamber of Commerce that he was being turned into "Boston's piñata" by the media and politicians. Frank, the ranking Democratic member of the House Financial Services Committee, first went public on the issue of executive compensation in April 2005 as business representatives were complaining to Congress about the costs of compliance with Sarbanes-Oxley. Speaking about executive behavior during a committee hearing, Frank said, "at least in one area of some importance to them – setting their own salaries – Sarbanes and Oxley might as well be Donald and Daisy Duck, because nobody lays a glove on these people when it comes to setting their own salaries. This is something we have to address."[26] In November, Frank introduced a bill to require direct shareholder approval of CEO pay and perquisites, including golden parachutes. Galvin, who had investigated the payout to Kilts, joined Frank at the press conference announcing the bill.[27]

---

[26] Block and Orol (2005).
[27] Reidy and Wirzbicki (2005).

Frank's bill never got out of committee, as the Democrats were in the minority in the House at the time. But, as in 1992, the SEC was not unaware what was being proposed in Congress.[28] Its proposals for reform, released in January 2006 and adopted in July, echoed some of Frank's proposals on more extensive disclosure as well as requiring a "plain English" standard for the publication of pay packages.

Frank's 2005 proposal to require advisory shareholder votes on executive pay – known as "say on pay" – died in committee. It would recur over the coming years. After the Democrats took control of Congress in November 2006, Frank dropped the measures on disclosure, which the SEC had addressed in its 2006 regulations, but he resubmitted a bill that would have required all public companies to hold an advisory shareholder vote on pay packages.[29] Business groups opposed the bill, with the president of the Business Roundtable testifying that "corporations were never designed to be democracies. . . . While shareholders own the corporation, they do not run it." The bill moved onto the Senate where it stalled in the face of managerial lobbying and opposition from the Bush White House, despite being cosponsored by then-Senator Barack Obama.

The economic crisis that broke out in the autumn of 2008 – which left several American and foreign financial institutions on the brink of insolvency – provided a vehicle for reinvigorated debate on the "say on pay" and clawback provisions proposed by Barney Frank. The Emergency Economic Stabilization Law, passed by Congress in October 2008, included a clawback provision and banned the use of golden parachutes for companies that received public assistance through the measure. Congressional Republicans successfully opposed a "say on pay" provision included in the original bill.[30] President Barack Obama took office in January 2009 amid rising press coverage of executive bonuses at many of the large financial institutions receiving public money, which the new president branded as "shameful." The large stimulus package his administration passed in February 2009 included a "say on pay" clause for companies that received any public money through the stimulus. Moreover, Barney Frank's counterpart in the Senate, Christopher Dodd, introduced tough pay limits on executives at these same companies, limits that went beyond even those demanded by the Obama administration.[31]

The cumulative effects of these measures, which were passed shortly before this book went to press, are not yet clear. They may well fail to rein in executive remuneration, just as the changes introduced by Bill Clinton did. But the continued high salience of executive pay since 2002 has at the very least coincided with an unprecedented expansion of the role of the American government in

---

[28] Cox (2006).

[29] HR 1257.

[30] Putnam (2008).

[31] Solomon and Maremont (2009). The Dodd-Frank Act of 2010 subsequently required that all publicly listed companies hold nonbinding shareholder votes on executive pay and on golden parachute arrangements.

regulating pay directly and in giving shareholders more tools to have input on managerial salaries. High political salience did not result in automatic losses for managerial lobbies. Frank's 2005 and 2007 proposals for "say on pay" were both defeated in Congress. The enduring post-Enron salience of corporate pay, however, left policy entrepreneur Barney Frank in a much better position than his counterpart Carl Levin had found himself in a decade earlier. Levin's attempt to control the expensing of stock options had failed after the concerted lobbying of business organizations, which secured bipartisan support for their opposition to Levin's measure.[32] By contrast, congressional Democrats after 2002 were no longer cowed by the claims of the Business Roundtable that managers knew best how to run American business.

For those Democrats, Enron was the scandal that kept on giving, in terms of skepticism about business autonomy in the area of pay setting. In the search of *New York Times* articles from 2005–2006, discussed previously, the Enron case was a regular feature in articles dealing with scandals on executive remuneration. Sometimes it was used as a clarifying example, such as in this quotation: "economists often argue that the best way to motivate managers is to link their pay closely to performance. But recent history (consider Enron and World-Com) suggests this idea works much better in theory than in practice."[33] Other times, Enron was a marker of fundamental change in shareholder–manager relations: "the most important issue that stands in the way of fully restoring investor trust – and eliminating the trust gap that was caused by the scandals of the Enron era – is the issue of executive compensation."[34] Finally, Enron not only became a shorthand for a sea change, but one former U.S. attorney noted that it had actually changed acceptable prosecutorial tactics, thereby bringing a whole new class of cases under legal (and thereby journalistic) scrutiny.[35]

The durability of Enron gave Democratic policy entrepreneurs a political incentive to care about executive pay while undercutting the plausibility of managerial claims to special expertise. The frequent references to the scandal in the press are likely to have led American voters to be more skeptical about the justice of high executive pay, and such references certainly focused the attention of enterprising political figures, such as Barney Frank, on the issues of pay and corporate malfeasance. As a result of this lasting increase in political salience, radical policy change became possible in an area where regulation had previously been stable for long periods of time.

The Regulation of Executive Pay in France

In the United States, the sharp increase in the political salience of executive pay in the post-Enron period created an incentive for politicians to intervene

[32] A resolution condemning the proposal to expense stock options had passed the Senate with a large majority (Cioffi forthcoming).
[33] Anabtawi and Stout (2005).
[34] Morgenson (2006).
[35] Creswell (2006).

with formal legal proposals, and political entrepreneurs in the Democratic Party responded to this incentive. In France, Enron did not have the same galvanizing impact on public opinion as in the United States, probably because it was perceived as a scandal of American-style capitalism. Only with the economic crisis of 2008 did the political salience of executive pay in France finally reach the level it had first reached in the United States in 2002.

This difference in the regulation of pay in France and the United States was partially a product of the different opportunities created by political salience. Yet there is also an element of partisan political competition that is relevant to the variation in policy outcomes between the two countries. Even as executive pay excesses in France first began to come to light from 2003, the French Socialist Party was less well positioned than were the American Democrats to take advantage of rising political salience to advocate reform. The presidency and the Parliament were both controlled by parties of the right during the entire period between 2003 and 2009. Whereas Democrats Barney Frank, Carl Levin, and Christopher Dodd were able to use their role in powerful congressional committees to push for reforms during moments of heightened public attention, the French Socialists had access to no such institutional levers of power. The corporate reforms observed in France since 2002 were the product of innovations of governments of the right.[36]

Each of these French reforms followed a characteristic path: government proposal; business counterproposal for self-regulation; and passage of government proposal only after the failure of self-regulation to solve the perceived problem. Executive pay in France has not been a high salience issue for most of this decade, and that has made the traditional power resource of informal regulation an important one in the political arsenal of organized managers. The fact that the recent periods of high salience have coincided with the domination of the French political system by the Gaullist UMP has removed the most obvious partisan source of political pressure on business.

There is one alternative explanation for patterns of French regulation and salience which we should consider first. Perhaps there was less regulation of executive pay, and less political pressure for such regulation, simply because French executives were not getting paid as much as American chief executives. If this were the case, any account based on the difference in salience would be excluding the variable that drove both press coverage and legislative action: high executive salaries. To consider this alternative, Figure 6.7 charts CEO remuneration relative to average worker pay in both France and the United States.

---

[36] A set of reforms known as the NRE (New Economic Regulations) was passed in 2001 by the Socialist government, which lost power the following year. This was an omnibus bill combining different proposals dealing with finance, corporate governance, money laundering, corporate social responsibility, and competition law. The corporate governance reforms included a measure increasing the transparency of executive pay.

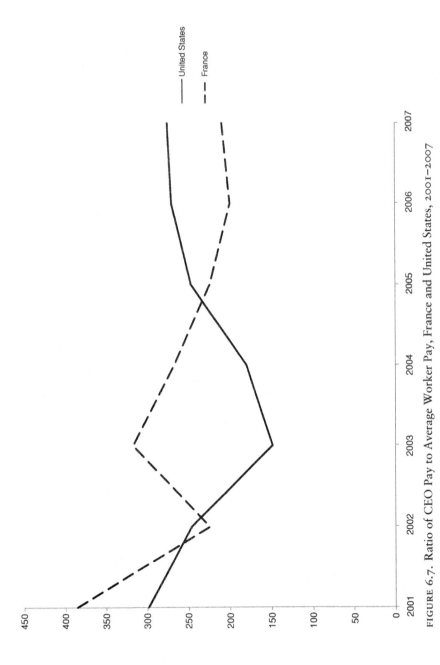

FIGURE 6.7. Ratio of CEO Pay to Average Worker Pay, France and United States, 2001–2007

These data emphatically refute the proposition that French lawmakers were passive because French executive salaries were not as high as those in the United States, relative to the pay of the average worker. From 2001 to 2005, when French laws governing executive pay were stable, CEO salaries in France were just as high as those in the United States, relative to average salaries. From 2005–2007, a period of constantly *increasing* press coverage of executive pay in France, executive salaries themselves were steadily *decreasing*, relative to average worker salaries. The level of executive pay accounts neither for the regulatory changes enacted by the government nor for the trends in the political salience of CEO pay observed in France during this period.

While Enron was not a highly salient event in French political life, both business leaders and politicians took note of it. The political organizations of French managers, the MEDEF and the AFEP, first established a joint commission of senior French executives to examine issues of oversight and executive compensation in April 2002, several months after the revelations from Enron. The committee's final recommendations, known as the Bouton report, endorsed the existing practices of executive pay in France, recommending against any increase in shareholder control over the compensation of senior executives. The first formal French response to Enron and Sarbanes-Oxley came in the National Assembly's Clément report, published in November 2003. The role of committee hearings led by Democrats in the American case was often to put pressure on the SEC to increase oversight of businesses. By contrast, in the French case the Clément report took as its target not regulators, but business itself, which the report asked to strengthen its own self-regulation.

←————————————————————————————————————

FIGURE 6.7. Ratio of CEO Pay to Average Worker Pay, France and United States, 2001–2007

Source: Data on the United States are from Economic Policy Institute. Data on France were assembled from Code de Commerce (2003), Comarmond (2002), Ducourtieux (2006), Gatinois (2007), L'Humanité (2000), Maurice (2008), Proxinvest (2005), Rosemain (2008), INSEE (2009), and Bessière and Depil (2009).

Note: To construct this graph, we assembled data from various sources in France to parallel the measures of executive pay relative to average worker pay maintained for the United States by the Economic Policy Institute. Proxinvest, a consultancy that advises shareholders in France, has maintained figures on CEO compensation in France for the CAC-40 index of the largest forty companies for the years 2001–2007. To estimate average worker pay for France, we used the data collected by INSEE on wages of *ouvriers* (blue-collar workers) and *employés* (lower-level white-collar workers), taking an average weighting of the two categories based on their respective shares of the overall French workforce. We were unsuccessful in discovering the size of the sample of CEOs the Economic Policy Institute uses to create its figures, despite repeated attempts to contact the EPI. It is possible that our figures somewhat overstate the level of French executive pay relative to that of American CEOs, if the EPI includes the incomes of CEOs from smaller companies, which are excluded from our French data. This should not affect the time trends observed in the French series.

The Clément report acknowledged that the Bouton report was an attempt by organized business to respond to the problems raised by the Enron crisis. It added also that in its legislative priorities in the area of corporate governance, "the Government [of the right] has not substituted laws for free contracts, and the legislator has followed this choice." Yet the report went on to suggest that in allowing business to continue to set its own rules, it would be under surveillance. "The global explosion of [executive] pay was both the symbol and the symptom of the crisis. The manner in which this question will be contemplated in the future by CEOs will be, therefore, a test."[37] The report did not advocate measures such as "say on pay," and indeed it went out of its way to underline that it was a call for self-regulation: on the issue of variable performance based-pay, the committee "once again leaves the question to contractual relations, and leaves the definition of these measures, entirely to the judgment of corporate leaders."[38] The determination of performance-based pay was not a subject on which the legislature would intervene, but it was watching. At the time of the Clément report, the French managerial organizations published a code of practice, which reiterated principles laid out previously in the Bouton report.

By April of 2004, Clément was convinced of the need for an additional law on transparency in executive remuneration. The government was unwilling to support a law in the absence of a strong popular push for it, and Clément's measure languished. In April 2005, however, the public outcry over, and press coverage of, CEO Daniel Bernard's retirement package from the retail company Carrefour, created a potential opening for Clément to reintroduce his measure on transparency for public pay.[39] Although senior figures in the government opposed any regulation of executive pay, there was a political incentive to respond to the wave of public anger created by the Bernard golden parachute. As summarized by the journalists of *Les Échos*, the leading French business newspaper, "For the parliamentarians of the majority, the difficulty is to react with a symbolically strong measure to the emotion provoked by the [golden parachute] of Daniel Bernard."[40] The amendment submitted by Clément required that the special pay associated with signing or leaving a firm (golden hellos and golden parachutes) be disclosed in plain language to shareholders. Prior to 2009, this was the only change to the regime of executive compensation enacted by the governing UMP party.

However, the UMP was not insensitive to the steady increase of press coverage of French executive pay in 2006 and 2007. By 2007, French press coverage had finally reached the same intensity as the American post-Enron coverage of the topic, as measured by proportion of articles in the press dealing with this

---

[37] Clément (2003: 18).

[38] Clément (2003: 21). Carrefour, which is part of the CAC-40 index of the largest French companies, is roughly the same size as the American company Wal-Mart.

[39] Orange (2005), Lechantre and Pécresse (2005).

[40] Lechantre and Pécresse (2005).

subject. The scandal over the high pay package awarded to Antoine Zacharias at French construction giant Vinci had led to his resignation in June 2006. The case also led Nicolas Sarkozy, the eventual presidential candidate of the UMP, to denounce "rogue bosses" (*patrons voyous*) and to call for greater executive pay restraint. Sarkozy would include this plank in his presidential platform of 2007. The response of the organized employers' groups, MEDEF and AFEP, was to release a new code of conduct at the beginning of 2007, just as the presidential race between Sarkozy and Socialist candidate Ségolène Royal began to intensify. The president of the MEDEF, Laurence Parisot, was also simultaneously head of the largest public opinion firm in France, and she was well informed about the rising unpopularity of exorbitant executive pay. The joint AFEP/MEDEF proposal was explicitly targeted to head off any new regulation. Parisot argued that a private set of rules would be more successful because "it will have been established and thought up by CEOs."[41] The report, though it suggested making clearer the elements of individual remuneration, mainly referred to earlier MEDEF reports and rejected any notion of shareholder direct control of executive compensation. And the managerial organizations picked up a theme that would be central to Sarkozy's campaign: that high pay, "even very high pay," was appropriate for those who worked hard in France.

This response to public opinion was apparently enough to forestall any legislative action by President Sarkozy's new government in 2007. It was only with the onset of the global financial crisis one year later that public attention returned in a concentrated way to this issue, and with it the pressure of the government on organized managers. The Franco-Belgian bank Dexia, which required a large infusion of public money to stay solvent at the end of September 2008, planned to pay its resigning CEO almost four million Euros. This "pay for nonperformance" scandalized French public opinion and drew the following threat from Sarkozy: "either the employers agree among themselves on acceptable practice [for golden parachutes], or the government of the Republic will resolve the problem with legislation before the end of the year."[42] The MEDEF published a new code of conduct within two weeks of the president's speech. This code held that the monetary value of golden parachutes should only be determined based on performance, not on contractually specified payouts. President Sarkozy immediately withdrew his threat to legislate, but warned that the government wanted to see concrete results in limiting golden parachutes.[43]

To understand the timing and content of Sarkozy's next intervention in the regulation of business, it is instructive to monitor monthly press coverage of executive pay in France during the financial crisis of 2008–2009. Figure 6.8 shows the percentage of articles in which executive pay was mentioned in both the leading general newspaper (*Le Monde*) and the leading business newspaper

[41] Delberghe (2007).
[42] *Tribune* (2008).
[43] Fressoz (2008).

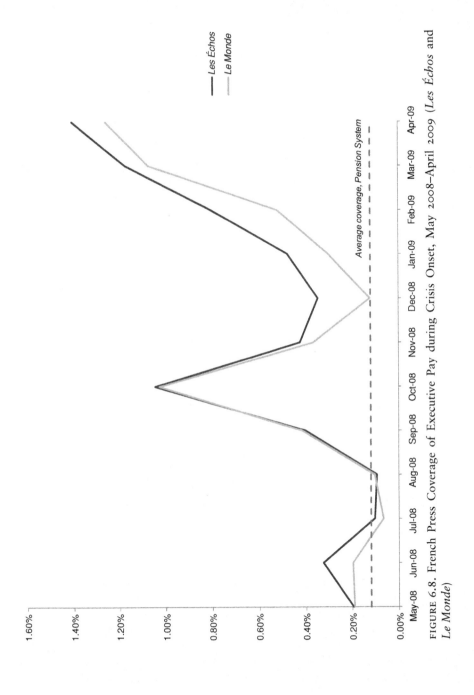

FIGURE 6.8. French Press Coverage of Executive Pay during Crisis Onset, May 2008–April 2009 (*Les Échos* and *Le Monde*)

(*Les Échos*). As in earlier chapters, the graph compares this coverage with the average level of coverage received by the pension system during the same period, which sets a baseline for high political salience. The 2008–2009 time period was one in which pensions were a hot topic in French politics. Even so, the coverage of executive pay was higher than the average coverage of pensions for most of this time, as illustrated in Figure 6.8. That figure shows there were two periods of especially intense press interest in executive pay. The first sharp spike in coverage took place immediately following the Dexia crisis in September–October 2008, to which the French president's threat was a direct response. The next jump in coverage was in March 2009, following the revelation of large payouts to executives at Société Générale and Valeo. As representatives of the banking and automobile industries – sectors that together had received more than thirty billion Euros in public money during the financial crisis – these two companies highlighted that executives of companies performing poorly were still getting generous payouts when they resigned.[44] Unlike previous examples, though, this media storm did not abate quickly, and indeed increased to unprecedented levels in April 2009, when nearly one and a half of every 100 articles in the French press dealt with the subject of executive remuneration.

Although Sarkozy's repeatedly stated preference was to allow business to regulate itself, French parliamentarians on the right began to break ranks with their president by the end of March, calling for legislation to respond to the public anger about executive pay scandals.[45] *Les Échos* reported in late March that the president warned members of the governing majority against new legislation. After threatening industry several times over the course of the month – during which time Laurence Parisot of the MEDEF emphatically rejected a hard limit on executive pay – Sarkozy's government announced it would issue a decree forbidding the issue of stock options or stock grants to officers of companies receiving state money (namely, the automobile and banking sectors).[46] Less than a week later, in a snub to the government, the parliament unanimously adopted a legal amendment to a supplementary budget that would substantially broaden the ambit of coverage. The amendment came from within the parties

←——

FIGURE 6.8. French Press Coverage of Executive Pay during Crisis Onset, May 2008–April 2009 (*Les Échos* and *Le Monde*)

Note: The y-axis refers to the proportion of all articles appearing in the French press that deal with executive pay.

Source: *Le Monde* and *Les Échos* were searched through the LexisNexis Academic database using the search terms "rémunération des dirigeants" OR "rémunération des patrons" OR "salaire des dirigeants" OR "salaire des patrons." There were 204 articles dealing with executive pay in *Le Monde* and 347 articles in *Les Échos* during this year.

[44] Guélaud and Michel (2009b).
[45] Cornudet and Lefebvre (2009).
[46] Guélaud and Michel (2009a).

of the right and it extended those affected by the rule from only chief executives to all senior executives and board members.[47] It included a ban not only on stock options and restricted stock grants, but also on golden parachutes and other payments on termination of contract of executives (*retraites-chapeaux*).[48] Outflanked by increasingly restive parliamentarians, the government had no choice but to incorporate these elements into its decree, which was finally published at the end of April.[49] Thus, the expansion of governmental control of remuneration in France, shown graphically in Figure 6.3 earlier in this chapter, was a product of legislation forced on a president of the right by parliamentarians of the right, in the wake of sustained public attention to the issue of executive pay.

Under conditions of very high salience created by a financial scandal, as obtained in March and April 2009, even a government favorable to business self-regulation could not keep its troops in line. The experience of Nicolas Sarkozy in 2009 was eerily similar to that faced by George W. Bush in the summer of 2003, when Republicans in the House of Representatives deserted him in the face of public anger over the Enron and WorldCom scandals. These Republicans, like the politicians of the right who generally supported Sarkozy, would have been willing to countenance the preferences of the president for self-regulation if their constituents were not clamoring for action. It is rare for corporate governance issues to cause large groups of citizens to demand legislation from politicians. But when they do, even when a government of the right is closely aligned with business, managerial organizations face an uphill fight.

Conclusion

The quiet politics framework implies that managerial organizations will exercise disproportionate influence in issue areas of high interest to them but of low general political salience. They will succeed under these conditions because of their expertise and lobbying capacity, the reliance by politicians on self-regulatory forums for rule making, and their potential to influence the tenor of press coverage. But these tools of quiet politics are much less effective under conditions of high political salience. Under high political salience, the expectation that political parties and broad political coalitions will drive processes of reform makes much more sense than under low political salience. This chapter has tested these expectations empirically by examining change over time in the political salience of executive pay and the government regulation of executive pay setting in France and the United States.

---

[47] Jean Arthuis, the centrist president of the Finance Committee in the Senate, proposed the amendment.

[48] Guélaud (2009).

[49] Delacroix (2009).

France and the United States were both led by presidents of the right between 2002 and 2008. Partisan theories of politics suggest, correctly, that business should win more often when its allies from political parties of the right are in power. Yet there is important variation between these two cases. The United States moved substantially further in the direction of regulating executive pay during this time than did France. The differences in the timing of reform initiatives and in these ultimate political outcomes are difficult to understand without reference to the variations in the salience of executive pay in the two countries. This is a story about partisanship, but the importance of partisan control of government depends on the level of political salience of an issue.

In the United States, the transformation of executive pay from an issue of low salience to high salience was a consequence of the Enron and Worldcom scandals. These scandals changed executive pay from a source of public fascination to a source of public outrage, and this change of perception had important political implications. It created incentives for political entrepreneurs like Barney Frank to develop expertise and expend political capital trying to legislate in this area. Frank lost some battles against managers, even during the high salience period. High political salience did not ensure that the managerial lobby would lose; it merely vitiated the special advantages that business groups enjoy during periods of low political salience, all of which derive from deference to managerial expertise. High salience forces managerial organizations to rely more directly on partisan political protection or to mobilize support in public opinion. During moments of extraordinarily high public resentment against CEOs – as in July of 2002 – even the protection of a Republican president and House of Representatives was not enough to protect business interests from sweeping legislation.

In France, executive pay became highly politically salient only during the international financial crisis of 2008. As we saw, France actually intervenes much less than the United States in matters of executive pay, a fact which will probably surprise both French and American readers. The lower salience of the issue for most of the decade, combined with the presence of a government of the right sympathetic to the prerogatives of business, allowed informal self-regulation of executive pay to persist far after it had been challenged in the United States. Only when a series of pay scandals in 2009 raised journalistic scrutiny of French executive pay to unprecedented levels of intensity did Nicolas Sarkozy lose the ability to keep his party on board in allowing self-regulation.

The full political ramifications of the international crisis of 2008–2009 are not yet clear as this chapter is being written. Yet the evidence we have so far demonstrates the promise of focusing on variations in political salience to understand the different vectors of managerial influence in politics. Crises and scandals focus popular attention on issues that can otherwise seem technical and arcane, their distributive consequences notwithstanding. When events like Enron and Worldcom take place, they change the calculus of politicians. The availability heuristic can change the way voters perceive high pay, creating a presumption of guilt because of one or two memorable scandals. American

CEOs after Enron went from being treated like movie stars, whose wealth is envied and fascinating but not questioned, to being treated more like ex-convicts, whose sudden wealth raises immediate suspicions. This change of public perception and political salience transformed the political terrain of corporate governance by denying business actors deference based on their expertise. When an issue becomes subject to such noisy politics, the best defense of managerial organizations lies in an alliance with a sympathetic political party.

If managers could choose between having a right-wing party in power and having executive pay disappear from the headlines, they would be wise to choose the latter. Political parties, even those ideologically sympathetic to calls for business to regulate itself, will eventually respond to the electoral incentives created by angry voters. The Enron effect, followed by the financial crisis of 2008, demonstrated this logic clearly.

The findings of this chapter should not be misconstrued as predicting that executive pay will be checked by a new, postcrisis government activism in the advanced industrial countries. Indeed, the prediction that emerges from the quiet politics framework is that governments in France and the United States will only intervene in this area so long as it remains of high political salience. The short history of state intervention in executive pay is one of government regulation that stimulates the remunerative ingenuity of managers and compensation consultants. Managers of large companies typically have more expensive lawyers than does the government. As scandals recede in the past, and as economic growth returns, there are many other issues that may crowd out popular outrage with executive pay. If and when that happens, government oversight of executive pay is likely to slacken.

7

Business Power and Democratic Politics

This book's main finding can be summarized in one sentence: the more the public cares about an issue, the less managerial organizations will be able to exercise disproportionate influence over the rules governing that issue. In other words, business power goes down as political salience goes up. So why spend an entire book developing an argument that could be communicated so succinctly? First, and most importantly, this fact has a significant impact on the lives of people around the world who live in democracies. The promise of popular sovereignty is only realized when politicians think voters care about issues and inform themselves about those issues. A second, related point also motivates this book: the explanatory power of this simple truth has been underestimated, even by many of those who study politics for a living.

Most of this book has dealt with a policy area of profound political importance for how capitalist systems operate: the rules governing corporate control. Some regimes of corporate control treat companies as mere commodities, free to be bought and sold at will by owners in search of the highest rate of return on their investment. Others, by contrast, view the company as a place where many important political and distributive compromises of capitalist democracy are struck. In these systems, rules restrain the buying and selling of companies on the assumption that a company is the site of many negotiated deals between management, labor, and other stakeholders, and that frequent and unpredictable changes of ownership challenge these firm-level bargains. These differences are fundamental to the distinction between different varieties of capitalism.

However, voters in most countries do not care about the rules of corporate control per se, although they care a lot about their observable consequences. And in this domain, organized managers have been extremely successful in advancing their preferred policy agenda and thwarting the agendas of their opponents, be they hedge funds or neoliberal governments. Corporate control is an area in which political parties play little role. Debates between scholars about whether it is parties of the right or of the left that are more likely

pport patient capital are simply misguided. Most of the time, political
ties do not matter in the regulation of corporate control.

Managerial groups have tools and resources that allow them to dominate
fights in low salience domains. It is costly for politicians or journalists to
acquire expertise about complex policy issues, and low public concern about
such issues reduces the incentive of either political parties or of news outlets
to expend the resources to develop that expertise. Managers, on the other
hand, do have expertise in this area, and they enjoy considerable deference as a
result of this expertise. Politicians do not want to risk messing up the economy
unless there is a big political reward for doing so. They are therefore likely to
respond favorably to the lobbying demands of managerial organizations for
changes in legal proposals. Alternatively, politicians may simply delegate the
details of complex governance issues to informal groups in which managers are
well-represented. These informal groups may write rules that are incorporated
into law, or their proposed self-regulatory codes may preempt the making of
law altogether, resulting in informal institutionalization. Either way, these are
avenues for managers to influence the rules of collective governance that depend
on their expertise and the deference of politicians to that expertise.

This asymmetry of expertise and the cost of redressing it structure the quiet
politics of low salience issues in other ways. Journalists, too, defer to managerial
expertise because they often lack their own sources of knowledge about a policy
area. Unlike politicians, journalists do not defer to managerial organizations
because of their concerns about hurting the economy. But they do need to
explain complex topics to readers simply, and so they are prone to rely on the
metaphors and analogies supplied by business leaders. This allows businesses
to influence the framing of political debates when they do occasionally receive
press coverage. As we saw in both the Dutch and the French press coverage
of the politics of corporate control, managers were successful in getting their
frames parroted in the press.

These tools of influence are fragile only because they are a function of public
inattention. When citizens do not care about an issue and are not well-informed
about it, the expertise of managers and the deference shown to them by politicians and the press are important. Yet the value of that expertise as a political
resource declines the more the public holds political parties accountable for
policy outcomes. Politicians do not want to disrupt the economy on whose
performance they remain dependent for reelection, but neither do they want to
risk the wrath of voters when voters are mobilized on a political issue. Journalists, less dependent than politicians on the state of the economy and therefore
less beholden to managerial expertise, will quickly seek other sources of information if it becomes clear that the public is interested in a policy issue. What
the changing value of salience does is convince politicians and the press to
invest in developing their own, alternative sources of information. That makes
them less dependent on managerial organizations, which makes managerial
organizations less influential than under conditions of low political salience.

One way that the public has come to care about issues of corporate governance is through accounting and pay scandals. The Enron scandal is the best-known of these, and I discussed the effect of Enron on American politics of executive pay in Chapter 6. Scandals are particularly bad news for managerial organizations because they not only make an issue highly salient; they also undercut the claims of privileged expertise on which business so often depends for its lobbying capacity. First, events such as Enron can draw the public's attention to an issue and thereby reorient the interests of politicians in such an area. This is what Frank Baumgartner and Bryan Jones call issue intrusion, when a previously inert policy area forces its way onto the political radar of the public.[1] Second, accounting scandals and market crashes highlight failures of business foresight and the potential for conflicts of interest. These failures lead politicians to rely less on business for their information, thereby undercutting one great advantage of managers under low salience politics. Most business organizations maintain formidable lobbying operations, but those operations are as much dependent on their reputation for expertise as on their direct expenditure of money. When this expertise is undermined, the influence of managers on public policy is likely to suffer.

The theory of quiet politics implies that the political power of organized business is insensitive to differences among the political institutions of advanced democracies. To put that point more provocatively, this argument suggests that the power of business in the United States is not a function of the large role of money in politics in the American political system. Institutions may influence what sort of things managers want from politics (i.e., business preferences), but they matter little in determining managers' ability to get what they want from politics (business power).

Previous chapters have considered how variations in political salience and in the character of institutional governance – formal or informal – influence the politics of institutional change and stability in the domain of corporate control. In this chapter I extend the analysis to speculate about how variations in political salience and institutional formality affect politics more broadly and how their interaction affects business power in particular. The intersection of the domains of salience and formality creates a governance space whose different quadrants feature very different political interactions and power resources. This governance space is the subject of the next section. The chapter then uses the governance space to reevaluate the current state of the literature on the scope and limits of business power in democracies. This discussion of how salience and institutional formality influences politics also yields useful implications for debates over the character of institutional change in politics and public policy. A final section reflects on how the recent international financial crisis may affect managerial influence in politics in the new, postcrisis environment.

[1] Jones and Baumgartner (2005).

Salience, Institutional Formality, and the Governance Space

Many current understandings of politics are premised on two questionable assumptions. The first is that politics in democracies takes place through the action of political parties, which take policy positions with an eye to what they think their potential voters want. The second is that all the important decisions about institutional rules are made in legislative arenas. This book has shown that neither of these assumptions accurately characterizes the politics of corporate control. Parties rarely matter in this domain because voters do not care about the issue enough for parties to invest in taking hard positions on it. Moreover, the discussions over institutional alternatives for regimes of corporate governance often take place in nonlegislative and nonregulatory arenas. Sometimes, as in France and Germany during the late 1990s, the real institutional decision makers about regimes of corporate control were actually private blockholders whose opinions showed little evidence of influence by public policy makers. Other times, as in Japan in 2004–2005, new rules of corporate control were drawn up in para-public forums in which managerial interests were well-represented, and in which the opponents to managerial preferences were unrepresented. When rules are made in arenas that are neither legislative nor regulatory, I refer to these as sites of informal institutionalization.[2]

Theories of politics that ignore these distinctions risk assuming that the world of political struggle is reducible to the dynamics we observe in formal institutional arenas when issues have high political salience. As we saw in Chapter 6 in the case of executive remuneration, politics looks very different once voters start paying attention to and caring about an issue. This insight allows us to build on a point emphasized by an earlier generation of political scientists, such as James Q. Wilson and Theodore Lowi: different sorts of policies create different sorts of politics.[3] Wilson focused narrowly on *regulatory* politics and Lowi more broadly on different areas of *policy making*, but both excluded the realm of informal institutions. If many areas of contemporary political struggle actually take place through informal institutions, then this is a serious oversight. We expect modes of political interaction to vary across the possible combinations of salience and formality of institutional governance. For example, where political battles take place through formal institutions under conditions of high political salience, as in some areas of fiscal policy, we expect

---

[2] Thus, this definition of informal institutionalization allows for such institutions to be interpreted and enforced by public authorities (e.g., courts), as in the case of the Japanese Corporate Value Report. Where rules are made in informal arenas but enforceable in formal ones, I argue that the interest of political scientists should be focused more on the locus of rule making than on the mechanism of rule enforcement. Both are, of course, important for social outcomes. But, if rules are indeed sticky, then it is the origin of their development and the arena in which they are recast that should most interest us. I owe this clarification to comments by Kathleen Thelen and Elisabetta Gualmini.

[3] Wilson (1980), Lowi (1964).

TABLE 7.1. *Political Salience, Institutional Formality, and the Governance Space*

	Informal Rules Primary	Formal Rules Primary
High Salience	Social partner bargaining	Partisan contestation
Low Salience	Private interest governance	Bureaucratic network negotiation

partisan contestation. Where political battles instead take place through informal institutions under conditions of low political salience, as in the issue area of corporate control, this book has shown we should expect private interest governance led by business organizations. Table 7.1 arrays the four potential intersections between salience and formality, which I call the governance space. Each quadrant of the governance space features a characteristic mode of political interaction. These four modes of political interaction involve different arenas of conflict, different sources of political advantage, and different central actors.

In the northeast quadrant of the space, where rules are laws and voters are interested in the outcomes, partisan contestation is the likely mode of political interaction. For high salience issues such as taxes and welfare spending, the rules that matter are formally inscribed as laws, and political parties fight over them in legislatures and through periodic electoral competition. The arena of struggle is the parliament as well as the court of public opinion, as parties battle to secure support in the electorate to be able to pass their preferred laws. The valuable power resources in this quadrant are legislative seats and public support. And the central actors are political parties, which are designed both to build electoral programs and facilitate the passage of laws. The importance of this quadrant is hard to overstate – it is where the rubber meets the road in democracy and where most of the titanic political clashes take place. Yet, much of the regulation of democratic capitalism happens in the other quadrants, and the characteristics of politics and policy change in those quadrants are likely to be quite different.

Corporate control, as we saw in earlier chapters of this book, is in most countries a low salience affair governed primarily by informal rules. That is to say, it is an area characterized by private interest governance. Managerial organizations tend to dominate in this quadrant because the arena of conflict often comprises a group of representatives drawn disproportionately from managerial interests. Thus, the outcome is simply derivative of the arena, in which managers are always the elephant in the room. Expertise is a preeminent power resource because of the deference extended to managers by politicians and reporters as a result of their expert knowledge. This deference is often what keeps informal institutionalization the primary mode of governance. The central actors are those with the resources and interest to acquire this information, namely large company representatives: their managers, their associations, and their blockholders. The concentrated interest of senior managers in the content of formal regulation in this area, combined with their informational advantage vis-à-vis politicians, has led other scholars to acknowledge the like-lihood that business interests are likely to prevail even when regulation is formal.[4] We have seen that institutional informality powerfully reinforces this tendency by further weakening the opponents of the institutional incumbents in private interest governance.

How does low salience politics vary between conditions of informal and formal institutionalization? In other words, what is the effect of moving from the southwest to the southeast quadrant of Table 7.1? From the perspective of social actors, moving from informal to formal governance under low salience has one advantage and one cost. The advantage is that formalizing negotia-tions through law may help to reduce problems of coordination and collective action.[5] Government bureaucracies gain in strength in this quadrant because they can become arbiters of disagreement among competing social actors. The ability to convince politicians and bureaucrats – lobbying capacity – is there-fore even more important here than in the southwest quadrant, where much negotiation happens beyond the reach of direct state authority. Because formal governance is happening under conditions of low salience in this quadrant, it has little to offer in terms of an electoral payoff. Politicians in the legislature are therefore content to delegate governance to bureaucracies. Social actors know this, and they work to establish ongoing ties with the bureaucracy in charge of regulating them. Expertise is the important power resource within bureaucratic policy networks, since most negotiations still take place out of the public eye. State bureaucracies prioritize the input of social actors by the expertise they bring to the table. Interest associations develop expertise, long-term ties with each other, and with state officials in the policy domains in which they are interested. Thus, the characteristic mode of political interaction in this quad-rant is negotiation among the members of policy networks organized around bureaucracies.[6]

An illustrative example of low salience formal politics is the making of vocational training policy in eastern Germany since German unification. Ever since the transition to capitalism, eastern German companies have not been able to offer enough apprenticeship places to absorb the number of would-be apprentices on the eastern German youth labor market. Much of the onus for experimenting with policies to convince these firms to engage in apprenticeship training has therefore fallen on eastern German state governments. Unlike western Germany, where many parts of firm-based training are devolved to corporatist negotiations between unions and employers alone, governments are deeply involved in the making of all aspects of vocational training in eastern

---

[4] Wilson (1980), Gormley (1986).

[5] Knight (1992).

[6] This quadrant of the governance space features not only the bureaucracy as the source of formal regulation, but also the courts. I concentrate in the remaining discussion on bureaucracies, but the point about expertise as an important power resource also holds, *mutatis mutandis*, for the case of courts.

Germany. In a comparison of several eastern German states, I showed in a previous book that employers' associations and unions in both states were involved in formal advisory bodies where they advocated the same sort of subsidy policies.[7] They converged in their policy preferences not because their interests were identical – they were not – but because both actors recognized that the best way to use state subsidy money was to target it at the firms that wanted to train but could not. The ties between these groups, and their credibility with state-level bureaucrats, were fundamentally a product of their ability to deliver expertise in a policy area. In a study of eastern German state-level economic governance, Stephen Padgett observed the same phenomenon: "a high level of policy expertise in most economic groups means that dialogue is constructed between policy specialists, rather than between policymaker and lobbyist. Technocratic exchange is largely independent of partisanship[.]"[8] Unlike in higher salience areas, where parties play a role in determining which policies get adopted because voters care about their policy positions, issues of low salience that are subject to primarily formal rule making are left to bureaucratic expertise. The influence of interest groups, including business groups, is in large part a product of their ability to bring expert analysis to the table, because that is the most relevant currency in convincing state bureaucrats.

In marked contrast, the quadrant combining high salience with informal institutions, located in the northwest part of the governance space, is a volatile political area because voters care about it but states do not directly intervene in rule making. Given high salience, it is difficult for the group with the most economic power – business – to capture issue domains lying in this quadrant. Voters care too much about the rules made in this area, which is what its high political salience denotes. Competing interest groups or associations are the likely actors in this quadrant. Only groups with claims to represent the important constituencies on either side of such issues have a plausible mandate to maintain private interest governance of this form. In most countries, the only groups with such claims are employers' associations and labor unions, which is why the characteristic mode of this quadrant is social partner bargaining. These social partners disagree on many points, but they both have an interest in limiting their conflicts in order to prevent state intervention. If the struggle actually moves to parliament, there is a risk the policy domain could be headed toward a permanently higher degree of formal regulation, with a consequent diminution of social partner influence.

The most noteworthy feature of high salience in combination with informal institutions is that it induces powerful private actors to compromise in order to avoid the possibility of unilaterally imposed state decrees. The tacit threat of state intervention changes the dynamic of negotiation, as Fritz Scharpf has observed.[9] The high salience of this area makes social partner bargaining

---

[7] Culpepper (2003).
[8] Padgett (1999: 161).
[9] Scharpf (1997).

conflictual, as organizational leaders are more likely to play to their base than they are under low political salience. This is because the mass members of social organizations care about high salience issues and hold their leaders to account for their positions on them, just as they do for political parties. At the same time, though, interest associations have a shared interest in keeping the state out of their regulatory arena in order to preserve their own bargaining prerogatives.[10] Thus, there are two distinct arenas of conflict, which have contrasting logics. On the one hand, social partners hold hard-line positions and challenge each other in the court of public opinion, just as do political parties. On the other hand, they are often involved in iterated negotiations with each other, through the informal institutions they jointly govern. The public posturing of the social partners is disciplined by involvement in a repeated interaction with their opponents – and, crucially, with a shared set of interests in maintaining institutional informality. The power resources of this quadrant are therefore two: support in public opinion is a powerful weapon in trying to force concessions out of a partner, but the mutual dependence on each other to keep private governance out of state hands is a resource that always helps the weaker bargaining partner. Social partner bargaining is almost always characterized by a joint preference to keep the state out – for which both partners need each other to justify their governance of such a high salience area.

Many of the institutional reforms orchestrated through social pacts in Europe in the 1990s fell in the quadrant that combines high salience and informal institutions. Although these social pacts often involved representatives of the state, alongside employers' associations and unions, they generally resulted in institutions based on social partner agreement, rather than new laws. In other words, they generated new informal institutions. And most such deals were front-page news, the epitome of high political salience. For example, in their respective national negotiations that led to social pacts that reformed national wage setting, Irish and Italian business associations both wanted to establish new institutions of bargaining that would deliver wage restraint.[11] Facing weak governments and unions hobbled by high unemployment, these employers' associations were unquestionably the strongest actors in the negotiations over new bargaining institutions. Yet they were unable to impose their preferred institutional solution on unions because of their commitment to informal governance in cooperation with unions. In both cases, employers' associations and unions carried on battles simultaneously through the press and through private negotiations. They eventually came to agreements recognizing shared understandings about the character of the international economy and the role of bargained wage restraint in supporting the competitiveness of

---

[10] Some social partners – especially those whose bargaining capacity is weak – may have more to gain by state intervention than they lose in conceding their autonomy in bargaining. They may then be willing to accede to greater state intervention on a permanent basis. Interest groups are aware, however, that state intervention may bring with it unexpected consequences.

[11] Baccaro and Lim (2007).

national companies. Once this common knowledge was established among the social partners, employers' associations were constrained by it because it tied them to shared assumptions about the nature of the unions as their bargaining partners.[12] Committed to keeping the governance of wage setting a negotiated institution among themselves and union leaders, Irish and Italian business leaders were unable to ignore the unions or capitalize fully on their power to impose tough terms on them because they, like the unions, preferred to keep institutions informal. Business leaders in the Irish and Italian cases were not in a low salience bargaining environment that would have allowed them to rely on their power resources to impose any agreement they chose. And the absence of formal rule making on this high salience issue meant that it was not located in the northeast quadrant of the governance space, and that political parties were unable to be the prime movers in the institutional agreements reached in these social pacts.

In short, different combinations of political salience and institutional formality will result in systematically different modes of political interaction. This book has assessed these propositions in depth only in the southwest quadrant of Table 7.1. A test of these claims for the northwest and southeast quadrants is far beyond the scope of this concluding discussion. Yet the following two sections of this chapter will illustrate the potential analytical utility of these dimensions for illuminating important, contested questions in the study of politics. The next section reconsiders the claims of the literature on business power in light of variations in salience and formality. The following section then explores current debates over the politics of liberalization and institutional change in comparative politics. In each of the two areas, understanding the political implications of variations in political salience and institutional formality helps make sense of abiding disagreements in these important areas of inquiry.

Political Science and Business Power

Scholarship in comparative politics has never before focused as heavily as it now does on the role of business in explaining national varieties of capitalism. Yet the study of business power is currently more neglected than it has been for the last half century.[13] What lies behind this paradox? On the one hand, past theories of the structural power of business have been marginalized in the face of careful studies showing how often business organizations fail to get what they want in politics.[14] On the other hand, most political scientists have followed the analytical stance adopted by Kathleen Thelen in eschewing

---

[12] Culpepper (2008).

[13] Robert Dahl published an article in the *American Political Science Review* in 1959 in which he reenergized the study of business in politics, claiming that the interaction of business and politics presented "no dearth of important and even urgent questions. But political scientists do not, by and large, seem to be searching for answers" (p. 34).

[14] Vogel (1987), Smith (2000).

"the language of 'power' in favor of identifying the interests and coalitions on which institutions are founded [because], unlike power, actors and their interests are more tractable empirically."[15] This choice has been highly productive in terms of understanding the coalitions that built and sustain modern varieties of capitalist institutions.[16] However, the concentration on business interests and their structural foundations has had an unintentional byproduct: a neglect of the mechanisms by which business converts its interests into policies. Does business get what it wants from politics because it forms coalitions with other groups and gets a majority in the legislature, as in coalitional theory? Or because political parties of the right protect it, as in partisan theory? Or by influencing public discourse in order to move the median voter toward its preferred position? Each of these positions has its proponents, but most of the analytical attention is on *why* business wants what it wants (usually a result of favored product market strategies and existing institutional endowments), not *how* business organizations go about getting what they want from politics.

I have argued that the arenas of political contestation depend on whether the political salience of a given issue is high or low and whether or not its institutions of governance are primarily formal or informal. This insight is relevant to debates on how business tries to exercise influence, because it suggests that such influence is dependent on the quadrant in which political activity is located. When business leaders try to influence tax policy, they have to work through political parties or by persuading public opinion. The tools of quiet politics do not work in the arenas of institutional choice dictated by high salience and formal institutions. When they want to influence issues of high political salience that are governed through informal institutions, their ability to get what they want is constrained by the threat of potential state intervention. Thus, they can bargain hard with unions or other interest groups, but the joint imperative for keeping governance informal dilutes their power. As a general rule, salience is more important for determining the degree of business influence than is institutional formality. Business has to work with allies in high salience arenas, and working with allies forces business organizations to make compromises.

Developing a theory of why some issues become politically salient and why others do not is well beyond the scope of this book. But given the important differences between politics in domains of high and low salience, a skeptical reader might well ask: if it is true that business is advantaged in low salience politics, why does business not strive to make the issues it cares about as low salience as possible? We have seen in earlier chapters that the organizations representing the managers of large companies prefer to work behind the scenes, knowing that is where their influence is likely to be greatest. The fact is, however, that business organizations have few tools to ensure low salience. If business organizations refuse to talk about an issue, that rarely stops an ambitious reporter

---

[15] Thelen (2004: 32–33).
[16] Katzenstein (1985), Crouch and Streeck (1997), Hall and Soskice (2001).

or politician from trying to exploit the issue to acquire either newspaper readers or votes. Business does not generally have the tools to keep the press from
covering issues in which people might be interested, except in Hollywood con-
spiracy movies. Business organizations can certainly spend money to try to
raise the profile of issues on which they believe voters will share their point of
view or to try to influence the way in which the press covers certain issues. Of
all the weapons in its armory, though, business organizations do not possess
the low salience magic wand.

These observations are consistent with the findings of scholars who have
investigated the effects of business power, particularly in the United States,
and have found it to be limited. The classic work of Charles Lindblom on the
instrumental and structural sources of business power is the reference point for
much of this discussion.[17] Lindblom argued that business possessed substantial advantages in the capacity to lobby and to influence public opinion, as the
result of the resources at its disposal. Lindblom's study is best remembered for
its notion of the structural power of business, in which the possibility of business disinvestment is sufficient to take certain issues off the table of political
consideration. Time and evidence have not been kind to this thesis. Lindblom's
critics have taken him to task for identifying both the power resources of business and its structural advantages, but not then explaining why, if business is so
powerful, it still loses so many legislative battles in the capitalist democracies.[18]
A successful theory of business power must explain why business loses as well
as why business wins, and Lindblom's work does not.

Studies of American business have not found the influence Lindblom
attributes to business organizations. One of the finest pieces of research in
this vein is Mark Smith's careful empirical study of the power of American
business since World War II. Smith demonstrates that the issues on which business holds an internally unifying position – that is, where companies are largely
united across different sectors on a given political issue – are also those which
tend to have high political salience. If these issues are big enough to unite the
diverse interests of the business community, they are often important enough
to attract widespread public attention. The high salience of these issues helps
mobilize other constituencies, and the incentive of politicians to follow the
votes does the rest, much as I have argued. Thus, Smith shows that a mobilized
public dampens the effect of the monetary advantage held by business in the
political arena.[19] The funding of political campaigns appears to have a weak
effect. This is consistent with the finding of other scholars that money spent
on lobbying is rarely predictive of which side will win in American legislative battles.[20] When business is unified, issues are likely of high salience, and
business loses in these arenas routinely.

---

[17] Lindblom (1977).
[18] Wilson (1980), Vogel (1987).
[19] Cf. Hacker and Pierson (2010).
[20] Baumgartner et al. (2009).

Smith's insight is undoubtedly correct. The structural power of capital is attenuated by the electoral incentives facing legislators. In the United States, where money is often thought to exert more influence in politics than elsewhere, even money spent on lobbying does not buy success for business groups in high salience environments. The structure of electoral democracy restrains business in these situations, more than the structural power of business restrains democracy. The greatest influence business exerted, in Smith's study, was in its attempt to shape public opinion more broadly by funding conservative think tanks in Washington: "a unified business community most effectively gains influence over policy not by working against citizen control of government but rather by working through it."[21]

Should we therefore dispense with the notion of business as being a special interest group in democratic politics? Is it just an interest group like any other?[22] The evidence in this book suggests not. Lindblom and Smith are both right. Organized business does benefit from the deference of politicians, when voters are not paying attention. And their lobbying capacity is a formidable tool in this circumstance. But, as Smith claims, the power of business must be exercised through different channels when an issue acquires high political salience. Business organizations must work through the democratic process, which means acquiring allies and persuading voters. Smith's methodological move – of looking at business only when it is unified – is a sound way to test the question, "Does business win when it is unified?" It is not, however, the only way to try to assess the political power of business. In this book I have focused on business interests as being the collective preferences of the senior managers of the largest companies. These managers have disproportionate impact on peak associations of employers – that is, those associations that combine small and large companies. They also have their own direct lobbying power as well as specialized organizations of large firms (such as the AFEP in France and the VEUO in the Netherlands). Even these associations have membership that is divided in its political opinion among different factions. But those factions that succeed in dominating the organizations have powerful political tools at their disposal, even though business was not unified behind a single position. And, crucially, they faced a very different playing field when issues were not of high political salience.

Expertise and lobbying capacity are the key resources in issue domains characterized by low political salience, whether they are governed by formal or informal institutions. As observed previously, the bureaucratic network negotiations that characterize domains of low salience and formal institutions involve ongoing exchanges among interest group representatives and representatives of the state. As long as the area is of low salience, politicians delegate these questions to bureaucrats. Business organizations are typically expert in the areas

---

[21] Smith (2000: 195).
[22] Vogel (1987).

of most concern to them and state bureaucrats tend to rely on this expertise. Governments in most industrial countries undertake a vast amount of activity; citizens pay attention to only a very small proportion of that activity. This means that most policy systems regulated by states are dominated by the members of the vested interests that are involved in the details of their governance, as Frank Baumgartner and Bryan Jones have shown in their work on the different policy subsystems in the United States.[23] Political salience draws the attention of politicians to a policy subsystem and can radically change it. Most subsystems, though, simply never receive this sort of attention. Given this situation, business interests are well placed to exercise important influence in these policy subsystems. This is not primarily because of the structural power to disinvest, which Lindblom emphasized. It is instead because they know the facts on the ground, and that expertise is extremely valuable in negotiating with other members of the policy subsystem. On the rare occasions when politicians turn their attention to typically low salience areas, they enter with an asymmetry of expertise vis-à-vis the representatives of business. Here, the tools of quiet politics are of great use to business organizations.

Of course, a bureaucratic policy network is still an area in which the state is the formal rule setter. Thus, informal institutions with low salience are even more likely to result in disproportionate business influence because these are arenas in which private interests make rules directly, without working through state regulators. Opponents to the existing institutional structure do not even have a chance to express their views because they are usually excluded from these forums. And, under the assumption of low salience, there is no credible threat of state intervention. Why challenge business about how best to run business if the public does not vote on the basis of these issues? This is a losing bet for most politicians and they rarely take it.

The foregoing considerations suggest that we can order the different domains of governance in a linear fashion to infer the likely political influence of business organizations versus political parties. Salience trumps formality because governing parties are often in a position to expand the ambit of formal regulation if voters demand it. Other things equal, we expect parties to be most influential the more we observe high salience and formality. Symmetrically, we expect business organizations to be most influential in domains of low salience and institutional informality. Figure 7.1 summarizes this relationship.

Figure 7.1 illuminates what most interest group actors and politicians already know: business is more likely to win political battles when voters are not paying attention than when they are. Similarly, political parties are more likely to intervene on the issues voters care about than on those voters do not care about. I have explored the ways in which the quiet politics of low salience differs from the noisy politics of high salience, and the reasons for which quiet politics makes business organizations more likely to succeed in achieving their political objectives. But the issue of corporate control is extreme, in that it is

---

[23] Baumgartner and Jones (1993), Jones and Baumgartner (2005).

Business Influence Increases

High Salience	High Salience	Low Salience	Low Salience
Formal Institutions	Informal Institutions	Formal Institutions	Informal Institutions

Political Party Influence Increases

FIGURE 7.1. Political Parties, Business, and Determinants of Political Influence

so rarely of high salience. Other issue areas are not so categorically either of high or low salience – their salience varies over time. Their governance may also shift between formal and informal institutions over time.

We therefore expect political actors to try to choose an arena of conflict that favors their strengths. In other words, this table highlights the likelihood of forum shifting: political actors trying to move from a less favorable to a more favorable box in this table. If business cannot win a dispute over new environmental regulations passed by a legislature – a conflict that takes place in the high salience, formal institutional box where business is least influential in comparison with political parties – perhaps it will fare better by shifting its attention to questions of implementation (through the bureaucracy) or judicial interpretation (through the courts). If increases in salience are only temporary, then business organizations should expect to do better by conserving resources spent on a legislative battle they are likely to lose, unless they have lots of allies. Instead, their ability to wield disproportionate influence – and so not to have to rely on allies – goes up if they can ride out the storm of public attention and shift to a technical battle over bureaucratic regulations that is uninteresting to newspaper readers. Similarly, policy entrepreneurs and interest groups will try to heighten the salience of an issue when they think they can mobilize broad support in the populace.[24] They are practicing forum shifting on the calculus that they are more likely to win when they can convince political parties that their potential voters care about an issue.

Conceiving of politics this way suggests a channel out of the cul-de-sac into which debates over business power have led. Business may indeed have a structural advantage, as Lindblom argued, but the value of deference is conditional on public attention and concern about an issue. Business power is a constant, but only in high salience, informally governed institutional arenas. Moving to other arenas causes business power to vary – and, other things being equal, the higher the salience of an issue, the weaker the hand of business. When political salience is high, the special advantages of business shrink to insignificance. Whether or not business gets what it wants or not under the

---

[24] Kollman (1998).

glare of the public spotlight is a function of beliefs in the general population and whether managerial interests are protected by a party of the right. The debates over executive pay in Chapter 6 revealed that even parties of the right will throw their business allies under the bus once the cost of supporting them becomes too high.

Yet Lindblom's arguments about structural power are all too apt for areas of low salience. Business brings a certain expertise in this area, and the expertise produces deference from politicians because politicians know their chances of reelection hang partly on the performance of the economy. Where the press has not invested in developing its own expertise, business also can influence press framing of issues of concern to it. Journalists seek out experts to make stories readily comprehensible to their readers, and when business has the most relevant expertise, it is likely to get press coverage that provides ample exposition of its point of view.

Taking business power as a variable, whose value depends on the quadrant in which political struggles are conducted, allows us to reconsider the influence of business in the United States.[25] It is often alleged in the popular press and by scholars that the role of money in American elections leads to an especially influential voice for business in politics in the United States, in comparison with other advanced industrial countries.[26] The argument about governance laid out here suggests that money spent on campaigns is merely an additional factor that reinforces the existing tools of quiet politics. When the public is not paying attention to issues, politicians will defer to business interests anyway,

[25] One very important recent debate in this field took place over the origins of New Deal social policy in the United States, and its protagonists were Peter Swenson (2004a and b) and Jacob Hacker and Paul Pierson (2002, 2004). Hacker and Pierson argued that the New Deal was a product of a steep decline in structural business power in the United States during the 1930s. Swenson argued contrariwise that the New Deal was a product of the shifting interests of American business with respect to the provision of old age insurance. Hacker and Pierson adopted a structural argument, in which business lost its exit option when the locus of social policy debate shifted from state capitals to Washington, DC. Swenson argued not about the mechanisms of employer power (*how* they got what they wanted from policy, in Washington or at the state capital level), but about how the *interests* of American segmentalists corresponded to the features of the old age insurance actually adopted through the New Deal, inferring that because their interests were close to the policy adopted, those business interests must have constrained policymakers.

Like Hacker and Pierson, I argue that business power is a variable, not a constant; like Swenson, I argue that political economic structures (in my case, works councils; in his case, labor markets) strongly influence the preferences of business groups. Such debates about business power are important for the analysis of democratic politics, and they can best be resolved empirically by identifying the key episodes of policy making and the tools of influence that different interest groups bring to bear. The theoretical expectation of my work is that business is likely to lose legislative battles when discredited by a high salience economic crisis, such as the Great Depression. The question one must investigate in this sort of dispute is whether the ability of business interests to influence policy through informal forums was great enough to counteract their weak influence in the halls of Congress during the New Deal.

[26] Hacker and Pierson (2010).

faced with business arguments that state intervention could adversely affect the economy. It is business expertise and lobbying capacity – rather than campaign donations per se – that give business this seat at the table. When issues acquire high salience, politicians in the United States will follow public opinion, no matter how much business has donated to political campaigns.

One hypothesis that emerges from this line of inquiry is that what makes the United States so friendly to business interests, in comparative perspective, is not its election campaigns, but the frequent use of courts to resolve disputes over public policy implementation. Courts, like bureaucracies, are informal forums in which actors battle over technical issues requiring both issue competence and legal expertise. In court battles, the monetary advantage of business is likely to pay big dividends, because the complex issues that are resolved through the court system may require thousands of hours of legal bills. American courts are aware of what issues are salient.[27] But they do not generally have the political incentives of parties to respond to public opinion when the public cares strongly about an issue. Courts usually resolve political struggles on questions of expertise and interpretation, not of public opinion. It is only when Congress threatens to make new laws in response to court decisions that the logic of high salience can reassert itself once issues have been thrown into the court system for resolution.

This is but an illustrative argument and these hypothesized relationships need to be subjected to careful empirical scrutiny. All too often, scholarship in political science pays close attention only to the quadrant of high salience and formal institutions. If these other quadrants have their own distinctive logic, political analysis needs to explore the less well-known features of political contestation in the remaining quadrants. At the very least, this framework of analysis promises to restart a productive discussion on the scope and limits of business power in contemporary democracies. It may well also shed some light on current debates over how institutions change in politics. That is the subject to which we turn now.

Political Salience and Institutional Change

The dimensions of salience and institutional formality structure political con-testation and the power resources available to social actors in predictable ways. Given the patterns of political interaction we expect across the different quad-rants of the governance space, we might also ask whether these quadrants are subject to different logics of reform. It is unlikely that each quadrant has a unique logic of institutional change. However, I argue that processes of institu-tional change that involve a shift from low salience to high salience quadrants are especially likely to be characterized by radical discontinuity. Where salience is stable, at either a low or a high level, I hypothesize that the gradual processes

---

[27] Epstein and Segal (2000).

of institutional change discussed by historical institutionalists are more likely to prevail.

The idea of punctuated equilibrium as a model of institutional change has been heavily debated in recent theoretical work in political science. Punctuated equilibrium describes a process by which long periods of stasis are broken by short, sharp periods of radical change. Political scientists have been attracted to the model because it corresponds to the notion that institutions structure politics in relatively durable ways and only change with difficulty. Both rational choice and historical institutionalists use institutional variables to explain the long continuities that we observe in politics. Rational choice institutionalists look to equilibrium arrangements in which political actors settle into a stable pattern of interaction from which they have no incentive to emerge, given the existing allocation of resources.[28] Historical institutionalists focus on path dependence, the process by which choices made in an earlier period make it difficult to switch paths in later years. Each quality should make institutions extremely resistant to change. Empirically, though, the real world offers much more change than these models would lead us to expect.[29]

Confronted by this gap between theory and reality, scholars in both analytical traditions have developed strategies for making their mechanisms of stability equally persuasive in explaining institutional change. Rationalists, confronting the critique that equilibrium analysis depicts a world in which change must be exogenous to the core model, have argued for a focus on quasi-parameters: variables that can be considered fixed and exogenous in the short run, but whose value over time may be affected by the implications of a given institution.[30] Changes in these quasi-parameters brought about by regular institutional functioning can reinforce or undermine an established rule, thus making the process of change endogenous. Historical institutionalists, whose characteristic concern has always been the unfolding of complex processes over time, zero in on the ways in which institutional layering leads to an evolution – an endogenous change – in the functions and implications of a given institution.[31] Thus, both sets of institutionalists seek the sources of incremental change within the same set of structural variables that lead them to predict long periods of institutional stability. Particularly among historical institutionalists, this has led to a disdain for models of change based on punctuated equilibrium: "equating incremental with adaptive and reproductive *minor* change, and *major* change with, mostly exogenous, disruption of continuity, makes excessively high demands on 'real' change to be recognized as such and tends to reduce most or all observable changes to adjustment for the purpose of stability."[32]

---

[28] North (1990).
[29] Thelen (1999), Crouch (2003), Weyland (2008).
[30] Greif and Laitin (2004).
[31] Thelen (2004).
[32] Streeck and Thelen (2005: 8).

The vogue within this school of analysis has been to characterize the myriad processes by which institutions can evolve incrementally and to show that these incremental innovations have a cumulatively transformative effect. Jacob Hacker, for example, has coined the notion of policy drift. Drift refers to "changes in the operation or effects of policies that occur without significant changes in those policies' structures."[33] For Hacker, the American welfare regime has not updated its policies in keeping with its original goals of socializing risk. The policy regime appears stable because drastic change has not occurred in the formal rules of the game, but patterns of private and public coverage of health and retirement risks have accumulated in a way that marks a significant increase, or "privatization," in the level of individual risk. Kathleen Thelen writes about two such processes in her analysis of how skill regimes have changed in several advanced capitalist countries over time.[34] One is the process of layering by which new institutional elements are grafted on to preexisting structures, thus changing their function over time.[35] The other is the process of conversion, by which old institutions are put to new ends. One prominent example in her study shows how the incorporation of organized labor as a partner in the governance of the German training system changed the functional and distributive implications of the system.[36] Through each of these processes, historical institutionalists find that apparently stable policy regimes in fact change in important ways.

The voting public is rarely an actor in such changes. This is strange, given the ample evidence that many policies respond to the preferences expressed in public opinion.[37] Most of these gradual institutional transformations appear to emerge instead from a set of deals whose ramifications only become clear over time. The implication in some of this work is that such changes take place because powerful actors want to avoid the veto points of political systems.[38] Incorporating political salience into such analysis would allow scholars to clarify two distinct political processes, which historical institutionalist analysis sometimes conflates. First, there is the issue of unintended consequences, where upstream changes to policy regimes have downstream effects that few actors initially foresaw. Because the effects of these changes are hard to anticipate, it is easy to understand why the public would not care about them. Yet this scholarship sometimes makes a second claim: that these institutional mechanisms are part of a deliberate political strategy of policy subversion, as in Hacker's argument that American conservatives have gradually undermined the public insurance of private risks through the mechanism of policy drift.[39] Particularly in cases involving important social policies, which are generally of high salience

---

[33] Hacker (2004: 246).

[34] Thelen (2004).

[35] Cf. Schickler (2001).

[36] Thelen (2004), Streeck and Thelen (2005).

[37] Soroka and Wlezien (2010).

[38] Hacker (2004 and 2005), Hacker and Pierson (2010), Mahoney and Thelen (2010).

[39] Hacker (2004).

to a large number of voters, institutionalist analysis needs to pay attention to the question of why public attention was *not* drawn to the issue, because such voter pressure can almost always stop reforms in their tracks. The political opponents of institutional change know the power of public pressure as well as anyone. So it is important to ask why they do not draw on their trump card of mobilizing the public against these changes. It is often true that institutions have an internal logic of their own that unfolds beyond the reach of voters. But institutionalist analysis would be more persuasive still if its practitioners were always attentive to the ways in which potentially blocking minorities were not mobilized around issues of high political salience.

Scholars of public policy criticize the structural premises of institutionalist models on similar grounds, and their analysis leads them to give a much more prominent role to radical change in their analysis.[40] These scholars observe that policy subsystems can have autonomous logics of functioning, but that public attention to issues can subject any area to the possibility of radical change.[41] For this group of scholars, punctuated equilibrium *is* the most accurate representation of democratic politics. The microfoundations of this work lie in cognitive psychology and behavioral economics and the focus is on how political systems process information.[42] Jones and Baumgartner's work on the American political system shows that punctuated equilibrium is exactly how we should expect political institutions to change because organizations update their information "with difficulty, sporadically and episodically."[43] When these systems finally react, they are indeed likely to overreact, as politicians rush to "do something" in response to a long ignored or discounted problem and new information. Thus, looking at the ultimate index of government action – the budget – Jones and Baumgartner find strong support for the proposition that most policy areas in the United States have been subject to substantial continuity, with a few outliers experiencing radical discontinuity. Kurt Weyland, examining the Latin American process of neoliberal reform, uses prospect theory to explain processes of "fitful reform." Politicians are risk averse until crisis strikes, which puts them in the domain of losses, where they suddenly become risk seeking and open to new ideas for policy reform. Here again, long periods of failure to reform are followed by bursts of radical change. The foundations of both models are not of stylized interest maximization, but of the empirical proclivities of human decision making. And they are consistent not with subtle change over time, but with episodes of radical change coupled with long periods of stability.

Some might say that these different perspectives result from different objects of study: Jones and Baumgartner write about the overall policy system of the United States, while historical institutionalists typically write about changes in

---

[40] Weyland (2008).
[41] Jones and Baumgartner (2005).
[42] Jones (1994), Weyland (2002), Weyland (2008).
[43] Jones and Baumgartner (2005: 17).

one policy area over a period of time. This is incorrect. Weyland, using similar analytical bases to Jones and Baumgartner, finds the politics of economic policy and liberalization in welfare states in Latin America to be characterized by punctuated equilibrium.[44] The contributors to an influential recent volume by Wolfgang Streeck and Kathleen Thelen are writing about patterns of liberalization in economic policy and welfare states in the United States and Europe.[45] These scholars are studying the same thing, albeit in different countries: the politics of liberalization. And the debate is an important arena for the democratic legitimacy of state decisions involving market regulation. As we have seen, institutional change that takes place in the formal, high salience arena involves the public: parties are disciplined by the fact that voters are paying attention to an issue area, and the strategy of party leaders is oriented around staking a claim that makes the party attractive to voters. By contrast, if the politics of liberalization shifts into the shadows of bureaucratic policy networks, there is a much greater risk of liberalization by "stealth."[46] This is the overriding normative concern that appears to motivate the work of the contributors of the volume by Streeck and Thelen and by other important contributions to historical institutionalist scholarship on liberalization.[47]

The missing dimension of political salience helps make sense of this disagreement. Debates over institutional change have been a highly fertile area for work by social scientists in recent years. Yet the concentration on the internal logic of institutions, and the way in which they may evolve over time, should not obscure how they interact with broader patterns of political struggle. When political scientists write books about institutional change within a given policy area over time, they have a natural tendency to consider these as *the* political dynamics of institutional change. If variation in political salience has the regular effects on governance domains that I have claimed, then the character of institutional change should vary when a policy issue moves from low to high salience. High salience institutional change in the formal domain is likely to involve political parties who are responsive to public opinion, as Jones and Baumgartner (and many others) argue. When public opinion creates incentives for these parties to deal with an issue, long-standing compromises can be shattered and radical change is easily imaginable. The stability of issue salience should instead involve glacially shifting power dynamics within apparently stable configurations, as Streeck and Thelen argue. There is no single politics of liberalization that unites these sorts of institutional change, because the arenas of struggle and the actors are so different.[48]

Rather than seeking a single logic of institutional change, institutional scholarship may best be served by incorporating the public as an actor in models of

[44] Weyland (2008).
[45] Streeck and Thelen (2005).
[46] Gordon and Meunier (2001).
[47] Streeck and Thelen (2005), Scharpf (1999), Hacker and Pierson (2010).
[48] Hall and Thelen (2009).

institutional change. If voters begin to care about an issue that has previously been off the political radar, then punctuated equilibrium is the most likely form of institutional change. This process will be driven by the intervention of vote-seeking politicians who, in combination with a politically mobilized public, are the ingredients of radical policy change. How these forces interact with the conventional institutional forces of inertia is likely to be an important area for future research.

Looking Forward: Business Power after the Crisis

As this book goes to press, organized business around the world faces a dramatically changed political environment. The systematic failures of risk assessment that contributed to the global economic crisis of 2008 highlighted shortcomings in managerial expertise. The realization that many of the financial institutions that had taken on outsized risks were in fact "too big to fail" has necessitated huge public outlays to keep these private companies afloat. These massive managerial failures went hand-in-hand with equally massive pay packages, which has put those pay practices under intense public scrutiny in all the major economies. Business has been rescued from errors largely of its own making, and its reputation for competence and efficiency is in tatters. In the United States and elsewhere, there are loud calls for a new regulatory framework, one that reinserts the state into markets from which it has been retreating for the past thirty years. The new social compact between business and government will look different in each country, of course, but most observers expect that large financial institutions and small hedge funds alike will have to face renewed regulatory oversight. Many indicators suggest that we are living through a period of radical renegotiation of the political status quo, and that organized business sits in a weakened bargaining position.

Do current models of politics help us to understand how we arrived at the present conjuncture, and what the determinants of collective choice in the next chapter of business-government relations will look like? The dominant theoretical approach in political science is to ask how these changes affect the median voter. If a recession makes the median voter poorer, we should expect more redistribution and more regulation of business. The findings of this book suggest that such a crude general prediction is worthless. In issues that achieve high political salience, such as whether the government should intervene in the executive pay setting of firms that receive public money, the prediction of more regulation is the right one. Even there, though, financial companies have rushed to find ways to elude these regulatory strictures, and the future effectiveness of these rules will depend on the extent to which executive pay remains a highly salient issue in American politics.

For issues of risk regulation of the finance sector, public outrage may have a much shorter half-life. If hedge funds are subject to greater regulatory transparency, will the economy lose some of the growth capacity associated with financial innovations introduced by that industry? The answers to such questions turn on expert knowledge, and it is hard to keep such questions in the public eye for long. We should expect much more stringent regulation of those issues that can tap into public outrage, such as CEO pay, than those issues that call for a complex new set of regulations. For this reason, we expect business power to bounce back much more quickly in low salience than high salience areas. There is not one model of politics, but four: depending on the mix of salience and formality involved, we expect business to have differential capacities to resist new regulatory initiatives.

These considerations raise a broader issue about how political scientists contribute to knowledge of politics. Namely, might it make sense to return to a more sustained discussion of power resources in politics? The institutionalist turn in comparative politics produced impressive achievements in how we understand the incentive systems that underlie national varieties of capitalism. We now possess very powerful theoretical elaborations of why certain production strategies lead companies in Germany to prefer different institutional arrangements than companies in the United Kingdom. What we understand less well, as a causal matter, is *how* business wins or loses in battles over institutional change. Structural theories of business power, such as Charles Lindblom's, ultimately failed because they could not provide a compelling account of why business loses as well as why business wins. But a focus on the power resources available to business, as well as to other interest groups, can allow political scientists to return to this question armed with the valuable insights of institutionalist research on capitalist economies.

Capitalist democracies are governed through the complex interaction of political parties, interest groups, and voters. This book has argued that the way to understand the relative power of parties and interest groups is through variations in salience and the formality of institutions in different domains of collective governance. These dimensions interact in predictable ways that privilege some of these actors and disfavor others. All democratic politics does not look alike, and power resources do not transfer easily across different quadrants of the policy space. A renewed attention to power resources seems a fruitful way to marry the advances of institutional political economy with the insight that policy domains have different politics. Ultimately, these political dynamics – and the power resources of different groups – will determine the new, postcrisis balance between states and markets in democratic societies.

Bibliography

Abescat, Bruno, and Corinne Lhaik. 1999. "Bébéar: L'homme qui tire toutes les ficelles." *L'Express*, August 26.

ACCJ (American Chamber of Commerce in Japan). 2005. Comments on the Ronten Kokai of the Corporate Value Study Group.

ACCJ (American Chamber of Commerce in Japan). 2006. ACCJ's Response to the Keidanren's Statement Regarding the ACCJ's Participation in the Triangular Mergers Tax Policy Debate.

Ahmadjian, Christina. 2007. "Foreign Investors and Corporate Governance in Japan." In Masahiko Aoki, Gregory Jackson, and Hideaki Miyajima, eds. *Corporate Governance in Japan: Institutional Change and Organization Diversity*. New York, Oxford University Press, pp. 125–150.

Ahmadjian, Christina L., and Gregory E. Robins. 2005. "A Clash of Capitalisms: Foreign Shareholders and Corporate Restructuring in 1990s Japan." *American Sociological Review* 70(3): 451–471.

Akkermans, Dirk, Hans van Ees, Niels Hermes, Reggy Hooghiemstra, Gerwin Van DerLaan, Theo Postma, and Arjen van Witteloostuijin. 2007. "Corporate Governance in the Netherlands: An Overview of the Application of the Tabaksblat Code in 2004." *Corporate Governance* 15(6): 1106–1118.

Albert, Michel. 1993. *Capitalism vs. Capitalism*. New York, Four Walls Eight Windows.

Allen, Franklin, and Douglas Gale. 2001. *Comparing Financial Systems*. Cambridge, MA, MIT Press.

Amable, Bruno. 2003. *The Diversity of Modern Capitalism*. New York, Oxford University Press.

Amedeo, Fabrice and Elsa Bembaron. 2006. "Nous sommes davantage un acteur qu'une cible." *Le Figaro*, March 24.

Anabtawi, Iman, and Lynn A. Stout. 2005. "An Inside Job." *New York Times*, March 27.

Aoki, Masahiko. 2001. *Toward a Comparative Institutional Analysis*. Cambridge, MA, MIT Press.

Baccaro, Lucio, and Sang-Hoon Lim. 2007. "Social Pacts as Coalitions of 'Weak' and 'Moderate': Ireland, Italy, and South Korea in Comparative Perspective." *European Journal of Industrial Relations* 13(1): 27–46.

Barca, Fabrizio, and Marco Becht, eds. 2001. *The Control of Corporate Europe*. New York, Oxford University Press.

Baron, David P. 1994. "Electoral Competition with Informed and Uninformed Voters." *American Political Science Review*, 88(1): 33–47.

Baum, Matthew A., and Philip B.K. Potter. 2008. "The Relationships between Mass Media, Public Opinion, and Foreign Policy: Toward a Theoretical Synthesis." *Annual Review of Political Science* 11(1): 39–65.

Baumgartner, Frank R., and Bryan D. Jones. 1993. *Agendas and Instability in American Politics*. Chicago, University of Chicago Press.

Baumgartner, Frank R., Jeffrey M. Berry, Marie Hojnacki, David C. Kimball, and Beth L. Leech. 2009. *Lobbying and Policy Change: Who Wins, Who Loses, and Why*. Chicago, University of Chicago Press.

Bebchuk, Lucian A., and Jesse Fried. 2004. *Pay without Performance: The Unfulfilled Promise of Executive Compensation*. Cambridge, MA, Harvard University Press.

Becht, Marco, and Ekkehart Boehmer. 2003. "Voting Control in German Corporations." *International Review of Law and Economics* 23(1): 1–29.

Bembaron, Elsa, and Jacques-Olivier Martin. 2005. "Grâce à l'Europe, notre pays compte plus de gagnants que de perdants." *Le Figaro*, October 28.

Benes, Nicholas, and Masayuki Katsuyama. 2006. "Flex System Finds it Hard to Flex." Unpublished Manuscript. November 18.

Berle, Adolf A., and Gardiner C. Means. 1932 (1991). *The Modern Corporation and Private Property*. Transaction Publishers, New Brunswick, NJ. (Originally published by Harcourt, Brace & World [1932]).

Bernhagen, Patrick, and Thomas Bräuninger. 2005. "Structural Power and Public Policy: A Signaling Model of Business Lobbying in Democratic Capitalism." *Political Studies* 53(1): 43–64.

Bessière, Sabine, and Stéphanie Depil. 2009. "Les Salaires dans les Entreprises en 2007: une forte progression." *INSEE Première* 1235, May (available online at http://www.insee.fr/fr/ffc/ipweb/ip1235/ip1235.pdf).

Block, Donna, and Ron Orol. 2005. "War on Section 404." *The Daily Deal*, June 6.

Börsch, Alexander. 2007. *Global Pressure, National System: How German Corporate Governance is Changing*. Ithaca, NY, Cornell University Press.

Buck, Tobias. 2006. "Doubts Grow on Efficacy of Takeover Directive." *Financial Times*, June 12.

Bunel, Jean. 1995. "La Transformation de la Représentation Patronale en France: CNPF et CGPME." Monograph, Commissariat Général du Plan.

Byrne, John A. 1991. "The Flap over Executive Pay: Investors, Employees, and Academics Are Asking, How Much is Enough?" *BusinessWeek*, May 6.

Callaghan, Helen. 2004. "The Domestic Politics of EU Legislation – British, French and German Attitudes towards Takeover Regulation, 1985–2003." Paper presented at the Conference of Europeanists, March 11–13, 2004, Chicago.

Callaghan, Helen. 2009. "Insiders, Outsiders and the Politics of Corporate Governance: How Ownership Structure Shapes Party Positions in Britain, Germany, and France." *Comparative Political Studies* 42(6): 733–762.

Callaghan, Helen. Forthcoming. "Constrain-Thy-Neighbor Effects as a Determinant of Transnational Interest Group Cohesion." *Comparative Political Studies* 44(8).

Callaghan, Helen, and Martin Höpner. 2005. "European Integration and the Clash of Capitalisms: Political Cleavages over Takeover Liberalization." *Comparative European Politics* 3(3): 307–332.

CCIP (Chambre de Commerce et d'Industrie de Paris). 2002. "Les OPA Communautaires: Propositions de la Chambre de Commerce et d'Industrie de Paris." Position paper.

Chong, Dennis, and James N. Druckman. 2007. "Framing Theory." *Annual Review of Political Science* 10(1): 103–126.

Cioffi, John W. 2002. "Restructuring 'Germany Inc.': The Politics of Company and Takeover Law Reform in Germany and the European Union." *Law and Policy* 24(4): 355–402.

Cioffi, John W. Forthcoming. *Public Law and Private Power: Corporate Governance Reform in the Age of Finance Capitalism.* Ithaca, NY, Cornell University Press.

Cioffi, John W., and Martin Höpner. 2006. "The Political Paradox of Finance Capitalism: Interests, Preferences, and Center-Left Party Politics in Corporate Governance Reform." *Politics & Society* 34(4): 463–502.

Cioppa, Paolo. 2006. "Executive Compensation: The Fallacy of Disclosure." *Global Jurist Topics* 6(3): 1.

Clément, Pascal. 2003. Report on the Reform of Company Law, Assemblée Nationale, October 4.

Clift, Ben. 2007. "French Corporate Governance in the New Global Economy: Mechanisms of Change and Hybridisation within Models of Capitalism." *Political Studies* 55(3): 546–567.

Clift, Ben. 2009. "Second Time as Farce? The EU Takeover Directive, the Clash of Capitalisms and the Hamstrung Harmonisation of European (and French) Corporate Governance." *The Journal of Common Market Studies* 47(1): 55–79.

Clinton, William J. 1991. "The New Covenant: Responsibility and Rebuilding the American Community." Speech at Georgetown University, October 23.

Code de Commerce, Article 225-102-1, [online] Available on legifrance.gouv.fr http://www.legifrance.gouv.fr/affichCodeArticle.do;jsessionid=05FE73D7D08ABFE9BA415ADD89CBA523.tpdjo07v_3?idArticle=LEGIARTI000006224809&cidTexte=LEGITEXT000005634379&dateTexte=20030801.

Comarmond, L. 2002. "Les grands patrons ont accru leur rémunération globale de 36 % en 2000." *Les Échos*, February 8.

Cooley Godward Kronish LLP. 2002. "Changes in NYSE and Nasdaq Listing Requirements Affecting Equity Plans and Executive and Director Compensation." December 12. http://www.cooley.com/news/alerts.aspx?id=37616020.

Cornudet, Cécile, and Etienne Lefebvre. 2009. "Rémunérations des patrons: l'Elysée envisage une première étape réglementaire." *Les Échos*, March 26.

Cowan, Alison Leigh. 1992. "Senators Fault the S.E.C. on Issue of Executive Pay." *New York Times*, February 1.

Cox, Christopher. 2006. Public Remarks at John F. Kennedy School of Government, Harvard University, May 9.

Creswell, Julie. 2006. "Investigations are Sifting Good, Bad, and Only Ugly." *New York Times*, July 25.

Crouch, Colin. 2003. "Institutions within which Real Actors Innovate." In Renate Mayntz and Wolfgang Streeck, eds. *Die Reformierbarkeit der Demokratie.* Frankfurt, Campus Verlag, pp. 71–98.

Crouch, Colin, and Wolfgang Streeck, eds. 1997. *Political Economy of Modern Capitalism.* London, Sage Publications Ltd.

Culpepper, Pepper D. 2003. *Creating Cooperation: How States Develop Human Capital in Europe.* Ithaca, NY, Cornell University Press.

Culpepper, Pepper D. 2005. "Institutional Change in Contemporary Capitalism: Coordinated Financial Systems since 1990." *World Politics* 57(2): 173–199.

Culpepper, Pepper D. 2006. "Capitalism, Coordination, and Economic Change: The French Political Economy since 1985." In Pepper D. Culpepper, Peter A. Hall, and Bruno Palier, eds. *Changing France*. Palgrave Macmillan, Hampshire, England, pp. 29–49.

Culpepper, Pepper D. 2007. "Eppure non si muove: Legal Change, Institutional Stability, and Italian Corporate Governance." *West European Politics* 30(4): 784–802.

Culpepper, Pepper D. 2008. "The Politics of Common Knowledge: Ideas and Institutional Change in Wage Bargaining." *International Organization* 62(1): 1–33.

Dahl, Robert A. 1959. "Business and Politics: A Critical Appraisal of Political Science." *American Political Science Review* 53(1): 1–34.

Davis, Gerald F., and Henrich R. Greve. 1997. "Corporate Elite Networks and Governance Gauges in the 1980s." *American Journal of Sociology* 103(1): 1–37.

Deeg, Richard. 2009. "The Rise of Internal Capitalist Diversity? Changing Patterns of Finance and Corporate Governance in Europe." *Economy & Society* 38(4): 552–579.

De Jong, Abe, Gerard Mertens, and Peter Roosenboom. 2006. "Shareholders' Voting at General Meetings: Evidence from the Netherlands." *Journal of Management and Governance* 10(4): 353–380.

De Jong, Abe, and Ailsa Roell. 2005. "Financing Control in the Netherlands." In Randall K. Morck, ed. *A History of Corporate Governance Around the World: Family Business Groups to Professional Managers*. Chicago, University of Chicago Press, pp. 467–515.

De Jong, Abe, Douglas V. DeJong, Gerard Mertens, and Charles E. Wasley. 2005. "The Role of Self-Regulation in Corporate Governance: Evidence and Implications from the Netherlands." *Journal of Corporate Finance* 11(3): 473–503.

De Kerdrel, Yves. 2003. "Pechiney, victime de la loi des privatisées." *Les Échos*, September 15.

Delacroix, Guillaume. 2009a. "Rémunérations: le code du Medef tarde à produire ses effets." *Les Échos*, March 12.

Delacroix, Guillaume. 2009b. "Les retraites chapeaux davantage taxées en 2010." *Les Échos*, April 23.

Delberghe, Michel. 2007. "Gouvernance après les affaires Forgeard et Zacharias, le patronat publie ses recommandations; Rémunérations des PDG: le Medef exclut toute loi mais appelle à la mesure." *Le Monde*, January 11.

Dew-Becker, Ian. 2008. "How Much Sunlight Does it Take to Disinfect a Boardroom? A Short History of Executive Compensation Regulation." CESifo Working Paper No. 2379, Category 4: Labor Markets. August.

Doering, Herbert. 1995. "Time as a Scarce Resource: Government Control of the Agenda." In Herbert Doering, ed. *Parliaments and Majority Rule in Western Europe*. New York, St. Martin's Press, pp. 223–246.

Dore, Ronald. 2000. *Stock Market Capitalism: Welfare Capitalism: Japan and Germany Versus the Anglo-Saxons*. New York, Oxford University Press.

Doyle, John M. 1991. "Senate Panel Probes Big Rise in Big Pay for Big Bosses." *The Associated Press*, May 15.

Doyle, John M. 1992. "Senate Panel Told Tax Law Not the Way to Fix Big Pay." *The Associated Press*, June 5.

Ducourtieux, Cecile. 2005. "OPA: la France modifie les règles du jeu." *Le Monde*, September 22.

Ducourtieux, C. 2006. "Un grand patron français gagne en moyenne 300 smics." *Le Monde*, December 14.

Dyck, Alexander, David Moss, and Luigi Zingales. 2008. "Media Versus Special Interests." NBER Working Paper No. 14360.

EBC (European Business Council Japan). 2005a. EBC Chairman Presents EBC views on Foreign Direct Investment to the LDP Corporate Governance Committee. Press Release, May 16.

EBC (European Business Council Japan). 2005b. EBC Position Paper: Foreign Direct Investments, May 25.

EBC (European Business Council Japan). 2006. EBC voices concern over government of Japan changing position on triangular mergers. Press Release, December 1.

Eberle, Dagmar and Dorothee Lauter. 2008. "Corporate Governance Codes and the 'Varieties of Capitalism', A Comparison between Germany and Great Britain." Paper presented at the Sixteenth International Conference of Europeanists, Chicago IL, March 6–8.

Edwards, Jeremy, and Marcus Nibler. 2000. "Corporate Governance in Germany: The Role of Banks and Ownership Concentration." *Economic Policy* 15(31): 237–267.

Engelen, Ewald, Martijn Konings, and Rodrigo Fernandez. 2008. "The Rise of Activist Investors and Patterns of Political Responses: Lessons on Agency." *Socio-Economic Review* 6(4): 611–636.

Epstein, Lee, and Jeffrey A. Segal. 2000. "Measuring Issue Salience." *American Journal of Political Science* 44(1): 66–83.

Estevez-Abe, Margarita. 2008. *Welfare and Capitalism in Postwar Japan*. New York, Cambridge University Press.

Fackler, Martin, and Henny Sender. 2004. "Tokyo Court Orders Halt in Planned Bank-Merger Talks." *Wall Street Journal*, July 28.

Fohlin, Caroline. 1999. "Universal Banking in Pre-World War I Germany: Model or Myth?" *Explorations in Economic History*, 36(4): 305–343.

Franks, Julian, and Colin Mayer. 1995. "Ownership and Control." In H. Siebert, ed. *Trends in Business Organization: Do Participation and Cooperation Increase Competitiveness?* Mohr, Tubingen, pp. 171–203.

Freeman, Laurie Anne. 2000. *Closing The Shop: Information Cartels and Japan's Mass Media*. Princeton, NJ, Princeton University Press.

Freeman, Richard B., and Edward P. Lazear. 1995. "An Economic Analysis of Works Councils." In Joel Rogers and Wolfgang Streeck, eds. *Works Councils: Consultation, Representation, and Cooperation in Industrial Relations*. Chicago, University of Chicago Press, pp. 27–50.

Frentrop, Paul. 2002. *A History of Corporate Governance: 1602–2002*. Brussels, Deminor.

Fressoz, Françoise. 2008. "Parachutes dorés: le gouvernement renonce à légiférer, dans l'immédiat." *Le Monde*, October 8.

Gao, Bai. 2001. *Japan's Economic Dilemma: The Institutional Origins of Prosperity and Stagnation*. New York, Cambridge University Press.

Garrigues, Jean. 2002. *Les Patrons et la Politique*. Paris, Perrin.

Gatinois, C. 2007. "Les patrons du CAC 40 gagnent de moins en moins." *Le Monde*, November 28.

George, Alexander L., and Andrew Bennett. 2004. *Case Studies and Theory Development in the Social Sciences*. Cambridge, MIT Press.

Gerschenkron, Alexander. 1962. *Economic Backwardness in Historical Perspective: A Book of Essays*. Cambridge, Harvard University Press.

Gilson, Ronald J. 2004. "The Poison Pill in Japan: The Missing Infrastructure." *Columbia Business Law Review*, pp. 21–44.

Gilson, Ronald J., and Curtis J. Milhaupt. 2004. "Choice as Regulatory Reform: The Case of Japanese Corporate Governance." ECGI – Law Working Paper No. 22/2004; Available at SSRN: http://ssrn.com/abstract=537843 or DOI: 10.2139/ssrn .537843.

Glazier, Donald. 2007. "Change is Here: The New SEC Disclosure Rules." *The John Liner Review* 20(4): 1–7.

Goergen, Marc, Miguel C. Majon, and Luc Renneboog. 2004. "Recent Developments in German Corporate Governance." European Corporate Governance Institute Working Paper, May 2004.

Goodijk, Rienk. 2003. "Partnership at a Corporate Level: The Meaning of the Stakeholder Model." *Journal of Change Management* 3(3): 225–241.

Gordon, Philip H., and Sophie Meunier. 2001. *The French Challenge: Adapting to Globalization*. Washington, DC, Brookings Institution.

Gormley, William T. 1986. "Regulatory Issue Networks in a Federal System." *Polity* 18(4): 595–620.

Gourevitch, Peter A. 1996. "The Macropolitics of Microinstitutional Differences in the Analysis of Comparative Capitalism." In Suzanne Berger and Ronald Dore, eds. *National Diversity and Global Capitalism*. Ithaca, Cornell University Press, pp. 239–259.

Gourevitch, Peter A., and James Shinn. 2005. *Political Power and Corporate Control: The New Global Politics of Corporate Governance*. Princeton, NJ, Princeton University Press.

GovTrack. 2002. Sarbanes-Oxley Act of 2002. January 23. Available online at http://www.govtrack.us/congress/billtext.xpd?bill=h 107-3763.

GovTrack. 2008. Emergency Economic Stabilization Act of 2008. October 1. Available online at http://www.govtrack.us/congress/bill.xpd?bill=h110-1424&tab= summary.

Goyer, Michel. 2002. "The Transformation of Corporate Governance in France and Germany: The Role of Workplace Institutions." MPIfG Working Paper 02/10.

Goyer, Michel. 2003. "Corporate Governance, Employees, and the Focus on Core Competencies in France and Germany." In Curtis J. Milhaupt, ed. *Global Markets, Domestic Institutions*. New York, Columbia University Press, pp. 183–213.

Goyer, Michel. 2006a. "The Transformation of Corporate Governance in France." In Pepper D. Culpepper, Peter A. Hall, and Bruno Palier, eds. *Changing France: The Politics that Markets Make*. New York, Palgrave Macmillan, pp. 80–104.

Goyer, Michel. 2006b. "Varieties of Institutional Investors and National Models of Capitalism: The Transformation of Corporate Governance in France and Germany." *Politics & Society* 34(3): 399–430.

Goyer, Michel. Forthcoming. *Contingent Capital: Short-term Investors and the Evolution of Corporate Governance in France and Germany*. Oxford, Oxford University Press.

Goyer, Michel, and Bob Hancké. 2005. "Labour in French Corporate Governance: The Missing Link." In Howard Gospel and Andrew Pendelton, eds. *Corporate Governance and Labour Management: An International Comparison*. New York: Oxford University Press, pp. 173–196.

Greif, Avner, and David Laitin. 2004. "A Theory of Endogenous Institutional Change." *American Political Science Review* 98(4): 633–52.

Groenewald, Edo. 2005. "Corporate Governance in the Netherlands: From the Verdam Report of 1964 to the Tabaksblat Code of 2003." *European Business Organization Law Review* 6(2): 291–311.

Guber, Deborah Lynn, and Christopher Bosso. 2007. "Framing ANWR: Citizens, Consumers, and the Privileged Position of Business." In Michael E. Kraft and Sheldon Kamieniecki, eds. *Business and Environmental Policy: Corporate Interests in the American Political System*. Cambridge, MIT Press, pp. 35–59.

Guélaud, Claire. 2009. "Rémunérations des patrons: sénateurs et députés préfèrent la loi au decret." *Le Monde*, April 4.

Guélaud, Claire, and Anne Michel. 2009a. "Rémunérations des patrons: l'Élysée mise toujours sur l'autodiscipline." *Le Monde*, March 26.

Guélaud, Claire, and Anne Michel. 2009b. "Les rémunérations des patrons encadrées à minima." *Le Monde*, March 31.

Hacker, Jacob S. 2004. "Privatizing Risk without Privatizing the Welfare State: The Hidden Politics of Social Policy Retrenchment in the United States." *American Political Science Review* 98(2): 243–260.

Hacker, Jacob S. 2005. "Policy Drift: The Hidden Politics of US Welfare State Retrenchment." In Wolfgang Streeck and Kathleen Thelen, eds. *Beyond Continuity: Institutional Change in Advanced Political Economics*. Oxford, Oxford University Press, pp. 40–82.

Hacker, Jacob S., and Paul Pierson. 2002. "Business Power and Social Policy: Employers and the Formation of the American Welfare State." *Politics & Society* 30(2): 277–325.

Hacker, Jacob S., and Paul Pierson. 2004. "Varieties of Capitalist Interest and Capitalist Power: A Response to Swenson." *Studies in American Political Development* 18: 186–195.

Hacker, Jacob S., and Paul Pierson. 2010. "Winner-Take-All Politics: Public Policy, Political Organization, and the Precipitous Rise of Top Incomes in the United States." *Politics & Society* 38(2): 152–204.

Hall, Peter A. 2003. "Aligning Ontology and Methodology in Comparative Politics." In James Mahoney and Dietrich Rueschemeyer, eds. *Comparative Historical Analysis in the Social Sciences*. New York, Cambridge University Press, pp. 373–406.

Hall, Peter A., and David Soskice, eds. 2001. *Varieties of Capitalism: The Institutional Foundations of Comparative Advantage*. New York, Oxford University Press.

Hall, Peter A., and Kathleen Thelen. 2009. "Institutional Change in Varieties of Capitalism." *Socio-Economic Review* 7(1): 7–34.

Hamada, Yukihiko. 2010. "The Informal Nature of the Japanese Business-Government Model." In David Coen, Wyn Grant, and Graham Wilson, eds. *The Oxford Handbook of Business and Government*. New York, Oxford University Press, pp. 330–345.

Hamilton, James T. 2004. *All the News that's Fit to Sell: How the Market Transforms Information into News*. Princeton, NJ, Princeton University Press.

Hancké, Bob. 2002. *Large Firms and Institutional Change: Industrial Renewal and Economic Restructuring in France*. New York: Oxford University Press.

Hansmann, Henry, and Reinier Kraakman. 2001. "The End of History for Corporate Law." *Georgetown Law Journal* 89: 439–68.

Hedström, Peter, and Richard Swedberg. 1998. *Social Mechanisms: An Analytical Approach to Social Theory*. New York, Cambridge University Press.

Heemskerk, Eelke M. 2007. *Decline of the Corporate Community*. Amsterdam, Amsterdam University Press.

Helmke, Gretchen, and Steven Levitsky. 2004. "Informal Institutions and Comparative Politics: A Research Agenda." *Perspectives on Politics* 2(4): 725–740.

Herrigel, Gary. 2008. "Corporate Governance." In Geoffrey Jones and Jonathan Zeitlin, eds. *The Oxford Handbook of Business History*. Oxford, Oxford University Press, pp. 470–500.

Hilzenrath, David S., Jonathan Weisman, and Jim VandeHei. 2002. "How Congress Rode a 'Storm' to Corporate Reform." *The Washington Post*, July 28.

Hirsch, Paul M. 1986. "From Ambushes to Golden Parachutes: Corporate Takeovers as an Instance of Cultural Framing and Institutional Integration." *American Journal of Sociology* 91(4): 800–837.

Höpner, Martin. 2003. *Wer beherrscht die Unternehmen? Shareholder Value, Managerherrschaft, und Mitbestimmung in Deutschland*. Frankfurt, Campus.

Höpner, Martin. 2007. "Corporate Governance Reform and the German Party Paradox." *Comparative Politics* 39(4): 401–420.

Höpner, Martin, and Gregory Jackson. 2001. "An Emerging Market for Corporate Control?: The Mannesmann Takeover and German Corporate Governance." MPIfG Working Paper 01/4.

Höpner, Martin, and Lothar Krempel. 2003. "The Politics of the German Company Network." MPIfG Working Paper 03/9.

(L')Humanité. 2000. "Au hit-parade des plus gros salaires de PDG." January 29.

INSEE. 2009. Database on nonagricultural sector wage growth, available at http://www.indices.insee.fr/bsweb/servlet/bsweb?action=BS_SERIE&BS_IDBANK=001567453&BS_IDARBO=0300000000000(downloaded September 30, 2009).

Iyengar, Shanto. 1991. *Is Anyone Responsible: How Television Frames Political Issues*. Chicago, University of Chicago Press.

Jackson, Gregory. 2003. "Corporate Governance in Germany and Japan: Liberalization Pressures and Responses during the 1990's." In Kozo Yamamura and Wolfgang Streeck, eds. *The End of Diversity? Prospects for German and Japanese Capitalism*. Ithaca, Cornell University Press, pp. 261–305.

Jackson, Gregory. 2007. "Employment Adjustment and Distributional Conflict in Japanese Firms." In Masahiko Aoki, Gregory Jackson, and Hideaki Miyajima, eds. *Corporate Governance in Japan*. New York, Oxford University Press, pp. 282–309.

Jackson, Gregory, Martin Hopner, and Antje Kurdelbusch. 2005. "Corporate Governance and Employees in Germany: Changing Linkages, Complementaries, and Tensions." In Howard Gospel and Andrew Pendelton, eds. *Corporate Governance and Labour Management: An International Comparison*. New York, Oxford University Press, pp. 84–121.

Jackson, Gregory, and Hideaki Miyajima. 2007. "Introduction: The Diversity and Change of Corporate Governance in Japan." In Masahiko Aoki, Gregory Jackson, and Hideaki Miyajima, eds. *Corporate Governance in Japan*. New York, Oxford University Press, pp. 1–50.

Jacobs, Lawrence R., and Benjamin I. Page. 2005. "Who Influences US Foreign Policy?" *American Political Science Review* 99(1): 107–123.

Jacoby, Sanford M. 2005. *The Embedded Corporation*. Princeton, NJ, Princeton University Press.

Jacoby, Sanford M. 2007. "Principles and Agents: CalPERS and Corporate Governance in Japan." *Corporate Governance* 15(1): 5–15.

Jenkinson, Tim, and Alexander Ljungqvist. 2001. "The Role of Hostile Stakes in German Corporate Governance." *Journal of Corporate Finance* 7(4): 397–446.

Johnson, Carrie. 2004. "'Enron of Kansas' Trial Begins." *The Washington Post*, October 12.

Jones, Bryan D. 1994. *Reconceiving Decision-Making in Democratic Politics: Attention, Choice, and Public Policy*. Chicago, University of Chicago Press.

Jones, Bryan D. and Frank R. Baumgartner. 2005. *The Politics of Attention: How Government Prioritizes Problems*. Chicago, University of Chicago Press.

Jones, Scott. 2007. "The Japanese M&A Market." Presentation at Asia Business Conference 2007, Harvard Business School, Boston, Massachusetts, February 10–11.

Julien, Anne-Laure. 2006. "Le dispositif anti-OPA de Bercy ravit les patrons du CAC 40." *Le Figaro*, February 18.

Katzenstein, Peter J. 1985. *Small States in World Markets: Industrial Policy in Europe*. Ithaca, Cornell University Press.

Keidanren, Nippon. 2004. "Reasonable Defense Measures against Takeovers Detrimental to Corporate Value Are Needed." Japan Business Federation, Policy Proposal, November 16.

Knight, Jack. 1992. *Institutions and Social Conflict*. New York, Cambridge University Press.

Kollman, Ken. 1998. *Outside Lobbying: Public Opinion and Interest Group Strategies*. Princeton, NJ, Princeton University Press.

Korpi, Walter. 1974. "Conflict, Power and Relative Deprivation." *American Political Science Review* 68(4): 1569–1578.

Korpi, Walter. 1985. "Power Resources Approach vs. Action and Conflict." *Sociological Theory* 3(2): 31–45.

Labaton, Stephen. 1992. "S.E.C. Approves Rules on Top Pay for Executives." *New York Times*, October 16.

La Porta Rafael, Florencio López-de-Silanes, Andrei Shleifer, and Robert Vishny. 1998. "Law and Finance." *Journal of Political Economy*, 106(6): 1113–55.

La Porta Rafael, Florencio López-de-Silanes, and Andrei Shleifer. 1999. "Corporate Ownership Around the World." *Journal of Finance* 54(2): 471–517.

Lechantre, Caroline. 2006. "La mesure anti-OPA du gouvernement examinée aujourd'hui au Sénat." *Les Échos*, February 21.

Lechantre, Caroline, and Jean-Francis Pecresse. 2005. "Parachutes dorés: la majorité cherche à rassurer les entreprises." *Les Échos*, April 26.

Lepetit, Jean-François. 2005. "Rapport du groupe de travail sur la transposition de la directive concernant les offers publiques d'acquisition." Official French Government Report, June 27.

Levy, Jonah D. 1999. *Tocqueville's Revenge: State, Society, and Economy in Contemporary France*. Cambridge, Harvard University Press.

Lindblom, Charles E. 1977. *Politics and Markets: The World's Political-Economic Systems*. New York, Basic Books.

Linden, Dana Wechsler, and Vickie Contavespi. 1991. "Incentivize Me, Please; Has the System of Incentive Pay for Chief Executives Turned into a Giant Pork Barrel?" *Forbes*, May 27.

Locke, Richard, and Kathleen Thelen. 1995. "Apples and Oranges Revisited: Contextualized Comparisons and the Study of Labor Politics." *Politics & Society* 23(3): 337–67.

Lohr, Steve. 1992. "Recession Puts a Harsh Spotlight On Hefty Pay of Top Executives." *New York Times*, January 20.

Lordon, Frédéric. 2000. "La 'Création De Valeur' comme Rhétorique et comme Pratique." *L'Année de la Régulation* 4: 117–165.

Lowi, Theodore J. 1964. "American Business, Public Policy, Case Studies, and Political Theory." *World Politics* 16(4): 677–715.

Lupia, Arthur. 1992. "Busy Voters, Agenda Control, and the Power of Information." *American Political Science Review* 86(2): 390–403.

Lupia, Arthur. 1994. "Shortcuts versus Encyclopedias: Information and Voting Behavior in California Insurance Reform Elections." *American Political Science Review* 88(1): 63–76.

Mahoney, James, and Dietrich Rueschemeyer, eds. 2003. *Comparative Historical Analysis in the Social Sciences*. New York, Cambridge University Press.

Mahoney, James, and Kathleen Thelen, eds. 2010. *Explaining Institutional Change: Ambiguity, Agency, and Power*. New York, Cambridge University Press.

Mauduit, Laurent. 2001a. "Les chefs d'entreprise redoutent de vivre sans cadre juridique commun." *Le Monde*, July 14.

Mauduit, Laurent. 2001b. "L'échec de l'harmonisation européenne sur les OPA inquiète les patrons." *Le Monde*, July 14, 2001.

Maurice, B. 2008. "Des règles pour la rémunération des dirigeants des grandes entreprises." *Note de la Fondation Terra Nova*, October 3.

McCargo, Duncan. 1996. "Political Role of the Japanese Media." *The Pacific Review* 9(2): 251–264.

METI (Ministry of Economy, Trade and Industry). 2005. *Corporate Value Report*. Corporate Value Study Group, April 27, 2005.

METI/MoJ (Ministry of Economy, Trade and Industry and Ministry of Justice). 2005. "Guidelines Regarding Takeover Defense for the Purposes of Protection and Enhancement of Corporate Value and Shareholder's Common Interests," May 27, 2005.

Michel, Anne. 2009. "La France va encadrer les bonus des traders." *Le Monde*, February 8.

Milhaupt, Curtis J. 2001. "Creative Norm Destruction: The Evolution of Nonlegal Rules in Japanese Corporate Governance." *University of Pennsylvania Law Review* 149(6): 2083.

Milhaupt, Curtis J. 2003. "A Lost Decade for Japanese Corporate Governance Reform?: What's Changed, What Hasn't, and Why." Columbia Law and Economics Working Paper No. 234.

Milhaupt, Curtis J. 2005. "*In the Shadow of Delaware? The Rise of Hostile Takeovers in Japan.*" *Columbia Law Review*, Vol. 105.

Milhaupt, Curtis J., and Katharina Pistor. 2008. *Law and Capitalism: What Corporate Crises Reveal About Legal Systems and Economic Development Around the World*. Chicago, University of Chicago Press.

Ministère de l'Economie. 2008. "Programme Confiance, Croissance, Emploi – Pour tout savoir sur les mesures mises en oeuvre. Mesure 7: Aménagement des parachutes dorés. " Available online at http://tepa.minefe.gouv.fr/me.php?id_rub=7&sec=1.

Miwa, Yoshiro, and J. Mark Ramseyer. 2006. *The Fable of the Keiretsu*. Chicago, University of Chicago Press.

Miyajima, Hideaki, and Fumiaki Kuroki. 2007. "The Unwinding of Cross-Shareholding in Japan: Causes, Effects, and Implications." In Masahiko Aoki, Gregory Jackson, and Hideaki Miyajima, eds. *Corporate Governance in Japan*. New York, Oxford University Press, pp. 79–124.

Morck, R., A. Shleifer, and R.W. Vishny. 1988. "Characteristics of Hostile and Friendly Takeover Targets." National Bureau of Economic Research, Cambridge MA, NBER Working Paper No. 2295.

Morgenson, Gretchen. 2006. "Investor Fills Annual Meeting Agendas." *New York Times*, April 27.

Morin, François. 1998. "Le modèle français de détention du capital: analyse, perspective et comparaisons internationales." Paris: Ministère de l'Économie, des Finances et de l'Industrie.

Morin, François. 2000. "A Transformation in the French Model of Shareholding and Management." *Economy and Society* 29(1): 36–53.

Morin, François, and Eric Rigamonti. 2002. "Evolution et structure de l'actionnariat en France." *Revue française de gestion* no. 141: 155–181.

Munsters, R., and Rients Abma. 2007. "De toekomst van corporate governance." In S.C. Peij, J. Koelewijn, and R. Munsters, eds. *Handboek corporate governance*, Deventer, Kluwer.

Nakamoto, Michiyo. 2005. "A takeover battle launched by the upstart Livedoor." *Financial Times*, March 22, p. 15.

Netjes, Catherine E., and Harmen A. Bennema. 2007. "The Salience of the European Integration Issue: Three Data Sources Compared." *Electoral Studies* 26(1): 39–49.

North, David S. 2001. "The Role of Managerial Incentives in Corporate Acquisitions: the 1990s Evidence." *Journal of Corporate Finance* 7(2): 125–149.

North, Douglass. 1990. *Institutions, Institutional Change and Economic Performance*. New York, Cambridge University Press.

North, Douglass. 2005. *Understanding the Process of Economic Change*. Princeton, Princeton University Press.

Nuttall, Robin. 1999. "Takeover Likelihood Models for UK Quoted Companies." Nuffield College, University of Oxford, Working Paper No. 6.

Olson, Mancur. 1965. *The Logic of Collective Action*. Cambridge, Harvard University Press.

Orange, Martine. 2005. "Thierry Breton veut soumettre les indemnités de départ des dirigeants au vote des actionnaires." *Le Monde*, April 26.

Osborn, Michelle. 1992. "Little Debate on CEO Pay." *USA Today*, March 4.

O'Sullivan, Mary. 2007. "Acting out institutional change: understanding the recent transformation of the French financial system." *Socio-Economic Review* 5(3): 389–436.

Osugi, Kenichi. 2008. "Transplanting Poison Pills in Foreign Soil: Japan's Experiment." In H. Kanda, K. Kim, and C. J. Milhaupt, eds. *Transforming Corporate Governance in East Asia*. New York, Routledge, pp. 36–59.

Padgett, Stephen. 1999. *Organizing Democracy in Eastern Germany: Interest Groups in Post-Communist Society*. New York, Cambridge University Press.

Pagano, Marco, and Paolo Volpin. 2005. "The Political Economy of Corporate Governance." *American Economic Review* 95(4): 1005–1030.

Patterson, Thomas E. 1993. *Out of Order*. New York, Knopf.

PEJ. 1998. "Framing the News: The Triggers, Frames, and Messages in Newspaper Coverage." *A Study of the Project for Excellence in Journalism and Princeton Survey Research Associates*, July 13. Available online at http://www.journalism.org/node/445.

Pempel, T.J. 1998. *Regime Shift: Comparative Dynamics of the Japanese Political Economy*. Ithaca, Cornell University Press.

Perotti, Enrico C., and Ernst-Ludwig von Thadden. 2006. "The Political Economy of Corporate Control and Labor Rents." *Journal of Political Economy* 114(1): 145–174.

Poutsma, Erik, and Geert Braam. 2005. "Corporate Governance and Labour Management in the Netherlands: Getting the Best of Both Worlds?" In Howard Gospel and Andrew Pendelton, eds. *Corporate Governance and Labour Management: An International Comparison*. New York, Oxford University Press, pp. 148–172.

Proxinvest. 2005. "Rapport 2005 sur la rémunération des dirigeants des sociétés cotées," November 2005.

Putnam, Adam. 2008. "H.R. 1424 – Emergency Economic Stabilization Act." Legislative Digest, House Republican Conference. January 3. Available online at http://www.govtrack.us/congress/billtext.xpd?bill=h110-1424.

Rajan, Raghuram G., and Luigi Zingales. 2003. *Saving Capitalism from the Capitalists*. Princeton, NJ, Princeton University Press.

Ramseyer, J. Mark. 1987. "Takeovers in Japan: Opportunism, Ideology, and Corporate Control." *UCLA Law Review* 35(1): 1–64.

Ramseyer, J. Mark, and Frances McCall Rosenbluth. 1993. *Japan's Political Marketplace*. Cambridge, Harvard University Press.

Raulot, Nicholas. 2005. "OPA: La France veut mieux protéger ses entreprises." *La Tribune*, September 22.

Raulot, Nicholas. 2006. "Le ministère de l'économie veut amender le projet de loi OPA." *La Tribune*, February 17.

Reidy, Chris, and Alan Wirzbicki. 2005. "Frank's Bill Seeks Greater Disclosure of Executive Pay." *Boston Globe*, November 11.

La Revue Fiduciaire. 2005. Comments on the "Loi pour la confiance et la modernisation de l'économie," July 29. Available online at http://revuefiduciaire.grouperf.com/article/3110/hb/rfiduchb3110loiloi01.html.

Roe, Mark J. 2003. *Political Determinants of Corporate Governance: Political Context, Corporate Impact*. New York, Oxford University Press.

Roe, Mark J. 2006. "Legal Origins, Politics, and Modern Stock Markets." *Harvard Law Review* 120: 460–527.

Rosemain, M. 2008. "La rémunération globale des patrons du CAC a légèrement baissé en 2007." *Les Échos*, November 21.

Schaede, Ulrike. 2008. *Choose and Focus: Japanese Business Strategies for the 21st Century*. Ithaca, Cornell University Press.

Scharpf, Fritz W. 1997. *Games Real Actors Play: Actor-Centered Institutionalism in Policy Research*. Boulder, CO, Westview Press.

Scharpf, Fritz. 1999. *Governing in Europe: Effective and Democratic?* New York, Oxford University Press.

Schattschneider, Elmer E. 1960. *The Semisovereign People: A Realist's View of Democracy in America*. New York, Holt, Rinehart and Winston.

Schickler, Eric. 2001. *Disjointed Pluralism: Institutional Innovation and the Development of the U.S. Congress*. Princeton, NJ, Princeton University Press.

Schmidt, Vivien A. 1996. *From State to Market? The Transformation of French Business and Government*. New York, Cambridge University Press.

Schneper, William D., and Mauro F. Guillén. 2004. "Corporate Governance, Legitimacy, and Models of the Firm." In Frank Dobbin, ed. *The Sociology of the Economy*. New York. Russell Sage Foundation, pp. 127–156.

Schnyder, Gerhard. Forthcoming. "Revisiting the Party Paradox of Finance Capitalism: Social Democratic Preferences and Corporate Governance Reforms in Switzerland, Sweden, and the Netherlands." *Comparative Political Studies* 44(2).

Schulten, Thorsten. 1999. "Vodafone's Hostile Takeover Bid for Mannesmann Highlights Debate on the German Capitalist Model." *EIRO Online*, November 28.

Schwert, G. William. 2000. "Hostility in Takeovers: In the Eyes of the Beholder?" *The Journal of Finance* 55(6): 2599–2640.

SEC. 2006. "SEC Votes to Propose Changes to Disclosure Requirements Concerning Executive Compensation and Related Matters." Press Release, January 17. Available online at http://www.sec.gov/news/press/2006-10.htm.

Shishido, Zenichi. 2007. "The Turnaround of 1997: Changes in Japanese Corporate Law and Governance." In Masahiko Aoki, Gregory Jackson, and Hideaki Miyajima, eds. *Corporate Governance in Japan: Institutional Change and Organization Diversity*. New York, Oxford University Press, pp. 310–329.

Smith, Mark A. 2000. *American Business and Political Power: Public Opinion, Elections, and Democracy*. Chicago, University of Chicago Press.

Sniderman, Paul M., Richard A. Brody, and Philip E. Tetlock. 1991. *Reasoning and Choice: Explorations in Political Psychology*. New York, Cambridge University Press.

Solomon, Deborah, and Mark Maremont. 2009. "Bankers Face Strict New Pay Cap." *The Wall Street Journal*, February 14.

Soroka, Stuart N., and Christopher Wlezien. 2010. *Degrees of Democracy: Politics, Public Opinion, and Policy*. New York, Cambridge University Press.

Streeck, Wolfgang. 1995. "Works Councils in Western Europe: From Consultation to Participation." In Joel Rogers and Wolfgang Streeck, eds. *Works Councils: Consultation, Representation, and Cooperation in Industrial Relations*. Chicago, University of Chicago Press, pp. 313–348.

Streeck, Wolfgang, and Kathleen Thelen, eds. 2005. *Beyond Continuity: Institutional Change in Advanced Political Economics*. Oxford, Oxford University Press.

Swenson, Peter A. 2004a. Varieties of Capitalist Interests: Power, Institutions and the Regulatory Welfare State in the United States and Sweden." *Studies in American Political Development* 18: 1–29.

Swenson, Peter A. 2004b. "Yes, and Comparative Analysis Too: Rejoinder to Hacker and Pierson." *Studies in American Political Development* 18: 196–200.

Tax Executives Institute. 1994. "Proposed Section 162 regulations on deductions for executive compensation – Tax Executives Institute Federal Tax Committee Employee Benefits Subcommittee." March–April. Available online at http://findarticles.com/p/articles/mi_m6552/is_n2_46/ai_14987890/.

Thelen, Kathleen. 1999. "Historical Institutionalism in Comparative Politics." *Annual Review of Political Science* 2(1): 369–404.

Thelen, Kathleen. 2004. *How Institutions Evolve: The Political Economy of Skills in Germany, Britain, the United States, and Japan*. New York, Cambridge University Press.

Tiberghien, Yves. 2007. *Entrepreneurial States: Reforming Corporate Governance in France, Japan, and Korea*. Ithaca, Cornell University Press.

Tifft, Susan E., and Alex S. Jones. 1999. *The Trust: The Private and Powerful Family Behind the New York Times*. Boston, Little Brown & Co.

(La) Tribune. 2008. "Sarkozy décide de légiférer sur les parachutes dorés." October 2.

Tsebelis, George. 2002. *Veto Players: How Political Institutions Work*. Princeton, NJ, Princeton University Press.

Tversky, Amos, and Daniel Kahneman. 1973. "Availability: A Heuristic for Judging Frequency and Probability." *Cognitive Psychology* 5: 207–232.

Vafeas, Nikos, and Zaharoulla Afxentiou. 1998. "The Association between the SEC's 1992 Compensation Disclosure Rule and Executive Compensation Policy Changes." *Journal of Accounting and Public Policy* 17(1): 27–54.

Van Den Berg, Annette, Yolanda Grift, and Arjen van Witteloostuijn. 2008. "Managerial Perceptions of Works Councils' Effectiveness in the Netherlands." Discussion Paper Series 08–05, Tjalling C. Koopmans Research Institute: Utrecht School of Economics, Utrecht University.

Verbraeken, 1996. "Wetsvoorstel beschermingsconstructies naar Raad van State." ["Draft bill protection constructions to Council of State"] *Algemeen Nederlands Persbureau*, December 20. Retrieved via LexisNexis Academic.

Vincent, Gregory. 2004. *Beyond 'Crony Capitalism': Financial Change and Elite Coordination in France.* D.Phil Thesis Manuscript, Oxford University.

Visser, Jelle, and Anton Hemerijck. 1997. *'A Dutch Miracle': Job Growth, Welfare Reform and Corporatism in the Netherlands.* Amsterdam, Amsterdam University Press.

Vogel, David. 1987. "Political Science and the Study of Corporate Power: A Dissent from the New Conventional Wisdom." *British Journal of Political Science* 17(4): 385–408.

Vogel, Steven K. 2006. *Japan Remodeled: How Government and Industry are Reforming Japanese Capitalism.* Ithaca, NY, Cornell University Press.

Voogd, R.P. 1989. *Statutaire Beschermingsmiddelen bij Beursvennootschappen* (Protective Measures in the Memorandum of Quoted Companies), Deventer, Kluwer.

Weir, Charlie, and David Lang. 2003. "Ownership Structure, Board Composition and the Market for Corporate Control in the UK: An Empirical Analysis." *Applied Economics* 35(16): 1752.

Weyland, Kurt. 2002. *The Politics of Market Reform in Fragile Democracies.* Princeton, NJ, Princeton University Press.

Weyland, Kurt. 2008. "Toward a New Theory of Institutional Change." *World Politics* 60(2): 281–314.

Whittaker, D. Hugh, and Masaru Hayakawa. 2007. "Contesting 'Corporate Value' Through Takeover Bids in Japan." *Corporate Governance* 15(1): 16–26.

Wilson, James Q. 1973. *Political Organizations.* New York, Basic Books.

Wilson, James Q., ed. 1980. *The Politics of Regulation.* New York, Basic Books.

Windolf, Paul. 2002. *Corporate Networks in Europe and the United States.* New York, Oxford University Press.

Wildstrom, Stephen H. 1991. "Executive Pay." *BusinessWeek*, June 3.

Witt, Michael A. 2006. *Changing Japanese Capitalism: Societal Coordination and Institutional Adjustment.* Cambridge, Cambridge University Press.

Wlezien, Christopher. 2005. "On the Salience of Political Issues: The Problem with 'Most Important Problem.'" *Electoral Studies* 24: 555–579.

Wójcik, Dariusz. 2003. "Change in the German Model of Corporate Governance: Evidence from Blockholdings, 1997–2001." *Environment and Planning* A 35(8): 1431–1445.

Woll, Cornelia. 2006. "National Business Associations under Stress: Lessons from the French Case." *West European Politics* 29(3): 489–512.

Wood, Stewart. 2001. "Business, Government, and Patterns of Labor Market Policy in Britain and the Federal Republic of Germany." In Peter A. Hall and David Soskice, eds. *Varieties of Capitalism: The Institutional Foundations of Comparative Advantage*. Oxford, Oxford University Press, pp. 247–274.

Yamamura, Kozo, and Wolfgang Streeck, eds. 2003. *The End of Diversity? Prospects for German and Japanese Capitalism*. Ithaca, Cornell University Press.

Yoshimatsu, Hidetaka. 2000. *Internationalization, Corporate Preferences and Commercial Policy in Japan*. New York, St. Martin's Press, Inc.

Zysman, John. 1983. *Governments, Markets, and Growth: Financial Systems and the Politics of Industrial Change*. Ithaca, Cornell University Press.

Index

CPSIA information can be obtained
at www.ICGtesting.com
Printed in the USA
LVOW04s2038140916
504613LV00006B/36/P

9 780521 134132